"Lorne Fitch writes from a lifetime of observing flowing water, whether it be barnyard runoff as a boy or free-running prairie rivers as a biologist. He describes the nature of a river and the landscape it creates in careful detail, sometimes technical, sometimes lyrical. Then he goes deeper to examine the effect human interference has on that flow and the creatures that live there. Given we humans are mostly composed of water, a better association with water and its stewardship seems logical. Fitch makes the case, and we would be wise to commit to it."

—VALERIE HAIG-BROWN, Canadian activist, author, and conservationist

"Reading *Conservation Confidential* is like taking a trip through Alberta's wilderness from the comfort of your living room. He describes the land and waterscapes with such intimacy that you feel as though you are there alongside him in the canoe or walking the trail. You'll leave this book wanting to get outside and appreciate it in any way you can, because you'll understand more of what is at stake in the constant battle to protect Alberta's water and wild places."

—SARAH ELMELIGI, carnivore biologist, wilderness advocate, and author of *What Bears Teach Us*

"Like his previous two books, Lorne Fitch's *Conservation Confidential* draws from his experience as a biologist and wildlife advocate to provide a primer on conservation. Like alchemy, Fitch's storytelling turns the simplest walk in the woods into an adventure and life lesson, revealing the interconnected web that binds our quality of life to maintaining the integrity of all that nature provides."

—CHERYL CROUCHER, journalist and broadcaster
specializing in environment and innovation

"In Alberta, the younger generation may start to think clear-cut forests, open-pit mines, and ploughed-under prairie are all the inevitable costs of doing business. But biologist Lorne Fitch is a passionate defender of the province's magnificent wildlands and also an elder with a long memory. He's here to tell you wilderness annihilation is not inevitable, and that there are still wild critters and landscapes crying out for our attention and protection. To read this book is to be educated, and to be educated is to be activated."

—SID MARTY, author of *Oldman's River: New and Collected Poems*,
The Black Grizzly of Whiskey Creek, and *Men for the Mountains*

"Lorne Fitch is a fine storyteller and a determined advocate, and he's as Albertan as the Okotoks 'Big Rock.' He writes to change the future, but he also leaves a legacy, documenting environmental concerns at a tricky time in our collective history. From masterful nature writing to clear, confident biological science, Fitch is at once folksy, embattled, sensitive, and optimistic. He's a good read, folks."

—JOHN ACORN, author, educator at the University of Alberta,
and host of *Acorn the Nature Nut*

CONSERVATION CONFIDENTIAL

Conservation Confidential

A BIOLOGIST INVESTIGATES THE CLASH
BETWEEN PROGRESS AND NATURE

LORNE FITCH, P. Biol.

RMB

Copyright © 2025 by Lorne Fitch
Illustrations copyright © 2025 by Liz Saunders
First Edition

For information on purchasing bulk quantities of this book, or to obtain media excerpts or invite the author to speak at an event, please visit rmbooks.com and select the "Contact" tab.

RMB | Rocky Mountain Books Ltd.
rmbooks.com
@rm_books
facebook.com/rmbooks

Cataloguing data available from Library and Archives Canada
ISBN 9781771607537 (softcover)
ISBN 9781771607544 (electronic)

Copy editor: Peter Midgley
Cover illustration: Liz Saunders

Printed and bound in Canada

We acknowledge the financial support of the Government of Canada through the Canada Book Fund and the Canada Council for the Arts, and of the province of British Columbia through the British Columbia Arts Council and the Book Publishing Tax Credit.

Canada   Canada Council   Conseil des arts   BRITISH   BRITISH COLUMBIA
           for the Arts   du Canada   COLUMBIA   ARTS COUNCIL
                                                                 An agency of the Province of British Columbia

DISCLAIMER
The views expressed in this book are those of the author and do not necessarily reflect those of the publishing company, its staff, or its affiliates.

Contents

Introduction

*We are a restless, dissatisfied novice
species, clamoring for rulership of a
planet to which we display not even
a rudimentary form of allegiance.*

—Robert F. Harrington

As a biologist I've had a long career of interacting with people who saw the world differently from me, obviously through completely different lenses. Standing in a forest, my forestry colleagues saw a crop of cellulose, in the form of potential dimensional lumber. People in the petroleum industry peered deep into the earth for exportable energy and profit, ignoring what was on the surface. Similarly, miners looked, not at the mountain, but what could be wrested from beneath it. Farmers, looking at native grasslands and prairie rivers, saw a waste of perfectly good land and water to raise superior crops of wheat, canola, or potatoes. You might guess my perspectives were different, almost always diametrically opposed to theirs.

I've observed that those who come up with development projects are applauded, sometimes for the most outlandish of schemes. Ironically, if biologists and conservationists suggest merely keeping a landscape intact, they are castigated for a lack of economic foresight, positive progress, and entrepreneurial spirit.

Who is to judge who is right? When developments are proposed, there are a welter of conflicting opinions on the economic, social, and environmental costs and benefits. There are equally spirited debates on the moral and ethical aspects.

Maybe we need to examine the word "development," and reflect on whether it is one of a noble endeavour, or one that has consequences beyond the initial hype and excitement. We have long operated on the principle that if something could be done, it should be done. Now we need to ask, just because something can be done, should it be?

The answer might focus on some basic questions. Is a forest an essential watershed, home to native trout that are the ultimate measurement of our ability to steward a place? Does extracting more oil and gas exacerbate our climate change woes? Can we blow the tops off mountains and not poison the water for perhaps centuries? Does an intact grassland ecosystem, admirably adapted to drought, have a role to play in our future? Are rivers more than just water for economic development?

Imagine Alberta (and Earth) is a business. We're all shareholders and benefit from the essential ecological services our "business" provides. It isn't a stretch to suggest future generations are entitled to a share as well as us.

These are essential questions, but perhaps not the most important one – how do we move forward when our beliefs are so different? It seems that our differing convictions, especially over development of our landscapes and resources, put us at odds over the human footprint we have built, and one that is rapidly expanding beyond natural limits. This leads me to the analogy that the radio of conservation is on, but the reception seems very weak in terms of an uptake (and understanding) on limits, consequences, and costs.

Kenneth Boulding, an economist quoted in the 1973 journal *Daedalus*, remarked, "Anyone who believes that exponential growth can go on forever in a finite world is either a madman or an economist." Harsh? Yes, but that is a belief system that fuels more development.

Constant growth with no consequence exists only in the world of belief, one where there are no limits. I exist in a state of near-permanent disbelief in the assertions from business and politicians that we can grow even more, even faster, even larger, and that we must grow to preserve our standard of living. Oh, and we can balance economic development with environmental protection and, if necessary, successfully fix the parts we inadvertently break. If you cannot believe corporate executives and politicians, who can you trust? You might as well put your faith in Santa Claus and the Easter Bunny.

We think we've made the great escape from the natural world and its lessons and limits. But we haven't. At best we've postponed the day of reckoning for a while.

If you are still skeptical of where an unrestrained development path leads, to cumulative effects and crossing ecological thresholds, try this simple at-home experiment – invite more and more people to live in your house, until the refrigerator is empty, the toilets are plugged, and the air reeks of sweat and old socks. Add a kid with a drum set to the mix. Then, ask yourself, was there a line beyond which it just wasn't a good living arrangement?

Seeing how callously and thoughtlessly we treat our natural

assets is sandpaper on my soul – abrasive, uncomfortable, and torturous. This is especially so listening to those in business or in government extolling the virtues of some economic development scheme but downplaying the consequences for the environment. It is similar to listening to a hostage reading a contrived and pre-written statement. No matter how the message is flavoured, or made to sound palatable, the taste is never quite right.

Psychologists tell us that the more you mistreat people, the more pressing your need is to rationalize why your victims deserve their fate. Look at the messages explaining why we have to over-exploit, pollute, and misuse the land and its resources. This is beyond wants – we *need* to keep the economy "firing on all cylinders," reduce red tape, increase employment, create services, bolster the tax base, and on and on. This explains and rationalizes why a development belief and the accompanying behaviour make sense, at least to those that stand to gain financially.

We see what we want to see and how we see reflects what we are taught, the limits of our perception, who we associate with, and, often, who employs us. As Robertson Davies, a Canadian novelist, observed, "The eye sees only what the mind is prepared to comprehend."

This is not to suggest the zeal for development is universal, or that a different belief system doesn't exist in some of the business community and in governments. However, there is a tendency on the part of the corporate sector to engage in the ruse of green-washing. Most governments spend more on subsidizing economic development that negatively impacts natural landscapes, ecological services, and biodiversity than they do on financing conservation. If much of that money was redirected from supporting fossil fuel extraction and harmful agriculture, mining, and logging to conservation, the end result would improve prospects for a more liveable Earth.

There is hope in the results of a national survey commissioned by the Canadian Parks and Wilderness Society in 2022. Results showed the majority of Canadians support protecting more land and sea for nature protection. Even in development-focused Alberta, Albertans support setting aside more land to protect wildlife habitat and prevent further declines, and that more land should be left as wilderness where human activity is minimal. At a national level, respondents felt that government should focus on conserving the environment over economic development and job creation. About eight out of ten Canadians agreed that protected areas support a healthy, sustainable economy.

Perhaps, if we treated natural resources more as gifts than commodities, we might be inclined to reduce the rate of exploitation and of pollution. This would dramatically increase our ability to maintain space, quiet, intact landscapes, and ecosystem resilience. As benefits, we would protect fertile soil, potable water, breathable air, and biodiversity. If we change the way we look at things, then the things we look at change.

If a different belief system can evolve, it might be one where we are more respectful than rapacious, more thoughtful than oblivious, more far-sighted than myopic, and more restrained than greedy. If you still think you are distinct from your surroundings, try reading the next three pages while holding your breath.

Prologue

If, then, I were asked for the most
important advice I could give, that which
I considered to be the most useful to
the men of our century, I should simply
say: in the name of God, stop a moment,
cease your work, look around you.

—Leo Tolstoy

I've got the handle in my hand, ready to flush. My eye catches an announcement in the paper I was reading, in the quiet room of the house. It's for a watershed meeting to be held here in town. As the noise of the toilet flushing echoes, I think, *Who, me? Part of a watershed?*

As I wash my hands I muse, *I live in town, and I don't live on a lake or next to a river.* Brushing my teeth, I say to myself, *I don't fish, and I don't raise cattle that drink out of the river.* The coffee noisily percolates, and I wait impatiently for that first cup. Fortified with a jolt of caffeine, I remark out loud, "I don't know what all the fuss is about. Water is water. It comes out of the tap."

That reminds me to mix up some orange juice. I turn the tap on, pour water into the juice concentrate, mix, and thirstily drink a glass. The water holds the sweetness of Florida sunshine in suspension. The last drops drain out of the glass and my answer is, *No, I don't know why I would be interested in a watershed meeting.*

Satisfied with my decision, I head off to work. It's a lovely morning and I linger beside the car, savouring the sunshine. Birdsong puts my ears on alert and a flash of yellow captures my eye. I think, *That's a funny-looking sparrow.*

I glance over and see my neighbour sitting on her porch peering through binoculars. She's a bit odd – there have been words over her yard. It's become a wild and untidy place with what looks like weedy plants springing up everywhere. She replanted her lawn to some native stuff and she never waters or fertilizes it.

This morning though, the differences over yard care seem to have disappeared and she is visibly excited. She shouts to me that the bird is a yellow warbler, the first of the year. "It's just flown up from South America, almost 9000 kilometres to get here."

Nine thousand kilometres! I think to myself, *How does a tiny bird manage that feat?* Despite the differences I have with my neighbour, this intrigues me and I have to ask how this is possible. "Even though these birds only weigh the equivalent of two 25-cent pieces, they manage that migration by stopping in the rich, treed areas along rivers and streams and around lakes and wetlands. They fuel up on insects and then make the next leap." I'm amazed! These wooded areas must be the bird equivalent of 7-Elevens.

The morning passes at work. My ears perk up at a news

report on the radio of a boil water order in some other community. "Boil water, I wonder what that's about?" says one of my co-workers. "It's not about childbirth, cooking corn, or canning," says another. "There's either too much mud in the water and it can't be cleaned, or some bug has got into the water and only boiling will kill it."

The thought of boiling water and mud reminds me it's coffee time and I head down to the corner café. The usual crowd is there, dissecting the events of the day. I sit next to the fellow that runs the water treatment plant.

When there's a lull in the conversation, I ask him about this boil water order. He replies that there are more and more of these to meet drinking water standards. One of the curmudgeons in the group snaps, "So what if the river is muddy and is covered by green scum – can't they filter and treat the water with something? Anyway, don't we get our water from a well?"

The treatment plant operator smiles at the opening he's been given. "Yes, we get our water from a well but most communities in Alberta get all of their water from surface sources like lakes or rivers. Even though we have a well you have to think about where that water comes from. It comes from the surface and slowly trickles down. That water comes from a huge area and even though a lot of stuff gets filtered out, there's an increase in some chemicals."

"What kind of chemicals?" snorts the curmudgeon. "Well," said the operator, "things such as pesticides, herbicides, and nitrates that come from fertilizer or animal manure. Even stuff such as the weed-and-feed you put on your lawn can sneak into the groundwater. All of these things, including mud, are hard to remove and can be awfully expensive, especially for our small town with a limited tax base. Our best, and cheapest, option is protection of the water at its source. That's why many towns are starting to work with the rural counties on watershed protection – it's where our water comes from."

"But," he continued, "there's another side to this – we treat our wastewater and put it into the river. There are at least three communities downstream of us that take water right out of the river." The curmudgeon snorts again and sarcastically retorts, "Should we flush twice for them?" That ended the coffee break.

The phone rings at work. It's a rancher north of town with a side of beef I ordered from him. We agree to meet at my place for lunch. Over sandwiches I tell him about my morning of water, watersheds, and birds. He listens intently, with a wrinkle on his brow. He starts to talk. "After 40-some-odd years of ranching I thought I knew it all. I'm embarrassed to say there are some things I should have known more about. Back in the '70s I went to a bunch of seminars where they told me I had to be more profitable and efficient." He spat the words "profitable" and "efficient" out, as if they had left a bad taste in his mouth.

"So I fired up the cat and bulldozed all the willows and poplars off my bottomlands by the big river. And they were right, for a few years I could graze more cattle and it was more profitable. Then the first flood came along. Without the willows and the trees to glue the riverbanks together the river just ate them up. I tried to slow down that erosion. I even got the government to help. We dumped rock, concrete slabs, and even old car bodies. Nothing worked. The river ate those up too. I figure I've flushed more than five acres of my best pasture down the river. I wish I had those willows back. If I had it to do again, I wouldn't touch that brush next to the river."

The beef is safely stored in the freezer, and I decide to walk back to work. Around the corner one of my neighbours, a retired farmer, is trimming his hedge. He's a quiet, thoughtful man and I share some of the day's events with him. "As I get older, I see more," he mused. "I grew up fishing, I suspect it kept me out of a lot of trouble," he said with a mischievous twinkle in his eye. "This river used to have walleye in it, and I once caught a 12-pound pike. It's hard to find a fish anymore and that worries me."

"But if you want fish, can't you buy fish sticks?" I say, prodding him a bit. "Can't stand them!" he replies, "Fish in the river tell me the place I live is healthy. That's why I'm worried." He's quiet for a moment, thinking about something else. "Fishing and being next to the river helped me see my place in the world. It's about making connections; something that eating fish sticks will never do for you. I want my grandchildren to be able to fish, to make those same connections I was able to make. How can they if we've used up all their chances?"

I almost miss the building where I work, I'm so lost in thought. Waiting for me is a county councillor and I apologize for being distracted by this watershed stuff. She waves off my apology. "Sometimes our thinking is pretty narrow," she says. "We're only interested in our own backyards. I used to think, So what if someone drains a mosquito-infested slough 50 kilometres from my back door? How is this going to affect me?"

She goes on to say, "The problem is that our backyards are hitched to everyone else's in the watershed. We've got a situation where the folks in the headwaters want more drainage, to get rid of those sloughs that hold all the snowmelt. The people in the middle, especially here in town, have more flooding and bigger floods because the water all runs off too quickly with the sloughs gone. Then, the people at the bottom end of the river complain there's no water left for most of the year."

I think to myself that I'm glad to be on higher ground, but I do remember the ban on lawn watering during the drought a couple of summers ago. "It's like we're all living in different areas with different ideas about what we want, but we are all part of the same watershed. We've got to figure this out together," she says.

After supper I take a short drive to clear my head. I cross what I thought was a drainage ditch and it strikes me, "No, this is the river!" There's no sign on the bridge and I'll bet many of my neighbours don't realize this is their river. No wonder it doesn't get any respect! We've ignored our river, turned it into one of the back alleys instead of a front street we could be proud of. It's been quite a day.

At the last flush of the evening I think, *Me, I'm part of a watershed! I'm going to go to that watershed meeting, meet my neighbours, and get educated about where I live.*

Illustration by Liz Saunders

1

Heartbeats of the Land

Nobody sees a flower really; it is so small,
we haven't time, and to see takes time –
like a friend takes time.

—Georgia O'Keefe

OF TREE RINGS AND TEA LEAVES

Towering above a windswept ridge in the Porcupine Hills of Southern Alberta is an ancient, gnarled Douglas fir. Its circumference is measured with multiple tree huggers. A lightning scar runs down the thick trunk to protruding roots, some bigger than your thigh. Some of its branches are larger than the trunks of lodgepole pine trees further down the slope. If you think the tree has been there forever, you are mostly right. If this tree and its cohorts could talk.

In a way, old trees do talk. Not the garrulous narratives of some people, but with ancient wisdom acquired with centuries of life experience. Dr. David Sauchyn, the director of the Prairie Adaptation Research Collaborative at the University of Regina, has "listened" to the stories of these ancient trees.

A tree grows in diameter with cell divisions in the cambium layer of the bark. Annual growth increments show up as concentric rings, with the earliest at the centre of the trunk spreading out to the recent additions just under the bark. A cross-sectional profile is the record a tree maintains, not just of its age, but how it prospered and faltered during its life.

David, his colleagues, and his students have scoured the ridges of Southwestern Alberta for the past few decades looking for the old trees. They have used increment borers, specialized tools designed to extract a section of wood from the trunk through to the centre of a tree. It allows researchers to count and assess the growth rings in the core sample.

Use of the increment boring tool is heavy work. Augering through a metre or more of tree trunk and hitting the centre is a job for patient people. Slowly, the team has uncovered pieces of history, as told by the trees. What the tree rings provide, from old trees, is a very large, long snapshot of time.

The growth increments are a measure of the year they were lain down, especially what moisture was available. Mark Twain famously said, "Climate is what we expect, weather is what we get." A tree ring is a measure of the conditions for that year, while the growth increments over time tell us about climate and how it changed.

Using the growth ring data from 196 trees of two long-lived species, limber pine and Douglas fir, researchers have been able to extrapolate the changing conditions of moisture and construct 900 years of streamflow information. The application of dendrohydrology to water resources management provides a window into our future and can tell us how to prepare for climate extremes – drought and flood – perhaps occurring back to back.

There are many nuggets in the dozens of research reports on what old trees told us. Although couched in the turgid language of research, the interpretation of the science should make us pause and reflect.

Foremost is the reminder we live in a land of recurring drought, which introduces substantial risk. This is immediately so for the South Saskatchewan River Basin, rated in a 2009 World Wildlife Fund report as one of Canada's "most threatened watersheds, with water supplies in most subbasins overallocated."

Results from David's team indicate that the drought characteristics over the past millennium have differed substantially from those that occurred over the past century. The infamous drought of the 1930s looks like a minor wet period in comparison to the recurring drought of the 1500s.

Yet we're planning our future endeavours in Alberta based on limited information. It's as fraught with risk as our recent history. John Palliser's expedition in the mid-1850s found the prairies were very dry, leading to the slightly ill-defined "Palliser's Triangle" and the sense this was a landscape not suitable for settlement. Less than two decades later, John Macoun reported on abundant moisture conditions and championed the farming capability of the prairies, leading to the settlement patterns of today.

Each had seen only one part of the climate elephant. For the federal government and the Canadian Pacific Railway, Palliser's observations were viewed as an aberration and ignored.

Generations of farmers would subsequently live with the enduring frustration of recurring drought.

Using historical data alone to define how to respond to drought could seriously underestimate the potential severity of it. We could be led down a path of building more storage reservoirs without enough water to fill them. The results indicate that the severity and duration of hydrological droughts with the same recurrence interval is substantially larger and longer than those observed in 100 years of settler historical records.

An octogenarian human would be viewed by an ancient tree as a stripling, without enough experience to warrant any attention. In that vein, researchers commented that "it is irrational to assume stationary climate in determining the frequency of severe droughts." This is where the paleo record provides such valuable insights.

Rapid population growth, economic development (especially irrigation agriculture and food processing), and climate change have exposed this region to increasing vulnerability to drought. This is especially so since longer periods of low flows have occurred in our paleo-past than have been recorded in historical records.

Diminishing streamflow from the Eastern Slopes, coupled with drought risk and high demand for surface water, means there will not be enough to sustain our expectations for economic growth. Given those expectations, we are set to sacrifice aquatic health, riparian areas, and biodiversity.

Old trees have given us a gift of insight into climate and of extreme variability, especially on the drought side. It's a cautionary tale about our future. Those ancient ones survived and might help us recognize the limits applied to a landscape of variable precipitation. "Adapt," they might say, if we had the ability to listen, "and don't think tomorrow is just a continuation of today."

Without looking back, way back, we can be fooled badly, lulled into complacency about the future. A rancher friend, with tongue in cheek, reminded me, "It always rains right after a drought." Some actually cling to that, but hope isn't a strategy. It's a capitulation to inaction and sometimes the wrong actions in the face of evidence.

The story of old trees gives us better goal posts than hope does. We have additional issues to confront. A pervasive one is the rate that our actions, especially the liberation of greenhouse gases from the burning of fossil fuels, exacerbate change in the climate.

Do we have the tenacity to weather years of drought combined with wicked storms and floods, all driven by climate change? Can we afford the insurance premiums for crops and our property in the face of drought, flood, and wildfire? Will banks continue to provide operating loans? Can we continue to push the envelope for irrigation, for urban expansion, for other water-thirsty economic endeavours, and for logging the headwaters, the source of our water?

All these encroach on and exceed ecological lines in the sand. Viewing tomorrow as just across another line in the sand doesn't strike me as a survival strategy. It seems self-destructive.

Old trees have imparted some wisdom, some reflection, maybe some advice to consider about our future. We should listen, reflect on the tea leaves provided, and reconcile that we can, we must do better and be smarter to prepare for the changes our climate will deliver.

Clinging to ridges with roots deep into cracks and crevices in the bedrock, ancient trees are the personification of patience and persistence. Their survival adaptations have been ones of hunkering down, not competing for scarce resources, enduring the bad times when water was mostly unavailable, and not expanding much when conditions were favourable.

It would have been uncharacteristic of old trees to push down hard on the accelerator of growth at their own expense. Old trees recognized limits and lived within them. That strategy has allowed them to survive for centuries.

IMMERSED IN WATER

Some people find inspiration in the water of a pristine mountain stream – I found mine in barnyard runoff.

I am drawn to water, perhaps because 65 per cent of me is composed of the liquid of life. The rest is just framing, plumbing, and wiring. Although there are times when I prefer my water flavoured with barley and hops, or enhanced with a smoky Highland Scotch, it is a fine beverage on its own. Because of its ubiquity we overlook it, dismiss it, or pander to some hydration merchandizing fad instead of a schooner of tap water. Rarely do we ask where water comes from, what its movement patterns are, or what we do to it on its journey.

I have a long association with water – we all do since we swam in amniotic fluid for the first months of our creation. The next stage of immersion, where my pathway of understanding started, was with water in the barnyard of the family farm. In retrospect the barnyard was a watershed, receiving snowmelt and rainfall from corrals and conveying that flow down a gently descending slope to another, larger drainage.

My father likely despaired of the barnyard ever drying out since I built multiple interlaced dams to capture runoff. I would often find a drained reservoir, with a large footprint overlain on a washed-out dam. I suppose this tinkering with flowing water could have led to a career in engineering, but I never was interested in controlling water, but rather watching how it moved and responded to my direction.

Barnyard water manipulation was an active series of experiments in fluvial dynamics. This was a formative, although primitive, grounding in the physical processes of streams and rivers. Several principles were revealed that I was able to confirm later in academic studies.

One of my first epiphanies about running water is it doesn't run straight and true. Even when I constructed a straight channel with a hoe to speed water along, it still twisted, turned, and meandered, like the undulations of a snake. This puzzled me, and it was much later I learned water has its own sinuous agenda that works to balance the gradient, volume of flow, and material carried by the stream. It is difficult to change that agenda, although people have tried (and often failed) to "train" running water.

What I did observe was that where the channel ran through grass, the roots resisted the agenda of erosion, slowing the rate at which a channel moved sideways. Vegetation introduced a dynamic balance, giving a little, resisting a lot.

It also became evident that no matter how many dams I built, or how high they were to enable the capture of more water, they always failed at some point. Runoff from the "watershed," especially after a soaking June rain, could not be contained, would overwhelm the storage capacity, and one dam would wash out. Other downstream dams would then fail, as in dominoes toppling. Bare soil was soon saturated; it could contain no more water and the excess would rush downstream, creating havoc along the way.

These "floods" gushing over unconsolidated, unvegetated soil would carve wide channels, eating away at the banks. My primitive drainage networks, built to trap and consolidate flow, would turn rogue, adding much more water more quickly and exacerbating the volume and the water's ability to erode. Minor gullies would appear, carving not only sideways but down. Once a gully was established, the flow would speed up since it could no longer avail itself of a wider floodplain to dissipate some of the flow and its energy.

Adding bits of wood and the occasional stone to shore up an eroding bank would prove fruitless, as the barnyard stream would either pick up the impediment and raft it downstream or move around it. Moving water is implacable – relentless, unstoppable and, for all intents and purposes, uncontrollable.

Deltas of mud would appear downstream at the barn entrance, sometimes over the top of one's rubber boots. My father would curse this new inconvenience. Once the damage was done there was nothing to do but to wait until things dried up. The situation repeated itself, year after year. So too did my father's impatience with my fluvial "experimentation."

Revelations from my barnyard watershed were profound. A key learning was that running water proved indifferent to my primitive engineering. Water has patience and power and is anything but passive in the long term. A genteel flow at one point can quickly turn angry and unresponsive to "control."

Another essential "ah-ha" moment was the condition of the barnyard made it a poor watershed to try and manage. Constant hoof action from cows churned up the ground, never giving grass much of a chance to establish and bind the soil. This meant the reaction of runoff was swift, with little retentive ability to hold moisture. With the essential pieces of watershed health missing, even at a small scale, all my attempts at managing water were ineffective.

The parallels between my childhood barnyard observations and the processes that play out in larger watersheds are striking.

Scaling this up, what we do in a watershed defines how streams and rivers react. Tinker with the absorptive quality of a watershed by clear-cut logging, excessive road networks, and other developments, and a river will run wild, eating stream banks, washing out bridges, and flooding downstream basements. Try to tame a river with concrete, channelization, rock rip-rap, channel impediments, and dams, and you will discover the secret of rivers.

That secret, evident to those who observe rivers, is this — they pay no attention to boundaries, especially those imposed by human construction. With infinite patience and time, these obstructions are ephemeral, such as the bedrock a river has cut through. John Vivian, a rancher near Salmon Arm, BC, once mused about his experience having land adjoining a river. He wisely said, "When you live on a bend in the river, you need to learn to bend with the river."

We are a hydrologic society with little understanding of what bending with or accommodating rivers means. In many ways it is unfortunate that others have missed a childhood opportunity to learn about water. Spending some time immersed at the scale of a barnyard, a backyard, or an empty lot provides insights. These would provide more respect for moving water and less costly and failed intrusions on our streams and rivers.

It seems we attempt to manage the aftermath of our activities rather than planning better to avoid problems.

RIVERS — FLOWS OF UNDERSTANDING

To contemplate a river is to slip from the present, to travel in time deep into the past to sense Earth in its primordial state. If the soup of ancient oceans is where we came from, rivers are how we got to where we are now. Rivers exhibit age, order, and expressive identity. They can tug at our heartstrings.

Not all streams are equal, but they were created equally, with glacial effects providing the template, especially ones flowing from the Eastern Slopes. Subsequent events created the variety. As Luna Leopold, a leading US geomorphologist and hydrologist, observed in *A View of the River*, "The river, then, is the carpenter of its own edifice." Rivers are the daughters of ice and the mating of erosion, flood, and drought.

Before human intervention there were beaver, fires, floods, ice jams, and the occasional landslide that defined the character of these streams. Adjustments were made, and even though these systems were dynamic, only rarely did they exceed a range of natural variability. Floods may have changed the channels, moving the stream back and forth across a valley. The compensation included the creation of deep pools, extracting new substrate from the banks and adding tree trunks that increased the complexity of the channel.

When a river carves its way downstream, there are places where the backbone of a mountain will not yield immediately. Over time that is inconceivable to us, rivers worry away at the resistant bedrock. The rock only budges minimally. The river has to compensate, for the flow is inexorable, pressing ever downwards. Go left, go right, or deepen are the choices to overwhelm the obstacle. It is here that the river is at its loudest, complaining at the hoops it has the jump through to deliver water downstream.

In stream rapids, the rocks and boulders intrude upon the flow of water so that it has to jump, dive, pivot, pile up, reverse itself, froth into bubbles of entrained air, and finally eddy into a quiet pool.

The river's fingers are its tributaries, especially the first- and second-order streams. These probe and provide the direct linkage with the watershed and the forest. There aquatic insects begin to convert leaves and sticks, the rich plant bounty, into fats and proteins, very scarce commodities. This detritus is the granola of rivers. These essential nutrients then flow through almost everything – birds, amphibians, and fish. You kill rivers and their living ecosystems by cutting off their fingers.

A river twists, turns, and flows – ancient yet ageless and unstoppable. Take it for granted and you will be rudely surprised. Dam it, dredge it, divert it, straighten it, smother its banks in concrete and it will still flood you. It is as if the river has an account to settle with those of an engineering mentality having delusions of control.

Rivers will always hold the mortgage on the land and will foreclose at a time and place of their choosing. Because of that, there should be a more intelligent framework for dealing with floods – protect, accommodate, retreat, avoid.

We are conflicted with rivers. We want them close, to take advantage of their waters. But we want them to move along quickly when flood flows threaten. Aldo Leopold, in *For the Health of the Land*, wisely observed, "To those who know the hills and rivers, straightening a stream is like shipping vagrants – a very successful method of passing trouble from one place to the next. It solves nothing in any collective sense."

Now the headwaters of rivers contend with logging clearcuts, multiple roads, seismic trails, well sites, the occasional coal mine, and a maze of motorized recreation trails. The original watershed architecture is thrown into disarray. It responds differently to snowmelt and runoff, increasing the frequency and intensity of flooding. These human footprints can also accentuate drought with the loss of headwater forests that store water.

Downstream, rivers can become liquid deserts, with too much sediment and other pollutants and too little flow because of diversions.

Study the river wisely, reflectively, and don't think for a moment you can tell from the surface what its inner state might be. Ecology and rivers could teach us there are limits and thresholds for our use (and abuse).

Thresholds define edges. Edges can be blades, precipices, stop signs, or markers. Some view these as goals to be attained. Others reject them as invisible and irrelevant. Scientists view thresholds as borders, beyond which travel is not recommended since further movement can be dangerous, unknown, irretrievable and, at the very best, risky.

There are several metrics to tell us when we are approaching the edge or have gone over it. Significant declines in water quality are one indicator. If you can't drink the water, recreate in it, or if it requires costly treatment for any commercial purpose, this is a signal of things gone seriously wrong. That tells us the human footprint has exceeded a threshold, and erosion, runoff from mine wastes, agricultural fields, and from industry are greater than the assimilative capacity of the river and beyond the range one would have encountered without those changes.

One would think it axiomatic that rivers need water and certain amounts of water to maintain ecosystem function and keep fish alive and riparian areas green. Yet we divert massive amounts of water from them, draining their ecosystem faculties. Metrics are available to let us know the critical inflection points for river flow, but we bypass those markers, thinking that if there is any water left, it must be enough to keep a river alive. Rivers are not good to the last drop.

Another clue is more and larger floods that occur more frequently. This indicates the absorptive capacity and storage capability of the watershed, primarily with intact forests, have been modified with a land-use footprint to the point where these abilities have been severely compromised. Headwaters are a sponge, collecting, storing, and slowly releasing water. Logging clear-cuts, roads, and mines allows faster melt and runoff, without slowing water so it can be absorbed in shallow groundwater reservoirs for later release, when flows are lower.

The most informative indicator relates to the presence, distribution, diversity, and abundance of native fish populations. Fish are the ultimate integrators of what happens in a watershed. It takes monitoring, but fish are an early warning signal of changes in watershed health. Any disruption in the integrity of a watershed can be manifested in changes to fish populations.

Understanding rivers is partly science, but it is also part of the heart. Rivers flow through our lives, livelihoods, and recreation. They also flow through our veins and are part of our identities. Understanding rivers is also a pathway to understanding ourselves. We should take that opportunity, both for our sakes and for rivers.

COMPREHENDING POWER

In moving water, the grinding and polishing of boulders, rocks, and gravel into finer and finer pieces is incessant. It is a relentless, gravity-powered belt sander capable of wearing down bedrock. If you put your ear to the water, the action is also audible. Rocks tumbling against one another is part of the stream's melody. It is an unharnessed melody, the purpose of which is to grind away at the banks, moving the flow from one bank to another, building up the opposite side with the deposited remains of ground-up rock.

The power to shift tons of soil and rock, to wear away even at bedrock, to periodically reoccupy and reshape a floodplain, and to outflank and find weakness in every human-contrived obstacle is, to many, incomprehensible.

Water moves under the influence of gravity and with considerable weight. A cubic metre of water is equivalent to the weight of a small car. Stream horsepower is the combination of water velocity and weight. We think nothing of wading into a stream but not stepping into the path of an oncoming car.

Yet that water has levelled mountains, spewing the remains far into the plains. Mountains are no match for the power of persistence. Nature abhors elevation as surely as it abhors a vacuum.

We have waged an endless war with water – dredging, diking, damming, diverting, draining, cementing, channelizing, and rip-rapping. All exhibit brute force to resist the influence of water. Yet nothing the human mind has invented, or could invent, can truly and forever tame moving water, render it a completely willing servant, or reduce its risk to us to zero. Gravity still makes its own decisions.

Yet plants can glue a stream bank together, knitting the stones and soil into a unified front to thwart erosion. A five-centimetre-deep mat of plant roots provides 20,000 times more erosion protection than unvegetated stream banks. This is nature's super glue. Native trees and shrubs, in particular, have hundreds of kilometres of multi-branched roots and hundreds of thousands of kilometres of root filaments, with much variation in the size of these roots. This is an extensive anchoring system – up to 15 metres across and sometimes as deep as ten metres for an individual cottonwood or willow.

A vegetated front of roots and above-ground growth may bend, flex, and occasionally be ripped but uses those virtues to be resilient and to rebound rather than be directly resistant to the power of water. Unlike rebar, which gives concrete rigidity and strength, plant roots bind soil and substrate together in a flexible matrix that is permeable to water. Roots grasp, cling, and unify unconsolidated stream banks. It is a front that is self-repairing once a rent is opened. No human-engineered structure has yet mastered self-repair.

Unlike the hard engineering of human designs, vegetation – green engineering – opposes rather than combats water. The welter of roots, trunks, and branches impedes flow, slowing water down. Vegetated banks are speed bumps – rough, rugged, and choppy – and that reduces stream horsepower since slowing water down retards its erosive capability.

The water that provides the motive force to move mountains comes itself from a mountain, the watershed that feeds the stream. Watersheds collect, store, and slowly release water to even the flow out throughout the year. That is, if the watershed is vegetated, especially with forests. An intact forest is a water regulator, a stabilizer for streamflow. The plumbing that allows for storage in shallow groundwater reservoirs is the reason streams flow over winter, when no surface runoff occurs. Think of forests as savings accounts for water.

Forests receive deposits of snowmelt and rainfall in seasons of excess, paying it back in seasons of want. Without intact forests forming the watershed, streams would have greater and extreme variability in flows. That translates into more stream horsepower and more grief for downstream recipients.

So where is the true power? What is the ultimate winner in the contest of might over the seemingly frail? It seems it is in the humble vegetation that regulates flow, passively resists erosion, and persists in the face of a seemingly implacable force.

A SHORT LIST ON THE VIRTUES OF NATIVE PLANTS

As humans we tinker and experiment. Those traits led us, in the fertile valleys of the Middle East, the terraced paddies of China, on the slopes of the Andes, and throughout valleys in Meso-america to domesticate cereal grains, rice, lentils, cotton, potatoes, and corn. All of these originated in wild plant stocks. The development of agriculture through plant crosses and breeding allowed humans to expand and increase in all portions of the globe, save the Arctic and Antarctic.

In the process we have forgotten, neglected, and overlooked the virtues of native plants. As colonizers of new lands, always from somewhere else, there has been a consistent feeling the land usurped needed "improvement." Stepping back from our origins in agriculture and the agents of change we have been for landscapes, it's time to recalibrate our expectations with a better sense of the virtues of native plants.

Native plants are adapted to local conditions of climate, soil, slope, aspect, and moisture variability. They were born in place with several thousands of years of trial, error, and adaptation that selected the ones with the inherent capabilities to survive and thrive throughout the range of natural variability. Their genetic material has stood the test of time and stands to continue to meet the challenge climate change brings. A native or indigenous plant is one that occurs within a particular landscape without direct or indirect human actions.

Native plants have adapted to a variety of soil chemistry situations (e.g., high salinity, calcium carbonate) and soil conditions (e.g., anaerobic sites, a variety of soil textures). Root systems of many native plants grow deep, tapping subsurface moisture at depth. This enables native plants to be resilient to drought conditions. The deep root systems of many native plants, especially trees and shrubs, are the essential "glue" that binds streams and riverbanks together, making them resistant to erosion.

There is a team aspect with native plants. Competition occurs for essential resources, but this is minimized to fill niches and to take advantage of the ebb and flow of moisture conditions, seasons, and life histories. There is redundancy and overlap in the roles native plants play. This creates ecosystems with resilience to change. Over time, native plants have developed natural defences against many pests and diseases. Native plants attract beneficial insects that prey on other pest insects.

Think of native plants as soil builders, energy recyclers, moisture conservers, and erosion preventers. They work in concert and synergy with soil microbes and invertebrates in many of these tasks, such as transforming atmospheric nitrogen to forms useful to plants. Nitrogen fixation with certain groups of soil micro-organisms, in symbiosis with native plants, provides a major part of the nitrogen in circulation on Earth.

These plants don't require artificial amendments, as domesticated agricultural species do, to maintain productivity. Over the long haul, over the range of natural variation, native plants are consistently productive and less subject to boom-and-bust cycles. They provide low, or no-cost, management.

Native plants are key to maintaining native wildlife species and form the basis of the food chain. The timing of flowering, fruit, and seed production is tied to the life cycle of many wildlife species. The structure of native plants is essential to nesting success, survival of young, thermal cover, escape cover, and essential winter food. Native plants are essential habitat for native pollinators, which provide benefits to many adjacent agricultural crops. The mechanism for recovery efforts for species at risk is often the availability, integrity, and scale of native landscapes available.

As part of a somewhat get-out-of-jail-free card, native plants successfully sequester large amounts of carbon and assist in moderating the human-caused emissions that are responsible for climate change. Native plants provide long-term economic and ecological stability. Conventional agriculture replaces free eco-system services with the requirement for costly, non-renewable energy to maintain production. Late successional plant species (of which most are native species) are more efficient than agro-nomic species at converting solar energy into biomass.

Native plants are an effective tool for land reclamation/res-toration, providing a long-term solution to issues of erosion, salinity, and non-native plant invasion. Biodiversity, a measure of ecological integrity, is greater on landscapes consisting of native plants. These species provide aesthetic appeal, diversity, and beauty. There are heritage, spiritual, and cultural values associated with native plants. Native plants are used in the de-velopment of new foods, medicines, and industrial products.

Native grasslands and forests supply a number of important ecosystem services, such as forage production, topsoil conser-vation, water capture, storage and purification, flood control, pollination, and carbon storage. These landscapes and the plants that make them up perform these services for free, with appropriate management.

Whatever the question is, the answer has to involve native plants!

IN PRAISE OF PRAIRIE

When asked why a child of the wooded aspen parkland became an aficionado of the prairie, I have to pause. It's tempting to be flippant and point out there are no trees or mountains to obscure the view. But there's no one good reason or clear rationale. As in questioning why you love your spouse, or favour the colour blue, choose chocolate ice cream over vanilla, there are a tangle of explanations.

I love people – mostly and in moderation – but prefer to see them as landmarks, spread well apart. The arid nature of prairie forces humans to maintain a low population density. Exceptions exist with major towns and cities that have been established beside rivers where water is more abundant. Our engineering propensities have diverted water from those rivers to make parts of the prairie bloom and expand our human footprint.

Irrigation agriculture has forced a semi-arid landscape to bend to our will and hew to the notions of abundant moisture, artificially provided. The entire plumbing of Southern Alberta, from the flanks of the Eastern Slopes to the sagebrush grasslands, has been altered to accommodate an agricultural dream of replacing self-sustaining, self-sufficient native grasslands with croplands of thirsty agronomic species. Skeptics of the practice might point out we've transformed a natural heaven into a manipulated hell.

Much of the prairie has thus been lost, fragmented, or abused. What remains, especially the portions privately held, and even some of the public lands, is wild country, but undesignated for protection from the plow, pipelines, powerlines, and persistent economic aspirations.

Prairie is an underdog, either out of sight or unseen in plain sight. The intact pieces are large and imposing, perfect yet vulnerable, of an uncertain future, defended by few and largely unguarded by negligent regulators. I cheer for underdogs and so prairie needs to have its praises and virtues sung to the uninitiated, the blind, and even to the deaf.

One appeal is emptiness, an apparent lack of attractions, a humbling vastness and, to some, a sense of nothingness. Samuel Beckett, the Irish novelist, said in *Malone Dies*, "Nothing is more real than nothing." He wasn't talking of prairie but about how exploration of an apparent void is to see reality, the significance of nothingness and the meaning of it.

Seeing and experiencing prairie is to understand a place where life can be whittled down to the bone and where we humans might see ourselves in a clear light. It might be said this was the kind of place that kindled Christianity. Many mystics, prophets, seers, and philosophers experienced a spiritual dimension and humility in such surroundings. Kilometres of open grassland, unimproved by a single visible work of humans, can accomplish that reality.

I marvel at the adaptations of wildlife and plants to the uncertainty of water availability. The kangaroo rat, a diminutive creature – nearly eight centimetres tall with 18 centimetres of tail – hoards liquids as would a miser counting pennies. It gets by on "metabolic" water produced from plant seeds through internal manufacture. Plant seeds contain only 4 per cent water, yet the kangaroo rat has perfected both the extraction of liquid and energy from them. Water produced is constantly recycled within the body to the point the animal seldom urinates. A nifty evolutionary trick I wish we humans had for long drives and interminable meetings.

Prairie plants, the majority of them, are water misers as well. Researchers had to dig deep to discern the rooting depths and hence the secrets of how these plants prosper in very dry conditions. Many had roots that went down at least a metre and sometimes much deeper to extract water well protected from high soil surface temperatures and extreme evaporation. The accumulated litter of previous years' grass growth insulates soil, preserving soil moisture and recycling nutrients.

Prairie plants are patient. When drought occurs, they bide their time and save their resources for another year. What they could teach us is water conservation and saving our energies for the opportune time.

Prairie defines community. It isn't a locality, a name on a map; it is a dynamic alliance of living plants, animals, birds, insects, reptiles, and micro-organisms. Together, all compete and co-operate, predate and parasitize, are symbiotic. Some are scavengers, and decomposers rule. This is a cosmopolitan place, more so than meets the eye. It is both utilitarian and beautiful – this is not a contradiction.

Prairie critters endure some of the harshest conditions Alberta has to offer. The prairie is a place universally hot and dry in the summer, bitterly cold in winter, windswept all the time, and subject to the most climatic variability and extremes of almost any part of Canada.

Short-horned lizards can survive variances that drop their body temperature from 32°C to below freezing. We complain over minor temperature fluctuations and tend to die if our body temperature varies more than 4°C. This dinky little critter, with its somewhat comical array of spikes and horns, has evolved the ability to withstand freezing to survive in the prairie's extreme winter environment. You have to stand in awe of evolution.

Antelope eyes are pools of deep, inscrutable velvet and protrude slightly from the skull, all the better to bring antelope their world. If you were to stare into those limpid pools, you might see where antelope came from, a networked community, an intact geography, and the prairie as once it was.

On the prairies one lives with the ghosts of what was, the hunger for what might have been and yet could be. Walking across the prairie toward a distant horizon one can get the sense that over the next fold, in the next coulee, around the next hill, will rise a herd of bison, antelope, elk, or maybe the full suite of Pleistocene critters.

As I say this, I still stumble over why prairie appeals to me. "There's something about it..." I might say. My explanation might get wrapped up in the clarity of the light and the colour of the sky. Part of it is the perception the landscape is soft and elegantly simple (at least until you hit a badland coulee). There is the endurance of the plant life and the admirable toughness of the wildlife. Maybe it is the relative scarcity of humans and their handiwork.

But it's more than those obvious things. It's not that anything defining the feeling is a secret so much as the elemental pieces have to be experienced, felt, and thus are hard to convey in so many words. When the wind tries to tear you apart, launch you, being there is essential. I can describe a salmon-red sunset with the dark pinnacles of the Sweetgrass Hills poking up into the hue of colour. Better to see it yourself after a long walk and be transfixed by the scene. As in the line in the timeless prairie song, "Home on the Range," "I stood there amazed..."

I'm back to where I started. This place called prairie appeals to me because there is something about it I can't fully explain.

Prairie is more of enormity rather than beauty, more of subtlety, originality, and humility. It's less about the *ooh* or *ahh* than the *hmm*.

Edward Abbey called those who revelled in the really arid areas of the southwestern states as "Desert Rats." Our grasslands are somewhat better watered and lack some of the starkness of the Sonoran, Mojave, and Chihuahuan deserts. But there is still congruity between those Desert Rats and our Prairie Faeries. I count myself as one of the latter group, named in response to the derision of a crusty rancher with no patience for prairie protectors.

We need to recruit more such devotees of prairie, to connect people better to this most imperilled, endangered landscape. There is no future for prairie unless more people really know, appreciate, care, love, and can't imagine an Alberta bereft of it.

FROM THE DEPTHS AND DEEP TIME — LAKE STURGEON

A monster prowls the depths of Alberta's prairie rivers. Not a malevolent one, but one of leviathan size and ancient origins. If you want to talk about big, old fish you need go no further than lake sturgeon. Lake sturgeon are only found in rivers in Alberta, but are also associated with lakes, including the Great Lakes. It is likely the name originates from the lake-dwelling ones.

Lake sturgeon have been swimming the waters of North America for about 136 million years. They swam while dinosaurs roamed, and then watched those "terrible lizards" disappear. If they had kept diaries, they could have recorded mountain building, multiple glaciation events and, finally, the erosion that created the landscapes of Alberta, including the river courses of their current residence. Only on the last page, maybe the last line, would there be a record of people appearing. If it were available, lake sturgeon would qualify for a senior's discount and be maxed out on a frequent swimmers program.

In a way, the fish is a dinosaur. Once lake sturgeon evolved to a certain point, essentially their current form, they said, that's good and workable – no need for more tinkering. Instead of a spine, it has a cartilaginous skeleton, pointing back to its ancient origins. Lake sturgeon have a torpedo-shaped body, covered not by scales but prominent rows of bony plates. These fish seem literally protected by body armour. This also gives a sense of a violent antediluvian past where a thick protective covering was a survival must.

An adaptation to water depths and poor visibility are barbels, two pairs of slender, whisker-like sensory organs near the mouth. Virtually anything edible on river bottoms is detected and vacuumed up into the mouth. These are not finicky eaters. There seems to be constant movement related to food. Radiotelemetry has shown long seasonal migrations to favoured spawning sites, over 200 kilometres in the South Saskatchewan and 500 kilometres in the North Saskatchewan watersheds.

There are no bigger freshwater fish species in North America than sturgeons. The largest of the five species is the white sturgeon, found in west coast watersheds. Lake sturgeon are a close second in size. The largest of the species on record weighed 141 kilograms, and was 241 centimetres long. It was caught in 1922 in Lake Superior. In Alberta, the largest on record was 48 kilograms. However, in 2020 a Lethbridge angler caught (and released) one that might have been much larger, maybe in excess of 60 kilograms. Angling for sturgeon isn't for the faint of heart. The angler suffered a broken rib and a gashed arm trying to land this monster.

Young sturgeon have sharp scutes, bony, diamond-shaped scales, to thwart predators. By virtue of their size adult sturgeon simply outclass and outweigh any potential predators (except us). These sturgeon mature even later than us humans – 15 to 20 years for males and 20 to 25 for females. I should point out this is sexual maturity, since in humans tangible evidence of other forms of maturity is still lacking. They can outlive us with records up to 150 years. In Alberta the oldest one was 62.

In a way, their body form and their ecology have served lake sturgeon well, from their origins in the primordial soup of a Cretaceous tropical world through to an ice age. They have persisted until modern times. It's these modern times that severely test them. In Alberta the population is now truncated into two, one in the North Saskatchewan River, the other in the South Saskatchewan. Gardiner Dam on the South Saskatchewan River divides and isolates one population from the other. The E.B. Campbell Dam in Eastern Saskatchewan isolates the North Saskatchewan population from downstream ones.

In Alberta, lake sturgeon historically swam in the Oldman River up to the confluence with the Castle River, in the Bow River up to near Bassano, up the Red Deer River to the confluence with the Medicine River and throughout the South Saskatchewan River. They were common in the North Saskatchewan River upstream to Drayton Valley. Strangely, the only record of them in the Sturgeon River is the harvest of 682 kilograms over the winter of 1916–1917. At one time the oil rendered from sturgeon was used to fuel lamps. Hopefully, we are more enlightened now about the value of sturgeon!

Currently, the province's fish sustainability index ranks sturgeon as low in the South Saskatchewan, very low in the Oldman, Bow, Red Deer, and North Saskatchewan rivers, and functionally extirpated in the upper portions of the Oldman and Red Deer rivers. Although the population has inched up from critically low numbers of the past century, which precipitated an angling closure from 1940 to 1968, they are by no means abundant today.

Not surprisingly, lake sturgeon are ranked as threatened in Alberta and endangered federally by the Committee on the Status of Endangered Wildlife in Canada (COSEWIC). Sustainability of lake sturgeon remains at risk, for a variety of reasons.

Very few people have ever seen a live lake sturgeon, or for that matter realize they exist in our prairie rivers. Sequestered in pools several metres deep, with water so opaque with sediment it makes your hand disappear from view only a few centimetres into the water, sturgeon are not part of routine fish watching. Angling for them would test the patience of Job, even for experienced sturgeon fishers. Because of their "at risk" status, fishing for sturgeon is strictly catch and release.

To be protected, a critter first has to be acknowledged, a challenge for biologists in a world that is ecologically ignorant. Biologically, any species that takes a long time to mature is at risk (except us humans it seems), since the Grim Reaper has a lengthy time period to exercise his scythe of death before reproduction occurs. Isolating the Alberta population into two separate groups does not aid in genetic exchange or in movement to bolster population sizes.

Ecologically, declines in water quality and quantity have had an influence on, and will continue to influence, the ability of lake sturgeon to move, spawn, rear, feed, and overwinter. The more pressure we put on prairie rivers to meet our needs, the less able they are to provide for sturgeon.

As climate change results in hydrologic shifts – less river flow, more variability in flow, and greater flood frequency – we respond with more water diversions, especially for irrigation agriculture. On top of less remaining water to keep rivers healthy, we have built dams and diversions, such as Bassano Dam, Dickson Dam, and the Lethbridge weir that block upstream movement.

To those existing impediments to movement have been proposed new dams on the South Saskatchewan River (Meridian Dam), lower Bow River, Red Deer River downstream of Red Deer, plus a new diversion from the lower Red Deer River (Special Areas Water Supply project). In Saskatchewan there is a proposal for a dam on the North Saskatchewan River near North Battleford (Highgate Dam). If built, these would further slice and dice sturgeon populations, putting the Alberta population at even greater risk.

The Alberta Lake Sturgeon Recovery Team laid out a rather frank appraisal of concerns and issues for the species in the *Alberta Lake Sturgeon Recovery Plan 2011–2016*. In as many words, perhaps not couched as bluntly, its advice was: retain and allow recovery of lake sturgeon populations, including proscribing the over-allocation of water that exacerbates many other issues for the species; don't build any more dams or diversions that impede movement; clean up the water in our rivers; and deal with some of the unanswered questions about sturgeon biology and ecology.

Terry Clayton, retired provincial fisheries biologist and chair of the sturgeon recovery team, responded to me with, "I worry most about the increasing water demands, especially for irrigation in the south and the cumulative effect on water quality of urban and industrial development in the North Saskatchewan. Failure to address these issues will undermine recovery efforts and our ability to retain viable sturgeon populations." Serious commitment to recovery would start with the province setting and adhering to ecologically relevant river flows that put water back into rivers and keep it there.

Lake sturgeon remind us of the past, a past of deep time, a fossilized past. That they have endured so much, for so long should fill us with admiration for their persistence. Instead, we have whittled down their opportunities to survive into the future, out of neglect, ignorance and, to a degree, greed.

If we saw sturgeon differently, not as impediments to further development but as a testament to heathy, intact rivers, we might be inclined to treat them and the rivers they exist in better. Even though lake sturgeon have been on the path longer, it is the same path as ours. We consistently ignore this reality.

Illustration by Liz Saunders

2

A Few Drops of Ecology

This curious world we inhabit is more
wonderful than convenient; more
beautiful than it is useful; it is more to be
admired and enjoyed than to be used.

—Henry David Thoreau

BATS IN YOUR HAIR AND OTHER WILDLIFE MYTHS AND MISCONCEPTIONS

———

We've come a long way from the time of Aristotle, who believed swallows and other birds hibernated beneath the mud in marshes. Others thought migratory birds flew to the moon and spent the winter there. Even so, science hasn't quite dispelled such notions.

There are myths and misconceptions about wildlife that still circulate. You might be familiar with some of them, like bats are blind and if they fly too close they get tangled in your hair. Wolves and coyotes howl at the moon. Hummingbirds migrate on the backs of Canada geese. A ladybug's spots tell its age. Snow buntings are sparrows that turn white in the winter.

Pike lose their teeth in the spring. Spiders sneak into our beds at night to bite us. Birds bang into windows to seek shelter indoors. Deer only cross roads at wildlife crossing signs.

These are humorous, even silly, misunderstandings and ignorance about wildlife. To a degree these are innocuous items that might not seem harmful to wildlife compared to the two fundamental myths that *are* harmful.

The first of these myths is that resources and space are inexhaustible. The second is we can do everything, everywhere, any time and all the time. These two myths underpin many of our land-use decisions. They have to a major degree become public and political realities, even though they are fiction. They aren't real, but the fiction becomes compelling because it sustains our economic systems.

Not necessarily a myth but a misconception is that wildlife is represented by the big, the furry, the feathered, the charismatic, the pretty, the pursued, or the photogenic. This gives short shrift to plants, fish, amphibians, and invertebrates; indeed, to most of the species that describe biodiversity fully. In fact, Dr. Dan Johnson, an entomologist, said to me once, "Compared to numbers of insect species, everything else is just rounding error."

The issues faced in Alberta bring into focus the old conundrum of too little land and too many expectations. With the discussion come all the old fairy tales, fables, fantasies, legends, and myths, along with partial truths, half-truths, and untruths. Inevitably, it will come down to ecological awareness and the courage to make decisions in the face of conflicting and overlapping aspirations.

Ogden Nash said, in a poem published in the *New Yorker*

magazine, "Progress may have been all right once, but it went on too long." With progress and all its benefits have come costs. One of the evident costs, with changes in landscapes, has been declines and losses of fish and wildlife, our biodiversity treasures.

The Wyoming Game and Fish Department categorizes impacts on wildlife from land use in these ways:

1. Direct loss of habitat.
2. Physiological stress and behavioural shifts.
3. Disturbance and displacement of wildlife.
4. Habitat fragmentation and isolation.
5. Alteration of ecological functions and process.
6. Introduction of competitive, predatory, or parasitic organisms.
7. Secondary and cumulative effects from increased access and additional development.

The impacts are real, based on research, evaluation, and empirical evidence. But facts have a hard time getting traction on a roadway paved with myth and misconception. J.B. MacKinnon writes, in *The Once and Future World*, "Denial is the last line of defense against memory. It helps us to forget what we'd rather not remember, and then to forget that we have forgotten it, and then to resist the temptation to remember...It fulfills...our need to be innocent of a troubling experience."

There are several misconceptions about the impacts of development on wildlife and the responses of wildlife to human disturbance that need to be addressed:

1. Wildlife just moves out of the way. There is no impact because wildlife relocates to unaffected, adjacent habitats.

This contradicts a fundamental axiom of population ecology. Populations of organisms increase to fill vacant, suitable habitat and then are regulated by the essential component of their habitat that is in the least supply. Examples of essential components would include winter range for ungulates, breeding, nesting, and brood-rearing areas for grassland birds, and spawning areas for native trout.

Existing populations of wildlife occupy the habitats that are suitable. Areas that are unsuitable are not used or are used infrequently. When development displaces animals from suitable habitats, they are forced to use marginal habitats (that do not meet all of their life cycle requirements) or they relocate to unaffected habitats where population density and competition for resources with an existing population increases.

Consequences of displacement, competition, and reduced habitat are lower survival, lower reproductive success, lower recruitment, and lower carrying capacity. All lead to population-level impacts.

Unlike us, who have developed technologies to live in many places, many wildlife species have evolved to be reliant on specific habitats. In the process they might have sacrificed other options and have accepted being profoundly linked to a particular landscape.

We forget, as we fiddle with the thermostat and wonder whether dinner will be roast beef or a pizza, that a wildlife species lives (or dies) with the immediacy of its habitat. There's no take-out on the wildlife speed dial. What wildlife species have done is rolled the storms, the floods, the droughts, the changes in water temperature, the good and the bad – the natural variability of their world – into their genetic material as a mechanism for survival. Unlike us, they are fine-tuned to the intricacies of their world and are on intimate terms with all the nuances.

2. Animals seen near developments indicate they have become accustomed to and are not affected by activity.

Individuals within populations show variable responses and tolerances to disturbance. Some animals may acclimate or modify behaviour in response to repetitious, non-threatening, or low-grade activity. Some species have adapted to human activity (none are in the species-at-risk category). Some species are habitat generalists and are not as affected by disturbance as other species.

However, other segments of the population may remain very sensitive to disturbance. This is particularly true of habitat specialists, which includes all of the species at risk. The health of the overall animal population depends on the ability of all segments of the population to effectively use, and have access to, limited resources.

Displacement is not necessarily evident if some animals remain visible in an area subject to disturbance or human activity. Presence of animals does not indicate that the animals are subject to no negative effects. Physiological stress may not be apparent.

3. Seasonal use stipulations, habitat protection guidelines, standard operating procedures, and reclamation practices are adequate mitigation for wildlife resources affected by development.

"Standard operating conditions" have not been researched or reviewed to determine efficacy at the stated objectives, especially at regional and local scales. Random reviews also show significant rates of non-compliance with standard operating conditions. Regulatory oversight is lacking. Guidelines for development are usually minimal requirements based on economic/political compromise, and subject to negotiation. Much of this attempt to mitigate the negative effects fails to account for cumulative effects, the additive feature of land-use activities and footprints.

Reclamation occurs at a much slower pace than development and there is a significant backlog, which adds to the cumulative footprint. The ability to restore land-use footprints to a comparable, pre-disturbance habitat function is inexact and problematic.

Research on the efficacy of mitigation is lacking and typical procedures are repeated without an empirical base to determine adaptive management and rates of success. At larger scales, many species at risk continue to decline in the face of an increasing development footprint, even with the application of a variety of administrative protection guidelines.

Mitigation has become one of those aggrandizing bureaucratic terms that assigns a human intent to compensate for a loss, without a clear statement about how the bargain will be struck. Mitigation is politically sound but ecologically risky. Mitigation might be thought about in the same way that technological solutions are employed in smoking, ostensibly to reduce the health risk but really to maintain consumption rates. The use of filtered cigarettes precisely fits this thinking. The tobacco company tries to solve a problem in a way that lets consumption of the drug continue without interruption.

Mitigation addiction is the affliction created in the vain hope everything can be done everywhere, anytime, and all the time, with our development footprint effectively erased behind us. At worst it creates the impression there is still room for expansion of development and biodiversity is protected.

4. The amount of physical disturbance is small in comparison to the land base and the impacts to wildlife are equivalent to the area affected.

The collective area of directly disturbed land may be small in relation to the land base, but the influence of the footprint and activity extends to a larger area where proximity causes stress, avoidance, increased mortality, and decreased use. Call this the extended collateral damage of a land-use activity. Avoidance and stress response impairs remaining habitat function by reducing the capability of wildlife to use habitat effectively. These impacts are especially problematic when they occur in or adjacent to limiting habitats such as critical winter ranges, hibernacula, and reproductive habitats.

There are varying degrees of avoidance, effects, and stress responses to sources of human noise and activity. These responses include reactions to humans on foot, to vehicles, off-road vehicles, equipment, roads, noise levels, timing of activity, and seasonal differences. An impact is defined as the impairment of the function of important wildlife habitat in ways that are discernible, increasing, or substantial, even though animals may still be present.

The thresholds start at the outer limits where a reaction or an impact on wildlife is undetected, undetectable, or there is no negative response. Between the outer limit and the disturbance is an increasing suite of reactions, responses, and effects on wildlife that represent a loss of habitat function and effectiveness. There is a gradient within this "buffer zone" and no explicit line beyond which it can be said wildlife populations are protected and there is no population-level effect. Within a buffer zone, in proximity to the disturbance, is found increasing avoidance, displacement, and physiological stress.

For grassland songbirds, effects can manifest themselves as failure to secure breeding territory, nest failure/predation/parasitism, and higher rates of mortality with less recruitment to the population. For species at risk, already at diminished numbers, this has a cascading effect.

5. Knowledge about the exact location of thresholds of change is insufficient so applying them now is unwarranted.

It is difficult to pin down in exact terms when and where the last wild animal will die as a consequence of land use and the effects on population integrity. What the last animal dying represents is exact precision and a failure to apply a threshold early enough to stave off their demise.

History does provide a mirror to view the list of extirpated and now extinct species whose populations developed a negative trend in the face of human intervention. History tells us that yesterday's abundant species can become today's imperilled ones. The use of trend information, especially for species at risk, is a useful distant early warning alarm about the effects on land use on populations and on intervention to avert population collapse. This speaks to adopting the precautionary principle that should guide targets and limits as research and monitoring fine-tune the lines that define thresholds.

6. Wildlife populations do not seem to respond quickly to land use – they persist – and that suggests protective measures are unnecessary.

The line of reasoning is if changes aren't observed in the short term, the effects are minimal and irrelevant to species protection. The conclusion might be that animals adapt quickly and positively to changes. The challenge is that many species react to changes in landscape structure and to disturbances with long response times. Current population densities may not reflect a response to current patterns of land use, but to earlier changes decades ago.

Populations may continue to decline even when the degree of landscape change does not increase. Negative impacts of landscape change (habitat fragmentation, plant species shifts, loss of connectivity, and habitat loss) only become apparent after lengthy time periods. Further population effects (and losses) will be incurred in the future as a result of the changes that took place in the past.

7. If some species are doing well in other jurisdictions, it is unnecessary to protect them in Alberta.

There seems to be a tacit assumption and rationalization that if these species survive elsewhere this is good enough. This assumes the level of concern and protection in other jurisdictions is sufficient to maintain these populations over the long term.

The line of reasoning sometimes follows this path – species at risk are often on the edge of their geographic range and this portion of the population is not important. However, outliers are key to population persistence, given things such as climate shifts. This argument ignores the possible genetic adaptations that are particular to Alberta and what that provides as a long-term survival strategy for the population.

In the maintenance of imperilled (and other) wildlife populations we should treat borders as the administrative lines they represent, not as range boundaries. Aldo Leopold wrote eloquently in *A Sand County Almanac* about the fallacy of thinking that someone else will protect imperilled species with, "Relegating grizzlies to Alaska is about relegating happiness to heaven; one may never get there."

8. Wildlife is abundant; how could biodiversity be declining?

Biodiversity isn't simply about numbers of commonly seen wildlife species. Abundant population sizes of Canada geese, mule deer, or robins do not signal that biodiversity maintenance is being achieved. Nor does an influx of English sparrows, starlings, brook trout, crested wheatgrass, or pansies indicate we can compensate for lost native wildlife or plants by substituting exotic, non-native species.

Some wildlife species can co-exist with us, even in urban settings and on landscapes largely used up for our economic pursuits. But those generalist species do not indicate the full suite of biodiversity maintenance, nor are they indicators of healthy, intact landscapes.

Wildlife may only seem "abundant" in the limited context of our memory span. Present wildlife diversity, abundance, and distribution may not equate to past conditions. The shift, the losses of spaces and species, occurs beyond our awareness and reckoning. This is the phenomena of "shifting benchmarks." We think the landscape and resources of today is the "full pie." It's part of our combined arrogance and ignorance.

The reality is today's pie is a mere slice of yesterday's pie. And so it goes – without an appreciation of the progressive thinning of the remaining slice, the pie can, and does, eventually wink out of existence.

9. *Absence of wildlife means no wildlife use.*

If we don't see wildlife, it must mean the area has little importance for wildlife. Failure to observe wildlife does not equate to wildlife absence. There was controversy over the proposed drilling of sour gas wells in the Whaleback in the early 1990s. The then minister of energy took a helicopter tour of the elk winter range, saw no elk, and concluded there were no wildlife issues. The flight was in August, not the best of times to survey ungulate winter range.

Not all habitats are created equal, are equally used year-round or between years, are equally distributed, or are equally critical. However, all habitats have to be present to ensure species survival over the range of variability. All habitats have to be connected to ensure species survival over the long term. Redundancy is important and shouldn't be viewed as surplus to a species's needs, or to ours.

10. My actions aren't a risk to wildlife; it's the activities of others.

The reasoning includes arguments such as: I don't hunt, fish, watch birds, visit parks, or care about polar bears and tropical rainforests. I don't kill wildlife (or much of it) or cause it any problems. The links between wildlife and personal choices to maintain wildlife have still not occurred in a major way. A Cows & Fish survey found almost no respondents felt they had any impact on fish and fish habitat. So no one who flushes a toilet, flips on a light switch, or lives in a home made of wood has any impact on fish? How do you spell "dissociative"?

Our settlement patterns, economic activities, transportation networks, recreational activities, and our homes have a footprint overlain on landscapes that have, or had, value to wildlife species. Even without direct mortality, we reduce or remove the productive capacity of the landscape for many species. The result is indirect mortality and a loss of biodiversity.

The list of myths could be longer, but the issues raised are in no small way related to our general lack of ecological literacy. Survey after survey demonstrates the value of environmental awareness and education in public support for environmental programs and actions. Yet Alberta's ecological IQ still seems too low to achieve progress on many species and spaces, especially the imperilled ones. Indeed, it may be too low to keep other creatures off the lists of the damned. We need a short course in ecosystem awareness, an Ecology 101, at all levels – individual, corporate, agency, and political.

Wendell Berry, the farmer/philosopher, captured this intent and exposed a fundamental myth with:

We have lived our lives by the assumption that what
was good for us would be good for the world. We
have been wrong. We must change our lives so that
it will be possible to live by the contrary assumption,
that what is good for the world will be good for us.
And that requires that we make the effort to know
the world and learn what is good for it.

Wildlife (the full expression of biodiversity) form part of our
stories, our history, our lives, and our landscapes. They are also
a measuring stick of the health of our world. We define ourselves by the same landscapes, the same sense of space, and the
same diversity of areas as do wildlife. They can slip to become
only a part of our memory and worse – we may forget them
altogether.

The last myth is we can do without biodiversity and the intact landscapes that support wildlife. We think we have broken
free of our ecological constraints, but the reality remains those
relationships endure and simultaneously place us within the
land and embed the land within us. We might consider moving
more slowly on the landscape, with a greater sense of humility,
and being more mindful of our fellow travellers.

ONCE THERE WERE TROUT

———

Once there were bull trout in this stream. There were cutthroat
trout too. Once the stream was clear and cold and overhung
with willows. With patience and stealth, you could see the
trout slowly sculling in the current. The white edge of their fins

focused your attention on the drab, torpedo-shaped bull trout. Cutthroat trout had an iridescent hue to them, so they flashed liquid sunshine as they squirted for cover.

In hand, after a short fight on the end of a fly rod, you could smell the forest, the moss, leaves, and other bits of detritus that reminded you of the magic of this place. The trout arched in your hand, a polished, muscular bit of torsional resistance to the air. On its sides were the dots and spots, the patterns of which displayed the beginnings of this creature – ancient, mysterious, and dynamic.

But we couldn't connect the dots from clean, cold water free of sediment to these trout, ones that had several millennia of struggle, survival, and evolution imprinted in their DNA. The trout in the hand was older than the moment. It was as deep as time. The ancestors of this fish were born when the land was new. We ignored and paid no attention to the natural maps and mazes in front of us – to what those trout told us, how they were an indicator and integrator of their watersheds, and what we might have learned, as people dependent upon water, as were they.

Now, sadly for this stream and similar ones, these trout are gone. The losses include Athabasca rainbows and Arctic grayling. Instead of the freshness of spruce and the tang of alder, these watersheds reek of greed and gasoline. The trout cannot be put back, made whole, made right again. There is little left of these streams, the habitat basics, to make them whole again.

An absence of trout has made the health of these streams seem less important, restoration less urgent, and more harm inevitable. As Andrew Nikiforuk, a prescient Canadian journalist, pointed out to me, "Vandalized landscapes, like homes with broken windows, tend to invite more abuse."

In those streams of the past, where trout lived, all was older than us, wiser, and more capable of enduring. We could have, we should have, done better.

In hindsight it is no mystery how so much of the cornucopia of native trout disappeared, declined, and deteriorated over time. Elderly anglers I interviewed in 1993, with memories of fishing before the Second World War, and one who could still recall the cool, curving world of trout before the First World War, regaled me with stories of a largely forgotten world of trout abundance and sizes.

One bull trout, they said, was so large it fed several hungry surveyors, with leftovers. Spawning runs of bull trout where none exist today. Cutthroat catches of several hooked per minute, leading to tired casting arms. Stringers of trout – yards long, pounds heavy.

But the world they described was foreign to me. The watersheds were largely devoid of roads and what roads existed had little traffic, logging was selective and small-scale, there were no dams and few diversions, oil and gas exploration and development was in a nascent state, and there were, relatively speaking, few anglers. Mining was concentrated, mostly to one major watershed, where the spectre of future trout declines was evident.

My uncle was a coal miner in that watershed, the Crowsnest. He was also an angler, with a metal telescoping rod strong enough to heave an anvil out of the water. My uncle didn't play a trout, nor did he practise catch and release, but he did look down his nose at those that netted, speared, and dynamited trout. I never heard him talk, though, about how the river would turn black with coal. Most people, including him, didn't see and couldn't see the cost to trout of doing business. This tendency, to be perceptually blind to the effects of economic and recreational pursuits, haunts us still.

But some, such as the elderly anglers I interviewed, watched and were able to comment on the juggernaut of development and the progressive, cumulative shifts in essential trout habitat that eroded the distribution, abundance, and sizes of trout they had experienced. They were clear on what had been lost, because they had seen it near its best.

Even so, before these anglers' memories of aquatic exuberance, trout ranged far from the mountains, through the foothills and onto the plains. As good as the memories of those elderly anglers were, even those benchmarks were fluid. Many more shifts in perception would occur before trout hit the wall and there was a recognition of the magnitude of loss. And so it goes. Every generation thinks it has the benefit of the best until the progressive and unnoticed erosion of the best turns it to dust.

We should not be confused about why native trout disappeared from some streams and declined in others. If confusion exists, it is about how to mount effective recovery efforts. We can use the predictive tools of science for guidance and choose the actions most relevant to a better outcome for trout. We can reach out to others who have confronted this dilemma earlier than us. From those experiences we can learn, avoid some of the pitfalls and blind alleys, and fast track other strategies. But to avoid the chiming of the trout doomsday clock, we must proceed with a sense of urgency.

Native trout aren't all gone, not all are memories, tantalizing us from stories found in old books and captured, frozen in time, in fading black and white photographs. But in our hearts, we must admit they are now a fraction of past numbers and sizes with distributions constrained by our human footprints. They are at a tipping point. Of those that remain we talk of them as threatened, maybe endangered, so perhaps the labels of imperilment confer some greater sense of responsibility to them and their future.

River, forest, climate, and time designed native trout. These are not simple ciphers, easily decoded, enumerated, and categorized, but are sensations of a complex, intertwined, and integrated system. The system has a pulse, a rhythm easily disrupted by the wheel, chainsaws, diversions, and non-native species introductions. For the eventual survival of native trout, we must reduce those human actions that increase their living costs.

We can waste time apportioning blame, or we can collectively agree that allowing native trout to wink out while we debate is untenable. If we continue to do what we've always done, native trout will be gone. It is a predictable pathway, one that sage-grouse and caribou are currently on. If we think time will change the outcome for native trout, we are delusional. Governments, industry, anglers, recreationalists, and a host of others have been part of the problem. Will everyone agree to be part of the solution?

Biologists are asking what elements are required to restore populations and what level of recovery will provide robust and self-sustaining populations. Politicians need to be asked whether recovery efforts are adequately resourced, especially to beat the rush to extirpation of some populations, in some streams. Is there the political will to stay the course of recovery, especially if it means slowing down the pace of economic development? Industry and other provincial government departments need to be asked if they have their collective shoulders to the wheel of recovery.

We conservationists (including anglers) need to be asking if recovery efforts are proceeding in a timely way and what our role is to ensure recovery efforts are successful. We might ask if we are willing to temporarily exchange some of our fun for native fish recovery. Albertans need to confront the reality that changes are necessary in the way public lands and resources are managed if we are to retain significant parts of our natural heritage.

How soon will the answers be provided? You tell me. Better yet – tell the trout.

IT'S A CUTTHROAT WORLD FOR THE CUTTHROAT TROUT

The trout is called a "cutthroat," not from personality or behaviour, but rather for a brilliant vermilion/orange slash on the underside of its jaw. In the clear streams of the upper Oldman and Bow watersheds seeing the flash of a cutthroat, a splash of liquid sunshine, is to experience a natural piece of art.

Duncan McEachran, a veterinary surgeon, travelled in 1881 from Fort Benton, in Montana, to Calgary along the foothills of the Eastern Slopes in search of possible ranch locations. Not only was he stunned by the potential of the foothills grasslands to support a livestock industry, but he also commented on the streams that ran clear and cold and were "full of trout...which are most delicious to eat."

Cutthroat trout were described by the North-West Mounted Police in 1890 as "speckled" or "brook" trout with, "the special mark is a red patch on each side of the throat, where it joins the mouth, and, in the fish of 12½ lbs and upwards, a reddish tinge along the belly." In living memory there are no examples of cutthroat trout of "12½ lbs and upwards."

A photograph from 1902 depicts two long stringers of cutthroat trout with an additional large pile of trout on the ground. There are over a hundred trout taken in what appears to be a day's fishing trip on Trout Creek, part of the Willow Creek watershed.

Later, in 1948, R.B. Miller, one of Alberta's first biologists to undertake systematic fisheries inventories, surveyed streams in the Willow Creek watershed. He commented on the productive nature of these streams and the overall abundant trout in contrast to other Eastern Slopes streams he had surveyed, including ones in the Bow River watershed. However, on Trout Creek, within the forest reserve and downstream, he observed sheet erosion from overgrazing and poor livestock salting locations. He was able to catch only a few cutthroat trout in the stream.

Another image from 1902 shows three anglers on the banks of Willow Creek near Fort Macleod holding large stringers of cutthroat trout. No trout, cutthroat or other, have swam in the lower portion of Willow Creek for decades.

From the June 15, 1903, edition of the *Calgary Herald* comes this insight into cutthroat populations in the Bow River watershed: "Two sportsmen went out after trout at Fish Creek one day last week and as a result brought back 400 fish."

Yes, anglers were greedy, wasteful, and even rapacious, but the bigger impacts that destroyed most of the trout habitat happened at a landscape scale.

Although now a dim memory in the minds of older anglers, the Spray lakes and the Spray River were renowned for the number and size of cutthroat trout produced. R.B. Miller reported that anglers caught 1,058 trout, many up to 60 centimetres long, from the Spray River in 1948. The cutthroat populations of this watershed were a unique blend of lake- and stream-dwelling species. All of this ended with the development of hydroelectric dams in the late 1940s. In *A Cool Curving World,* Miller wrote,

> One great dam converted them [two natural lakes]
> into a vast, barren reservoir, fifteen miles long and
> two hundred feet deep. The beautiful cutthroat
> trout that formerly made them famous has already
> vanished, and in place of the green wooded slopes is
> the now familiar desert of mud, trash and stumps.

At the very least, when we flick a light switch on, we might consider the trout that died so we could illuminate our homes. A dramatic change in cutthroat waters was dam development. In the Bow watershed, ten hydropower dams and four irrigation dams in the Oldman watershed have irrevocably changed these systems and dramatically reduced the cutthroat populations that used to exist.

The combination of overfishing and industrial land uses depleted cutthroat populations until a cry rose from sport-fishers to restock lakes and streams. Although cutthroat from the Spray system were used initially, non-native rainbow trout, which were easier to obtain and rear, became the species of choice for stocking efforts. Cutthroat populations, already hit by overharvest and habitat issues, were overwhelmed by the new, foreign neighbour in their midst.

Pouring rainbow trout into cutthroat streams resulted in unsafe sex because the species are so close on the trout evolutionary tree. Hybrids result from these interactions. The loss of genetic purity among cutthroat populations may seem insignificant, but there is a problem.

Native cutthroat trout have evolved in streams of the Eastern Slopes for over 12,000 years. Their genetics contain the code that has allowed them to thrive and prosper in spite of the variability of these aquatic systems. They could have survived long into the future. Rainbow/cutthroat crosses have mixed and diluted genetics, untested in the crucible of time. They lack the "right stuff" for persistence. The remaining, remnant pure strains of cutthroat are precious.

Although Alberta still has not completed a comprehensive inventory of all cutthroat waters to determine the status of the species, it is apparent that perhaps less than 5 per cent of historical habitat is currently occupied in the Bow watershed, somewhat more in the Oldman. Cutthroat trout are now designated as threatened.

Early examinations of the fishery resources of the province undertaken by the Alberta and Saskatchewan Fishery Commission in 1910–1911 led to the statement about cutthroat trout, that "of all the indigenous fish of the western streams none are more worthy of preservation."

In spite of this sentiment, according to the *Alberta West-slope Cutthroat Trout Recovery Plan (2012–2017)*, in all of the streams of the Bow and Oldman watersheds where this species used to be numerous, there are only 51 genetically pure populations left.

That is approximately 5,500 fish remaining in both watersheds, which is about the present human population of the Crowsnest Pass. Not so very long ago, cutthroat trout outnumbered people in Alberta.

IT'S A BEAR MARKET FOR BULL TROUT

Bull trout resemble baseball bats with fins, torpedo-shaped and similarly dangerous. Think of bull trout as the aquatic version of a grizzly bear – a summit predator, except with fins and gills.

And, as with grizzlies, the range of the bull trout has shrunk drastically.

Historically, bull trout ranged throughout the Peace watershed nearly to the Peace–Athabasca delta. In the Athabasca watershed they were commonly found in the confluence with the Pembina River and occasional catches were made downstream to beyond Fort McMurray. The North Saskatchewan watershed had bull trout well below present-day Edmonton, to perhaps the confluence with the Redwater River. The range of bull trout in the Red Deer River watershed extended to almost Drumheller. In the Bow and Oldman watersheds the range extended to the confluence of those two rivers near Bow Island.

The huge geographic range in bull trout distribution isn't surprising when one considers that adults will drop down from their home ranges in the upper reaches of watersheds into more productive waters to feed on other species of fish.

Sam Steele, the famous member of the North-West Mounted Police, wrote in his memoir, *Forty Years In Canada*, of the building of Fort Saskatchewan, a police post east of Edmonton on the banks of the North Saskatchewan River, in the spring of 1875. One of his memories was, "Our food at this time consisted of pemmican and mountain trout. The smallest trout weighed 5½ lbs., and many were over 12 lbs. These fish have a flavour quite equal to salmon, but one does not soon tire of them."

He could have only been speaking of bull trout, since no other salmonids would have been present (other than mountain whitefish). Steele was born and raised in Ontario and would have known trout from experiences there. Bull trout were likely caught out of the river, since there would have been no way to transport them from distant upstream locations.

In 1890, the NWMP became interested in fish stocks in the rivers of Southern Alberta and asked officers posted at various detachments for reports on the status of populations. Officer McIllree's response, from the records of the Calgary post and summarized in *Fishing in Southern Alberta*, was "When I fished this section about fourteen years ago [1876], the rivers and streams teemed with fish. Now, it is very different." One infers that he was talking about trout populations, especially the bull trout. That a decline in fish populations was observed so early suggests the beginning of a negative trend that persists to current times.

An image from 1893 exists in the Glenbow Archives, showing two anglers on Callum Creek, a small tributary to the Oldman River. Arrayed around them are no less than 60 trout, several of which are bull trout. If McIllree's observations of change are correct, imagine the catch those two anglers would have had a decade or so earlier. Today, there are no trout in Callum Creek.

Anglers were catching bull trout in Waskasoo Creek, within the city limits of Red Deer, in 1916. Wherever bull trout were caught there was antipathy if not outright aversion toward them. Red Deer anglers would catch bull trout because there were no others, but would not recognize them as "official" trout. Fish yes, trout no.

In the meetings held by the federal Alberta and Saskatchewan Fishery Commission of 1910 and 1911 there were almost universal recommendations to get rid of bull trout, because of their "predatory" habits and perceptions they were a "weedy fish, unworthy of protection." One local fish and game association suggested in an early article in the *High River Times*, "these fish [bull trout] should be destroyed by dynamiting the places they are known to infest." As a consequence, it wasn't until 1927 that bull trout were offered the same regulatory protection as other trout and gamefish species had since the 1890s.

Elk Creek is a tributary of the Clearwater River west of Rocky Mountain House. In the early 1900s, when this area was the back of beyond, it was reported to have large numbers of bull trout and mountain whitefish. Roads and trails were few, and in contrast to today, the Alberta Forest Service kept these roads gated and locked, allowing no vehicle access. This was the domain of the horseman and the very determined hiker.

In the early 1950s the Forestry Trunk Road was constructed through the foothills of the Eastern Slopes, eventually connecting Coleman to Grande Prairie. Much of the previously unroaded, undeveloped portions of forest reserve watersheds became subject to new roads, recreational traffic, logging, mining, and petroleum exploration and development. All of these roads produce sediment, and many deliver sediment to streams containing native fish.

According to early fisheries inventories, Elk Creek supported a self-sustaining population of bull trout along its length in the 1950s and 1960s. By the late 1970s a combination of overfishing, overgrazing, and other land uses, including the close proximity of the Forestry Trunk Road to most of the stream, had reduced the bull trout of the lower section to a few individuals. Bull trout were few and far between when I fished the creek in the late 1960s.

In the upper sections of the stream there were 80 bull trout/ km in 1968; 13/km in 1979; and by 1987 only one bull trout was caught. Since it takes more than one fish to make a population, one might have considered bull trout in Elk Creek as missing 40 years after the Forestry Trunk Road crossed it in the early 1950s. But bull trout are resilient.

More recent inventories in Elk Creek by provincial fisheries biologists have shown the positive effect of more restrictive angling regulations. In 1985 the bag limit was severely reduced and at the same time the minimum size of fish that could be kept was increased. This was followed in 1995 with a zero-bag limit, which is the case currently. Bull trout have responded positively to a high of 316/km in 2008.

Since the rigour of fisheries science wasn't applied in earlier times, it is difficult to know whether the increased numbers of bull trout found in recent inventories represent the full potential of Elk Creek or are only a fraction of historical abundance. While the trend is encouraging, issues such as sediment from logging, roads, and recreational vehicle use still present bull trout with challenges.

One might be tempted to conclude that overfishing stemming from better road access is the primary problem confronting bull trout. The extirpation of a unique bull trout population in the upper Crowsnest River tells another story. The trout survived a long time against the combination of overfishing and illegal fishing with nets, spears, and dynamite. However, the cumulative effect of logging, mining, urban development, river channelization, and blockages to critical spawning sites on streams tributary to the Crowsnest River wiped out bull trout in about one human lifespan. Bull trout might have coped with fishing, but they were unable to overcome compounding, multiple, watershed-scale issues.

Bull trout have now been eliminated from the Redwillow and Beaverlodge rivers, the North Saskatchewan River below Drayton Valley, the upper Crowsnest watershed, including Crowsnest Lake, the Willow Creek watershed, the Red Deer River downstream of Dickson Dam, the Rosebud River, the lower Bow River, the lower Oldman River, and the lower St. Mary, Waterton, and Belly rivers. In many watersheds bull trout may have gone missing before we recorded their presence.

Even within the current range of bull trout there are substantial contractions and more to come. In 2005, Travis Ripley, then a provincial fisheries biologist, predicted extirpation of bull trout from 24 to 43 per cent of streams in the Kakwa River Basin subject to logging and roading in as little as two decades. If the prediction proves correct, time's up for many of these populations.

There are a few examples of bull trout reoccupying former

range. The late Wayne Roberts, past curator of the Zoology Museum at the University of Alberta, found them again in the North Raven River, where they had been missing for more than 80 years. Overfishing, habitat changes, and competition from introduced brown trout likely contributed to the demise of bull trout in this stream. But restoration of riparian habitats with stream bank fencing, starting in the 1970s, coupled with protective angling regulations, has provided bull trout with the spark to resettle in old homes.

The jury is still out on other recolonization efforts. Bearberry Creek, a small tributary to the Red Deer River, once had an abundant population of large bull trout. Long-time residents interviewed by Rocky Konynenbelt, a provincial fisheries biologist, recalled bull trout large enough to be "cut up and fried like salmon steaks" in the 1920s. The population dwindled and was reportedly gone by the 1950s.

In the 1960s the stream was channelized downstream of Highway 22 and a weir installed in 1980 to deal with chronic flooding issues in the town of Sundre. The weir was a barrier to upstream fish movement. A fish way around the weir was installed in 2004 and, almost as if they were waiting for the gate to open, bull trout moved upstream into Bearberry Creek.

It is doubtful whether bull trout moving back upstream will find much resembling their former homes. In 1951 R.B. Miller and Martin Paetz surveyed Bearberry Creek and reported, in *Preliminary Biological Surveys of Alberta Watersheds 1950–1952*, "The banks are...mostly overgrown with a heavy tangle of willows and shrubs." In an overview flight of the watershed in 2005 this expression of riparian health was the exception. Substantial riparian recovery will have to occur to provide necessary habitat conditions, to moderate stream temperatures, and to filter sediment from farm fields before bull trout can truly be said to have reoccupied their former range in Bearberry Creek.

The provincial government's recent *Bull Trout Conservation Management Plan (2012–2017)* summarizes population status for the species. Remarkably, the report escaped the spin doctors of the province's Orwellian Ministry of Truth. Its authors clearly make the case bull trout are in trouble. No wonder the species has been designated as threatened. Population trends indicate that 61 per cent of bull trout core areas (there are 51 in the province) show declines and 39 per cent are stable or increasing.

However, tucked into the tables and turgid narrative of the management plan are a series of red lights flashing out danger signals to be interpreted and decoded. "Stable" populations are still below their historical levels and the word doesn't imply the population is healthy, only that there have been no changes in survey results over the short time of monitoring. A handful of populations were shown to have increased in numbers over time, but most exist in areas protected from industrial land-use pressures. A close examination leads to the conclusion that 94 per cent of the provincial bull trout population is still in trouble.

In many ways the detractors of bull trout got their wish. Bull trout have been virtually extirpated in many watersheds. George Colpitts, writing on trout conservation in the early years of Alberta in *Fish Wars and Trout Travesties*, concluded that bull trout "faced the brunt of pioneer vigilantism, the harassment of interbreeding foreign bullies and only a modicum of protection by fisheries officials."

It's a "bearish outlook" for bull trout, a pessimistic future given their range has shrunken and continues to do so, and numbers are declining.

VILLAIN OR VICTIM –
THE BLACK AND WHITE OF MAGPIES

My grandparents weren't birdwatchers; they were homesteaders carving out a living in a new land. When they settled west of Red Deer in 1900, even if there had been spare time and they had been observant birders, the resplendent, obvious magpie would not have made the bird list.

It's not that magpies were ever totally absent from the native wildlife assemblage of western Canada, but some did go missing for a while. Magpies were part of the bison ecosystem and they too all but vanished along with the bison. With the extirpation of bison from grassland, parkland, and boreal landscapes, the food they provided – dung, insects, and their carcasses – disappeared. So too did many of the wildlife species associated with this food resource, such as coyotes, wolves, bears, ravens, crows, and magpies.

In step with the collapse of the bison economy, by the late 1880s there were no magpies left in Central Alberta. The bird was unknown to early settlers (such as my grandparents) in the Red Deer District according to Frank Farley, an early Camrose hunter/naturalist. A remnant population survived in the Cypress Hills of southeastern Alberta.

As my grandparents and other farmers began raising crops and livestock, some vestiges of a substitute food source for magpies were established. With agricultural expansion, magpies began to reappear around the time of the First World War. By 1939 their range had extended north to Grande Prairie, and they became a much more commonly encountered bird.

The phoenix that was the magpie did not seem to receive rave reviews for their reappearance. Fine proportions and colouration, coupled with intelligence, did not make magpies friends with farmers. Even Kerry Wood, the famous Red Deer naturalist who observed reasoning ability among magpies, contended in *A Nature Guide for Farmers*, the birds were "devoted to evil pursuits at all times of the year." Magpies were seen as implacable foes and, if not the devil incarnate, at least his standard bearers.

In the farming community I was raised, it was taken as the gospel that magpies were evil. Didn't they pick out the eyes of newborn calves and lambs? They competed with livestock at feed troughs, raided farm poultry yards, killing young chicks and other valuable, insect-eating birds. When I worked for one of the neighbours, he became apoplectic at the thought of magpies eating some of the grain put out for cattle. I was instructed that the rusty pump shotgun in the pumphouse was to be used liberally and without mercy to shoot magpies.

In an ecologically deficient age, when random observation and stories trump evidence, wildlife deemed as nuisances are persecuted. Magpies had started to develop a bad reputation even as early as the late 1920s, and by the 1940s had become defined as "vermin" in popular opinion and among government agencies, hunting groups, and conservation interests. The invective was based on poorly informed but well-established notions that led to a variety of "control" programs.

Bounties were established, with cash rewards for egg collections and legs of birds. One can only speculate on the stench from rotten eggs and putrefying legs turned in at collection depots. Bloodthirsty and cash-poor children, me included, raided nests for eggs, chopped off legs, and destroyed nests (not realizing that in the process we were eliminating the source of wealth).

Military-style armed marches, with gunners lined up in formation along the four sides of a hunt area, were organized to kill coyotes, crows, and magpies. No records exist of any of the participants being shot as the circle of excited gunners tightened. Advice was provided on shooting magpies over bait, especially in the winter. Designs for magpie traps were provided. One of my early mentors and I built these and learned magpies were smarter than us. In 1959 the government of Alberta began to set out strychnine poison baits to control magpies.

Hunters, seeing a decline in waterfowl and upland game birds beginning in the 1930s, saw magpies as part of the array of enemies of sought-after quarry. Something had to take the blame and although overhunting, drought, and changes in habitat from agriculture were the most evident causes, magpies and their ilk took it on the beak.

In this full-scale war on birds like magpies, there was a split. Farmers and many hunters saw only the black side of the bird. Others on the white side, perhaps more enlightened, argued the birds created a net benefit to society by consuming more insects and weed seeds than cereal grains, poultry, and game bird eggs.

Beginning in the 1960s, the ardour for bounties and control

programs diminished. Rational reviews of engaging and recruiting children to kill thousands of gophers, crows, and magpies deemed this was unethical and those practices stopped. Science began to provide evidence about the futility of control programs on predators and nuisance wildlife.

Bounties and other methods of population control have proven to be mostly a triumph of activity over progress. Removal of too many animals undermines population stability, the ability to self-regulate. It can and has resulted in not less but more of the problem species.

Removal of some species can cause cascading effects down the food chain, increasing populations of wildlife species that were not a problem before control programs. Killing coyotes to benefit game birds allowed fox numbers to rise, since they were no longer suppressed by their canid cousins. Game birds declined even faster under fox predation.

The net effect of the war on magpies (and others) was the reality this was improving the lot of those remaining birds, allowing them to raise larger families. The birds were able to easily fill the void created by our feeble efforts at population control. In effect, magpies won the war.

We still harbour ill will toward magpies. If I were defending magpies in a court of law, in front of a dispassionate judge, I would turn to the plaintiffs. "If you so dislike this bird for its predatory habits and waking you up early with its raucous racket, why did you create such ideal conditions for it to live?" Because that is the case, the evidence.

With our urban landscaping, fruit trees, gardens, and especially our garbage, magpies have hit the motherlode, a nirvana of habitat conditions. In country settings, with livestock and cereal crop production, we have done the same. We have become the new bison for magpies.

If ever there was a time for reflection on wildlife that share space with us, it is now. The magpie is an elegant, immaculately attired bird with a saucy attitude. They are smart and resourceful and will profit from living with us, no matter what we do to thwart their efforts. We might as well resign ourselves to being in this together.

THE ANSWER IS BUFFALO. WHAT WAS THE QUESTION?

———

After virtual extirpation in the declining years of the 1800s, now in the 2000s bison reintroductions have become all the rage. Recovery of such a totemic and symbolic species has great promise. But in the enthusiasm of the moment there is also the potential for getting ahead of what might be the prime directive, the goal that bison are thought to help achieve. As well, goals differ, from landscape restoration to farmed bison.

There are many reasons for bison repatriation (or rematriation as Indigenous Peoples view it), and it would be good to separate them to discern the different motives and the role bison might play. The many bison dreams fall into one or more of the following categories:

- **Ecological bison** – an integral part of biodiversity protection is understanding and keeping the drivers of ecosystems, especially keystone species.

Bison were a keystone species in grassland ecosystems. In *The Ecological Buffalo*, Wes Olson makes a compelling case for the integral part bison perform in maintaining and supporting grassland ecosystems.

- **Cultural bison** – bison were the epicentre for Indigenous plains tribes for millennia and were a driver of their culture. As Leroy Little Bear, University of Lethbridge professor, observed about culture in *The Buffalo Treaty*, "Bison are a symbolic, iconic notion that strengthens and nurtures these beliefs." Loss of bison was a significant, devastating cultural loss – restoring populations is a visible step toward regaining part of a driver of culture. This might include the availability of bison meat as a tangible link to the past and a culturally appropriate meal for the future. Putting bison back could be seen as reconciliation, righting past wrongs done to Indigenous Peoples.
- **Symbolic bison** – in the same way that the Canadian beaver, the American bald eagle, and other species are viewed, bison are an icon of grassland ecosystems and their absence is a motivator for re-establishment. Bringing back bison shows we have the will and ability to restore missing species. Those actions are an indicator of our environmental and stewardship commitment. Restoration of bison in Banff National Park is an example.

- **Socio-political bison** – restoring wild bison populations is viewed as a way to re-establish all of the wildlife species that existed in the 1800s on landscapes that have proven difficult to farm economically, especially with the spectre of climate change. An example is the Buffalo Commons, a controversial concept to create a vast nature reserve in parts of ten states in the western United States. It was envisioned that bison would replace conventional agriculture, which is viewed as unsustainable in a semi-arid landscape. A smaller-scale example is the American Prairie initiative, focused on eastern Montana.

- **Economic bison** – as an alternative to cattle, bison are touted as a high-value source of lean, nutrient-dense, naturally grown meat. Bison can be marketed to people concerned about the intensive factory aspect of the livestock industry. As a species with a long evolutionarily fit to grasslands, bison can provide low input costs (once appropriate fencing is built), don't need shelter, and can maintain themselves on native range (as long as the carrying capacity of pastures isn't exceeded).

Each of these reasons has bison as a tool to reach an outcome, but the outcomes can be quite different, maybe even mutually exclusive. In their original setting, bison were not impeded in their movements by any human infrastructure. Sustainability of bison populations was a function of scale, the ability to move to new foraging opportunity, and of long periods of intervening rest for the grasslands between bison visits.

Today's landscapes do not generally provide that flexibility. There are few places left with sufficient space to allow movement patterns that keep bison grazing below the carrying capacity of the system. Bison may be the answer to many dreams, but if there isn't sufficient space, the dream can become a landscape nightmare.

To accomplish the maintenance of grassland ecosystems requires disturbance regimes within the range of natural variation. This recognizes that natural disturbances (such as fire, flood, drought, and grazing) have built many of the landscape features and created the opportunities for plants and animals to find appropriate niches and thrive. This happens at both temporal and spatial scales. We have little influence over most natural disturbances, with the exception of grazing.

A major part of grassland integrity and biodiversity is maintaining native vegetation species diversity, differences (heterogeneity), and structural attributes as key elements.

Native grasslands and especially their grasses were forged out of natural disturbance in a climate of extremes. Lose the native grasses and you might be able to replicate some of the structural attributes of the grassland with agronomic (tame) species. What is difficult, maybe impossible, to restore would be the interactions, complexity, and integrated nature of a diverse native plant assemblage. It might resemble native grassland, might have some of the representative wildlife species, but is still a superficial shadow of the real thing. Just adding bison doesn't change this.

Scale is a key ingredient. While we think big about our developments, we are small thinkers about the one attribute that maintains many species – that of big space, really big space. For any bison dream that is focused on grassland integrity and biodiversity, big space is required. Otherwise, the goal of grassland protection might be churned into dust by overgrazing.

Chris Helzer, with the Nature Conservancy in Nebraska, observed in the *Prairie Ecologist*, "Among some prairie enthusiasts, there seems to be a perception that plains bison are magical creatures that live in complete harmony with the prairie."

Bison were an integral part of native grasslands, and helped forge them and their rich biodiversity. They still do in places such as Grasslands National Park, the Nature Conservancy of Canada's Old Man On His Back Prairie and Heritage Conservation Area and Elk Island National Park, where space provides much flexibility. However, unlike Wood Buffalo National Park, all the others still have space limitations and lack natural regulatory mechanisms (especially predation) that require (or will require) bison management. Populations of organisms increase to fill vacant, suitable habitat and then are regulated by the essential component of their habitat that is in the least supply and by other limiting factors.

When the space shrinks, the number of animals increases and the long rest periods for the range are eliminated. It's very difficult to see any differences between a small bison-grazed pasture and a small cattle-grazed pasture. Bison have been shown to be as prone to overuse of their range as cattle can be when inappropriately managed.

The realities of research indicate there are conservation benefits to using bison, but this happens more so in very large pastures. Even at such scales there are cattle management practices that can be appropriate to the goal. Grazing to achieve a grass-land management impact is the outcome – not necessarily what animal does the grazing. Adaptive management to meet conservation goals may be much easier to accomplish with cattle than with bison. Both cattle and bison are tools to an end – what's key is how they are managed.

First, though, we should sort out what the question is – is it managing for ecological integrity, farming bison, aiding in cultural resurgence, iconic species restoration, or long-term options for arid landscapes in the face of climate change? While bison could be a tool for all of these, it is not a one-size-fits-all approach. Inevitably, there will be ecological limits and thresholds to be addressed. Pragmatically, bison may require higher levels of investment in infrastructure and very different approaches in management than do cattle.

Our enthusiasm for bison shouldn't blind us to the practical realities of today's landscape management. Bison are a part of but not the complete answer.

Chris Helzer summarized the discussion in the following way: "In very large prairie settings, bison may be the best fit – assuming the logistics and costs of owning bison make sense. In other situations, however, deciding whether bison or cattle are most appropriate is not a simple matter. It's a decision that should be based on facts and management objectives – not on aesthetics or mythology."

ECOLOGY FOR DUMMIES

"An investment in knowledge always pays the best interest," said Benjamin Franklin in *The Way to Wealth*. If you can comprehend how something works, how the pieces fit and what this does for you, it is less likely you'll break it. Creating awareness of ecosystem functions, processes, and relevance to humans is the first step to attitudinal and behavioural shifts at individual and community levels.

In *A Sand County Almanac*, Aldo Leopold said, "Every profession keeps a herd of epithets, and needs a pasture where they may run at large." There are some basics in the "herd" of descriptions to help people grasp the ecological underpinnings of our world.

Landscape integrity is the key to sustaining biodiversity. Maintaining native vegetation diversity, differences, and structural attributes are some key elements. To accomplish this requires disturbance regimes within the range of natural variation. This recognizes that fire, flood, drought, and grazing have built many of the landscape features and created the opportunities for plants and animals to survive and thrive. This implies change is necessary and desirable within a range – a dynamic equilibrium – to keep options available.

In one respect, we humans crave stability, which is contrary to the habitat needs of many species. Alternately, our footprint and activities increase the range of variability beyond what is natural. Dividing up the landscape into smaller and smaller pieces results in some species failing to find what they need for their life cycle requirements. Species can't cope and evolve fast enough to survive landscape changes and the new and ever changing normal.

Scale is important. While we think big about our developments, we are small thinkers about the one attribute that maintains many species, that of big space, really big space. Landscape integrity occurs at both temporal and spatial scales. Creatures needing big space that is currently truncated by all of our development zeal can't wait for us to finish and move on, hence our need to think both in time and in space.

Connectivity, the requirement to move easily and safely between habitats, occurs at different scales (local, regional, provincial, national, and global) and implies a much higher level of human co-operation than we currently display. Think of a bird species that nests in the Arctic but overwinters in the tropics. How many different geopolitical areas does it fly through to meet its life cycle requirements?

Fragmentation, through our roads, pipelines, fences, and other linear disturbances, results in habitats of decreasing size, value, and utility. The islands of intact habitats left may not be big enough or well connected enough to sustain many species. This is why cumulative effects are crucial to measuring and modelling the consequences of our economic aspirations. Modelling, although a surrogate for reality, is nonetheless important, because we don't want to turn everything we want to do into an experiment with the high risk of failure.

There are limits and thresholds. Ecological lines in the sand define the ability to survive, or not. They include us humans. This is surely the hardest one for us to grasp, with our unrealistic expectations, recurrent frontier mentality, and the irrational belief that technology will continually nudge the threshold further away. The reality is there is a minimum viable population and habitat size for species – we can't change those rules. Beyond those lines the risk of a species disappearing ratchets up considerably.

Monitoring, over space and time, is a key tool for determining status, trends, and failures. We need to use both tools, cumulative effects modelling and monitoring, to evolve to a more effective ecological accounting practice that aids our decision-making capability. Currently, it seems we base decisions more on coin tosses than on science and predictability.

We need to keep the pieces, keep the connectors, and connect the pieces. Not all habitats are created equal, are equally used year-round or between years, are equally distributed, or are equally critical. However, all habitats have to be present to ensure species survival over the range of variability. All habitats have to be connected to ensure species survival over the long term. There is a need for redundancy, like there is a need for spare parts.

A population is only as safe as its weakest link. The identification of limiting factors and ecological bottlenecks is in its infancy for many species. The acquisition, the discovery in many cases, of that crucial knowledge seems imperative if we are to predict effects on species of our development. Below certain critical thresholds, species are at risk from variations in habitat or from influences from other sources (such as weather, predation, disease, and human-caused mortality). Prudent management of species entrusted to our care implies we know enough to at least cause no more harm, an ecological Hippocratic oath.

Keeping both ecosystem drivers and passengers is an integral part of biodiversity protection. Drivers can be keystone species such as beavers, or predators, pollinators, and recyclers. Drivers can occur at the community level also. Think of riparian areas, native plants, and wood in stream environments. These provide the essential structure for critters to make a living. Ecological processes are drivers – fire, drought, and floods periodically reset the biological clock. Of course, we still don't know all of the drivers of the system, even though we are mounting un-intentional experiments with no monitoring, which could be eliminating both drivers and their passengers.

We don't want to lapse into thinking that many (or any) of the passengers are surplus to ecosystem function. There is a web of interaction and interdependence that can't be discount-ed. Some of it is barely understood, such as the mycorrhizal interactions between plants. And, of course, bad driving by humans can affect all of the passengers, even us, as we are pas-sengers along with wild plants and critters.

Blundering along, unaware of the ecological underpinnings of the world is untenable, even suicidal. Clearly, we need both the tools of science and help from other quarters to assist in attitude shifts and of values. This would provide answers to the consequences of our decisions and allow us to make course corrections.

This suggests that one of the fundamentally important jobs of biologists and conservationists is to develop some level of ecological literacy and create a constituency that knows and cares. Very simply, human decisions can have a disproportion-ately greater impact by changing, sometimes irreversibly, the playing field, and the dynamic equilibrium of the ecosystem is thrown off by the additive effects of our actions.

All of this is important, as a bureaucrat once said to me, "For those who live in the environment." I'm assuming he meant all of us since I can't think of anyone living outside the environment. Maybe some think they do, and they are magically immune to the ecological principles affecting the rest of us.

There is an ancient Buddhist and Taoist proverb that says, "Knowledge is a treasure, the practice is the key to it." The more you know, the greater the obligation is to act.

Illustration by Liz Saunders

3

A Country Almanac

It seems clear beyond possibility of argument
that any given generation of men can
have only a lease, not ownership, of the
earth; and one essential term of the lease
is that the earth be handed on to the next
generation with unimpaired potentialities.

—Roderick Haig-Brown

ERRATICS AND RELICTS

———

Boulders sprinkle the ridgeline of the northeast quarter of section 36. Not of this place, these glacial erratics are hundreds of kilometres from their origins in the mountains of Jasper National Park. Part of the 930-kilometre-long Foothills Erratics Train of quartzite boulders, they trace a glacial conveyor belt from both Cordilleran and Laurentide ice sheets. The end of the belt is not far south of this ridge.

The remaining boulders, now lichen-covered, and with edges rubbed smooth by bison, tell us this is new land, geologically speaking. Some have shattered, likely from freeze-thaw actions.

Exactly when these boulders were deposited on land emerging from beneath ice cover isn't exactly clear. Each, like an aging beauty, is cagey about their birth date.

The erratics blend with the exposed sandstone outcrops, an indication of the intervening years of wind and water erosion scouring some of the ridgeline free of vegetative cover. Droughts, fires, and herds of grazing bison and elk probably started the exposure of the underlying sandstones. With winds that can be gale force, persistent, and coupled with freeze-thaw action, one might think it was hard for even the hardiest of plants to get and retain a toehold on these exposed ridges.

It is on sheltered lee sides of boulders that saskatoon and rose bushes find tentative homes. In the cracks and crevasses grow moss phlox and beardtongue. In one is the weather-beaten dead trunk of a limber pine that succumbed to the elements. This is a tough place, even for the toughest of trees.

Even so, there are 11 limber pine seedlings with their roots driven into the sandstone outcrop. How they established is a bit of a mystery, although limber pines are present upwind on another ridge a kilometre or so away. Maybe a Clark's nutcracker cached some seeds in these sandstone cracks and then forgot about them. These trees must understand that in the prevailing ecological coin toss, heads they win, tails they must flip again.

Where the ground-up remains of bedrock aren't blown away, there are the grasses of rough fescue and Parry's oat grass, creating soil from glacial grindings. This is when the land first developed a memory through the colonizing efforts of grass and forbs, then trees and shrubs.

Grass allowed bison, elk, deer, and even bighorn sheep to find lunch, then home. Once these meals on legs prospered, so did

First Peoples. In the winter, when these animals fed on the cured native grasses, perhaps an Indigenous hunter crouched behind one of the erratics, bowstring taut with a stone-tipped arrow at the ready.

Our friend John Dormaar could find no evidence of Indigenous Vision Quest sites on our ridge, despite its commanding view of the mountains from Chief Mountain north to the Livingstone range. The south-facing slopes, free of deep snow, harbour wintering elk now, and surely did in the past, as well as bison. This place would have been remembered by those to whom meat was fuel and hides and bones were tools of survival.

Perhaps some of their arrow heads, maybe even their bones, are still entombed in the roots of prairie grasses. On the ridgeline lie the scattered ashes of two of our beloved dogs. There, too, will our ashes be scattered to meld with the grass and the earth, to return some of the basic building blocks of life to the place that has given us much joy and inspiration. The fertilizing effects may be insignificant, and the protection of the land into the future with some legal covenant more important.

Sitting on one of the erratics, on a day when the sunshine warmed both from above and up through the heated rock, I thought of others who must have sat there. An early visitor was likely focused on hunting, or watchful for enemy sign. When I think of that early watcher, I realize my time, indeed most the tenure of the current population, is reduced to a mere shrug.

Wildlife holds my attention, whether it is a red-tailed hawk, a mountain bluebird, or the chance to see a grizzly. For watchers, the landscape provides information, key to understanding.

That we can understand the mechanisms, time spans, and evolution that created the landscape initially is a credit to our innate curiosity. However, when I look east to the cultivation of former native grassland and west to the footprint of industry, I see not curiosity, but elements of control. In such settings of resource extraction and exploitation introspection is viewed as a waste of time and memory is made malleable to match today. We resist looking back, yet it is the brink upon which we stand.

When place is transformed into property there seems little choice between preserving a pristine landscape and developing it into one whittled, dug, plowed, and otherwise changed into something denatured.

This place is not free of human manipulation – fencelines, a pipeline right-of-way, a power line, a cabin, and non-native grasses in the lower, moister areas – but it is relatively intact compared to much of the surrounding landscape. As time passes and development pressures continue, the risk is this dab of native landscape, with its ecological processes still functional, will become more and more of a relict – separate, disconnected, and shrinking.

It is irrelevant that we, as temporary owners, are remembered, but there is hope the northeast of 36 will remember its time-tested patterns if some aspect of the wild survives. In a landscape context, change is both inevitable and inexorable; however, our human footprint outpaces any natural evolutionary pressures. This is already evident beyond the boundaries of this small bit of wild.

As in the erratics that remind us of a previous ice age, a largely intact northeast of 36 can be a reminder, maybe even a measure, of the virtue of wild places. It may become an island in a sea of human-tossed change, an indicator of what has passed, and a geography of what might yet be possible. If such places cease to exist, how will anyone know that the wild things formerly seen, felt, and experienced have been subtracted from them? It might be the land is still there, yet the *whole* is dead.

In their rarity, wild places might be considered sacred objects, esteemed and venerated but untouchable by most. Or we could ensure they do not shrink to become relics by treating them with respect and restraint now. I don't think we can afford to abandon these last remnants of the geography of hope.

TRANSITIONS ON THE NORTHEAST OF 36

This quarter section, a place in the foothills of Southwestern Alberta, is in transition, as it has been for millennia. We, the current stewards, have only a fragmentary sense of the waves of change. Wetter periods when the aspen forest marched out onto the fescue grassland, drought and fire that favoured grass over trees, coupled with bison that beat back the encroaching forest and settlement that brought fences, non-native grasses, and a pipeline right-of-way that unleashed a phalanx of invasive weed species, have driven these changes.

When we acquired the land, and it started to own us, a rectangular dugout a little bigger than a basketball court was the only permanent water body. It swelled into a somewhat larger pond in wet years and retreated into its unnatural form in the dry. We took little notice of this until beavers moved in, refurbished a dam, the existence of which we had not realized, and the dugout was flooded to form a larger, jellybean-shaped pond bigger than a football field. Suddenly, the line of old willows made sense. They were the historical shoreline of a former pond.

What we had perceived as a low, marshy area was, indeed, an older pond made by beaver that had been bereft of them for decades. As is the case with many infrequent "wet" spots, they are in fact old beaver ponds of variable shapes and sizes that held spring melt on the landscape. These created glades and doughnuts of aspen and willow growth. Extensive beaver trapping and drainage for cultivation dried out the land, erasing the places of warblers and moose.

As with an occupying army, the beavers soon razed the aspens and willows along the shoreline, reducing them to sharpened stumps. We watched, bemused and alarmed as the woody growth we had protected from grazing with a fence around the pond was logged to build a lodge and a food cache in front of it for winter dining. They did entertain as we watched the leafy branches float to the lodge on a watery conveyor belt in dawn and dusk light. This was often accompanied by a tail slap as they seemed to assert their ownership of the place.

The shallow portion of the pond, formerly a cattail marsh, owned by yellow-headed blackbirds, sora rails, and coots disappeared with the summer foraging of beavers, with muskrats riding the coattails of their larger, furry neighbours. On the island in the pond, a layer of sandbar willow, potentilla, and non-native sweet clover was nibbled down to that of a severely overgrazed pasture.

Shoreward, the aspen forest retreated up the slope, leaving behind a litter of fallen and discarded tree trunks, too big to buck up and move to the lodge. A count of the stems harvested at the end of the first year of beaver residency showed the number to be the average indicated in the scientific literature – about one tree per beaver per day. The barbed wire fence took a terrible beating from falling trees.

Beavers are a force of nature and we did not step in to police them. As we watched through the years, the old forest of aspens began to be replaced with regenerating seedlings and saplings, liberated from the shade of their parents' foliage. These were not chomped, likely because these younger trees have a bitter taste to dissuade beavers. For those that mourn the loss of "their" trees, a little patience is prescribed as new forests emerge.

As logging proceeded, the source of new materials got further from the shore, ratcheting up the risk of a beaver running afoul of a coyote, or larger predators. A strategic shift occurred when beavers began damming up an intermittent tributary, creating a cascading system of ponds, down which new wood could be safely floated. These new ponds kept water on the landscape longer and added a new diversity to the aspen forest, which was appreciated by chorus frogs, shorebirds, and secretive white-tailed deer.

All the ponds attract wildlife, especially in the summer. On a hot August day, a bundle of fur cannonballed down the slope into the main pond, followed by two more. A sow grizzly watched her three cubs swim, splash, cavort, wrestle, and mouth discarded beaver logs and aquatic vegetation. She eventually succumbed and bathed more discretely, having a soak and cooling off.

It's tempting to think of such places as the peaceable kingdom, where all the inhabitants get along and there is no drama such as death. We might have been lulled into that sense with the beavers until one spring when we noticed the lodge, protected as it was with a watery moat around the island, had a huge, gaping hole in its roof. An amateur forensic analysis did not discern the agent of destruction, although our neighbour had noticed bear tracks nearby.

Even with scant evidence, only a bear, probably a grizzly, could have excavated the roof of the lodge, seemingly bomb-proof under two feet of soil and logs. Alpine meadows with ground squirrels, a favourite diet choice of big bears, often look as if a cultivator has gone through them. Grizzly bears have a distinctive hump on their shoulders, and long claws up to four inches long. Both the hump and the claws are traits associated with an exceptional digging ability. For a hungry bear, emerging from hibernation, a beaver (or two) would be viewed as fat on four feet, worth a bit of digging.

Months of observation have confirmed the beaver are gone. In the transition, the pond mourns their passing, as do we. But the cattails have reasserted their dominance of the shallows. Red-winged blackbirds have a set of new perches on a moat of water, safe from predatory coyotes. The aspen forest breathes a sigh of relief. Canada geese could care less, but as vegetation grows taller on the island, their squabbles over territory are more muted as they are visually shielded from one another. Such is the ebb and flow of a beaver pond.

Life will go on; the chorus frogs will sing in the spring, warbler music will resonate from the willows, deer will drink from the pond, and a coyote will walk across its frozen surface in winter, hoping for a muskrat dinner.

As it was, the pond will be again, if we allow natural transitions to occur. In the fullness of time, another beaver or two will find the pond, recognize the advantage of the island for relative safety and the abundant food supply of aspen and willow. They will set up shop, shore up the dam, build a new lodge, raise successive families, and boot them out to find their own ponds. Nature's sequences, patterns, and designs will continue.

I'm not a Bible reader, but the first lines of Ecclesiastes 3 have a resonance: "To everything there is a season, a time for every purpose under the heaven: A time to be born, and a time to die; a time to plant, and a time to pluck what is planted."

If we humans could pay attention, we would see that dreams of stability are illusionary and the reality is that even our lives are in constant flux over time, as is the pond.

WEEDING IN PARADISE

Who knew that paradise has a cost? On our quarter of land there is a cost to the appreciation of nature, of serenity, and of inspiration. Keeping nature natural is an ongoing struggle.

We marvel at the irrepressible life force of plants – the adaptation, the tenacity, and the mobility. With Velcro-like stickers, spear-like skewers, and windblown parachutes, some plants are adept at seed dispersal and seem to march quickly. They establish on bare patches of dirt, on sheltered spots, and in damp areas. I'm speaking mostly about weeds – the noxious, invasive, uber-competitive, and nasty ones, such as creeping thistle (inappropriately named Canada thistle), hound's-tongue, and burdock. Paradise has a weedy garden.

How did these plants get a foothold in paradise? None are native. We brought many plants from other geographies, sometimes with intent, but in the case of weeds, often inadvertently. In their native habitats, these plants had natural controls – here, we are the only control agent. They're akin to a lingering house guest, and if we don't terminate them (the weeds) with extreme prejudice, they prosper.

I would single out burdock to vent my spleen after having picked seeds from the dog and blistering my hands digging out the plant. The plant has ruined a simple, indolent stroll through the forest. There it establishes as advance, single-plant invaders on cow trails and expands, if left undiscovered, into patches of up to a hundred plants, with large, heart-shaped leaves, resembling rhubarb.

As a burdock seed germinates in the spring, it forms a rosette. The leafy solar collector gathers energy for the plant and stores it in the root. As the next spring rolls around, this store allows the plant to burst forth in a tall, leafy form, flower, and set seed. Lots of seed. This biennial strategy is an adaptation to thrive under extreme weather conditions. Marshalling energy over two years rolls the dice for prolific seed production, the driving force for the plant.

We mount regular search and destroy missions to wrest plants from their lair by the roots. Digging them up removes the root, the energy source for continued growth. Finding and destroying the first-year rosettes ensures they will not survive to grow the following year. Doing the same for the second-year growth ensures they will not set seed, if caught early enough in the spring. Constant vigilance is key.

Burdock is known for its clinging burrs that attach indiscriminately to animals, gloves, and pant legs. Anything that moves will move a seed to another location. In particularly infested areas, cattle and other livestock can have so many burrs attached to them, it can affect their health and reduce the value of the animals at market time. Wildlife can be similarly affected.

A Swiss inventor, tired of pulling the burrs from his dog's fur, was inspired and came up with the idea for Velcro fasteners.

Many plants produce similar seeds with grasping, clinging, and sticking features, but burdock gets credit for the invention. It's not enough for me to warm to burdock.

Health advocates, especially ones favouring natural remedies, extol the virtues of burdock. The root, which we painfully dig out, has a natural dietary fibre that improves digestion. Those roots we discard contain considerably stronger antioxidant activity than common fruits and vegetables. Recent studies also confirm burdock root has prebiotic properties useful in improving health. So why aren't people flocking to our place to dig up our burdock? It seems the only health benefit we are achieving is the exercise to remove it from the land.

We term our surveillance patrols "recreational weeding." It gets us out of bed and off the porch. In the recesses of our minds, we know we can never win, completely, against weeds like burdock. Somewhere on the quarter is a plant that has escaped our scrutiny and scorched earth policy. The northeast of 36 will never be a weed-free island in a landscape containing many invasive plants.

With a bit of sweat equity, we can exert a level of control over these plants. This ensures they will never dominate the native plant assemblage and negatively affect biodiversity values. It is part of our stewardship pact with the northeast of 36.

A PALETTE FOR PLEASURE

———

"You can't eat scenery," growled the crusty old rancher. "It's hard to get a fork into it." I reluctantly agreed, but pointed out beauty has a message we can't ignore. Aldo Leopold's answer, more insightful than mine, in *A Sand County Almanac*, was "Our ability to perceive quality in nature begins, as in art, with the pretty. It expands through successive stages of the beautiful to values as yet uncaptured by language."

If you remain ignorant of the native floristic exuberance, especially in spring, you miss an important lesson, not only in beauty but in diversity. An ecological axiom is that in diversity is strength, resilience, and quality. This is something a monoculture of wheat can't give us, although there are economic benefits.

There are some, when gazing at a mountain, a forest, or a grassland, who can only see money. Despite standing in a field of flowers with their subtle scent, or beside a clear-running stream, or in a shady forest with a thunderstorm in the background, all they can hear is the sound of a looney in a cash register, smell only the diesel fumes of a feller-buncher, or feel the vibration from their off-highway vehicle.

A spring wildflower bloom may not fill the pocketbook, but it does excite and inspire thoughts of a landscape intact and healthy. This is something that overwhelms me every spring on the ridgeline of the northeast quarter of section 36, tenuously held by us under legal title. As a spring breeze ripples through the flower heads there is a calm serenity that envelopes me.

If you were to paint the spring wildflowers on the ridge of the northeast of 36, it would require a rainbow palette. Mauve to deep purple are the crocuses, fading to an off-white in the bright spring sun. The shooting stars are a shocking pink, a splash of brightness in patches. Subtle pinks are the Townsendia. Ground-hugging phlox are wedding dress white, as are the diminutive rock cress. Double bladderpod, golden bean, prairie parsley, and balsam root blossoms are Crayola lemon yellow, butter yellow, mustard yellow, and highlighter yellow, respectively. The regal penstemon is royal blue. Three-flowered avens are a deep ruby, resembling a merlot. Anchoring the frame, the backdrop, and the filler are the deep green shoots of rough fescue.

Timing is everything to drink in this feast for the eye and solace for the soul. In wild landscapes there is a time for everything, but everything doesn't last. It seems spring blossoms happen all at once. The scene becomes vibrant with colour and then it's gone. Blink and you miss the rites of spring.

I wonder how many people take in this rite of spring, celebrating the shrugging-off of winter. This is a reminder we are still governed by the seasons, even if we think we are isolated from the vagaries of weather. Spring blossoms are a plant's ultimate gamble against odds of snow, freezing temperatures, and uncertain rain. They remind us that beauty is not only good for the soul but for contemplation. Our survival is as dependent on the same variables as those facing these tenacious plants.

A FIERCE GOLDEN EYE — THE GREAT BLUE HERON

———

It glared at me with huge golden-yellow eyes. I think the bird was sizing me up, calculating if I could be swallowed. One of those golden eyes stared right through me, appraising my bulk as a possible edible. I doubted it, but the great blue heron seemed resolute in the concept. To this bird, everything is a possible heron food unit. I'm glad herons stand only a metre tall. If they were as big as their dining aspirations, we would be in danger.

If it can't swallow me, it can gulp down several stocked rainbow trout from the beaver pond. I don't actually begrudge the bird its due, although I hope by late fall there are enough trout left for us to warrant the cost of stocking.

For most of the summer it waited patiently, or not, for a trout to venture into shallow water close to shore. Patience personified is the great blue heron. Motionless for long minutes and not missing any movement. Delicately tuned radar for prey. With a slight turn of the head, to better calculate the angles and trajectories of the prey, a dart of the bill, and another fish or frog becomes heron food.

This is a bird designed to kill. When a potential meal comes near, the heron folds its neck back. One leg moves in the direction of the prey. In an action too fast to see, the whole body unbends, the bent neck straightens, giving more velocity and power to the stab of the spear-like bill. A specialized neck vertebra acts as a hinge for the forward stab. The prey is either impaled by the bill or grasped in it. Then a gulp, and the energy embodied in the prey becomes the bird's.

Silhouetted in early morning light, the heron took on the appearance of an undertaker, appropriate enough given the amount of death the bird administers. Nothing in a hatchery trout's experience prepared it for the lightning stab and being impaled on a sharp bill and swallowed whole. By the time the event happens, it's too late for the learning. Nature is a hard teacher.

To me, this bird is the modern personification of the avian dinosaur *Archaeopteryx*, although the ancestors of the modern great blue heron never shared the landscape with such creatures. The oldest heron fossils are from the later Pleistocene era, not the older Mesozoic era. Although evocative of an early bird prototype, the modern heron's prehistoric appearance has more to do with successful adaptations – a long, spear-shaped bill, a curvaceous and powerful neck, and long legs.

Despite the loss of an expensive fish, I am intrigued and entertained by the heron. I'm assuming it was the same bird, one that runs a trapline of suitable places to scrounge a meal. We're not friends, or even nodding acquaintances, but I have grudging admiration for the evolution, the strategy, and the patience of the great blue heron. I probably annoy it as it has to keep both an eye on me and on possible prey. Sometimes it's too much and the heron lifts off with an exasperated squawk and heads off to places with less human scrutiny and interference.

Seeing a heron standing motionless beside the pond or methodically striding in the wetland provides a sense the world is functioning as it should, with many of the key pieces in place and an elegance to the way creatures array themselves. A great blue heron is a reminder that the world is made of many parts; none are redundant, and in biodiversity protection lies our salvation. It's worth a few trout and a stare that reminds humans a great blue heron might view us with gustatory interest.

Maybe that appraising eye on us is analogous to the greedy eyes we fix on much of Earth's resources.

THE 14 SEASONS OF THE NORTHEAST OF 36

———

We are blessed (or cursed) with not four but 14 seasons. These are sometimes indistinct, erratic, and the pattern only appears after years of observation. In contemplation of these seasons, there is enough distinction and variation that splitting, rather than lumping them into just four, is necessary. There could be even more seasons, but we haven't discerned them yet.

By the calendar it's spring, but which one? In *tentative spring*, snow flurries, drifts, and a frozen pond say otherwise to the formal seasonal announcement. A lone Canada goose raucously contests the calendar as it circles, fruitlessly looking for an open-water landing spot. There is a small fringe of open water on the wetland's edge. It's enough for one chorus frog to bravely give a raspy, if not somewhat frozen, croak.

A killdeer circles the frozen pond, beseeching it to thaw. It seems to know there must be a pond under that snow and ice. Perhaps a memory from previous years' successful foraging. It lands in the snow, shortly followed by two more birds. They explore on their little stilt legs, jerky and skittering, like the motion in a 1920s film.

We already had one *false spring*, weeks ago, with temperatures on the cabin porch in the high teens. Snow melted away, the pocket gopher mounds were an ooze of black mud, and there were signs of green grass on the sunny side of the cabin.

This is often followed by *rude winter return*, a pounding snowstorm with big wet flakes driven by a wind that turns a quiet drive into a polar expedition. Wind-driven snow is mesmerizing as it hurtles past you on a horizontal plane. It is also the time of the mud-ice-snow transition where no footwear or clothing choice is appropriate.

By the time the crocuses are fully in bloom, even though they might be flanked by snowdrifts, we call it *full spring*. That's not to say another snowstorm (or two) might not blanket them temporarily. This season might linger through the first spring rains, even deluges, until the aspen have sent forth the first light green leaves. We are still uncertain when spring ends and summer officially starts.

We call this period *looks like summer* since we have some heat, and every plant seems to lunge upwards toward the sun. A rainbow of blossoms provides an uncertain sense of the season and then a frost hits and we fear there will be no saskatoons to harvest that year.

The only sure sign that it's summer, other than occasional heat domes, baseball-sized hailstorms, and furious aerial pyrotechnical displays, is how we can read on the porch until late evening amid swarms of mosquitoes. Tree swallows and bats are on active duty, but as is the case in a Russian missile attack, a few biting insects always find their way through the protective wildlife cordon to us.

It's a progression from *tentative summer* to *memory summer*, as we think summer should be but almost always isn't, to *smoking summer*, when we cling to the shady side of the cabin to escape the heat, watch the occasional piece of ash fall, and start inhaling wildfire smoke to begin the equivalent of our pack a day habit.

We recognize the waning of summer and the onset of autumn with cooler nights, but not necessarily cooler days, except for the exceptions when we are caught short weeding on the far side of the place without a jacket. If we've had a hot, dry summer, most plants have given up, closed shop, and retreated to their roots. Greens give way to browns, tans, and whites as the first snow surprises everyone. That would be *surprise autumn*.

Then, as a reward for not running screaming from the place in weather frustration, there is *summer autumn* – what we expect in summer, but rarely get. Beautiful temperatures, cool nights, few insects. At this time, we bookmark that this is an exceptionally fine place to be. It is a season to forget all the other vagaries, frustrations, and issues with other seasons. It is also a time when a false belief sets in that this will not end. Then it does.

A screaming northerly storm, or an easterly one, puts pause to those thoughts of Elysian fields, with freezing temperatures and a snowfall that screams, "Get out of here while you can!" This is *warning winter*. Then the snow goes, temperatures increase, and we enter the *waiting autumn*, when we know winter is impending. It's akin to a child impatiently fidgeting in the interminable period before Christmas. You know it's coming, but waiting for it wears away at you.

When winter does come, it is inconsistent and inconvenient. There is *fleeting winter*. A chinook lays in with those tropical-feeling winds. Snow disappears, going from a solid to a gaseous form without the intervening step of a liquid. It's a relief to the deer and elk. South-facing slopes bare off and the rough fescue is available without the effort of pawing. What's good for them bodes ill for the mice and voles, whose protective snow cover is rudely removed. Suddenly, the rough-legged hawks have the upper hand.

Advantages and disadvantages ebb and flow, especially during *false fleeting winter*. Warm western winds bring not promise but falsehood. A partial melt is immediately followed by plunging temperatures, sometimes within hours. This creates a frozen, cruel crust. Blood on the deer trails shows how the ice lacerates deer legs. But rodents find themselves with a bombproof cover from the predatory hawks and coyotes.

Polar winter can set in multiple times. A polar vortex

descends with sub-zero temperatures that seem to persist for an eternity. The cabin stove requires regular stoking and a trip to the outhouse takes on aspects of an Arctic expedition. Outside, life is cruel. Fat reserves melt away as metabolism tries to moderate the cold. Even the normally chatty chickadees go quiet. Only the croak of ravens breaks the silence.

And then, almost as if by magic, there is water dripping off the roof. Sandhill cranes and swans have apparated, as have robins, all expecting spring of some variety or another.

MUSINGS FROM THE PORCH

There is an ominous hum on the porch, punctuated by sharp pings, as hail sounds on a tin roof, but the sky is cloudless. Part of this strange noise signals it is fall. You don't need a calendar to perceive this – the aspen trees give it away with their golden tones. As days shorten, chlorophyll production slows and then stops. The green that is chlorophyll is destroyed and the carotenoids and anthocyanins that have always been present in the leaf now are unmasked and show their colours. Aspen leaves land on the metal roof of the woodshed with a thud, maybe a whimper or a murmur.

Another sign of autumn is the insect activity, especially the clouds of houseflies on the porch. The hum comes from hundreds of them, all focused on one thing – getting inside the cabin. They probably perceive, in their tiny fly brains, what is coming and want inside to lay eggs for the spring. Some of them seem to overwinter, coming into a buzz when the woodstove heats up the interior.

You know the season of easy living is coming to a close as hornets and wasps swarm over every piece of meat that comes off the BBQ. It's hard to wield both knife and fork as you attempt to repel their incursions with one hand. Mice, too, are disposed to being snug in the cabin, raiding our larder, rather than outside, firmly clenched in the talons of a great horned owl.

Then there are the bears – coursing over the landscape from one chokecherry or buffaloberry patch to another. We shy away from putting on weight; bears require it at this time of year. This is the season of hyperphagia for bears, an intense search for calories to lay on reserves of fat for a long hibernation. There is an urgency in the air, related to declining temperatures, perhaps a touch of frost, and waning daylight hours that triggers an innate, inner switch in wildlife. There are three positions on the switch – eat, store food, or migrate.

There was a time we humans were part of that fall rhythm. We would routinely engage in similar fall patterns. It was a ritual, harvesting and putting food by – canning, smoking, pickling, freezing, and drying essential winter foods. I suppose we still do it to a degree, but the supermarket has become our provisioner, with fresh produce from around the world available at our beck and call. This has freed us from the rigour of preparing for winter and the cornucopia of food items has made us forgetful of the seasons. The red strawberries of winter from California that have the texture and flavour of cardboard should remind us there is no substitute for a locally ripened berry.

I think we have lost something in our inability to recognize and get ready for winter. I don't mean just remembering to put the winter tires on and raking the leaves. My father was a farmer and I think he looked forward to winter without all of the labour, worry, and concerns about the onerous cycle of planting, harvesting, and livestock management. It was a time of quiet, of rest, of contemplation, and of recuperation from a season of watching the clouds for hail, waiting for the next equipment breakdown, and the endless tasks. Autumn signalled that time was close at hand.

No, unlike bears, we humans are in a constant state of hyperphagia, consuming, hustling, being driven, and hyperactive. Beyond the clinical definition of hyperphagia, an excessive compulsion to overeat, we are engaged in an extreme, unsatisfied, unrestrained, and persistent drive to consume. The articles of our consumption are endless. It's not surprising we are exceeding the limits of Earth.

No wonder we are unhealthy, excitable, irritable, unfulfilled, and worried. We've neglected the lessons of the seasons, especially the one of autumn. For most of us there is no seasonal preparation for winter followed by rest and a season of chilling. As a wise colleague, Janna Wowk, observes, "Our biggest mental health challenges today are not that we are too busy, but rather that we are not busy enough doing things worth doing."

Our woodshed is full. The sticky fly strips are up. Every hole a mouse could wiggle through is tamped full of steel wool and sealant. Our shelves groan under the accumulated weight of preserves. Soon smoked trout will join the butchered remains of an elk. We will be ready to enjoy the accumulated pile of books, the companionship of friends over a home-cooked meal, and the sense that our season of preparation has paid off.

We feel bonded to nature, are inspired by it, but the flies and mice can stay outside.

Illustration by Liz Saunders

4

The Progress
of Conservation

A thing is right when it tends to preserve
the integrity, stability, and beauty
of the biotic community.
It is wrong when it tends otherwise.

—Aldo Leopold

CONSERVATION SUCCESSES –
LIGHT AMID THE GLOOM

———

There is criticism, sometimes valid, that there are more conservation doom and gloom stories than ones profiling successes. Unfortunately, the reality is that the former outnumber
the latter. In a *mea culpa*, it is easy to concentrate on the issues
rather than on the solutions. But in my defence, without providing insight on environmental challenges, we can be drawn
into a false sense of progress, even complacency, and assume all
is well outside our doors.

But perspective is important, as in focusing on the Herculean efforts to restore habitats and maintain the ecological and biological processes key to fish and wildlife populations. Part of this is also recognizing the population recovery of some species that required no particular effort on our part, other than to get out of their way.

The test of conservation is not how many projects have been done, how much has been spent on them, or regulatory changes enacted, but rather which ones have worked to remove bottlenecks, leading to population increases to levels where the species is no longer at risk. Examples include conservation efforts for Canada geese, pronghorn antelope, and walleye.

When I started my career as a biologist in the early 1970s, many wildlife biologists were consumed with restoration efforts for Canada geese. Populations had dwindled to levels of concern. Programs such as the goose nesting bale program, promoted in rural Alberta, coupled with transplants of geese to unoccupied habitats, seemed to bring populations back from the brink. With more open water available through the winter, more geese began to overwinter on Alberta rivers. This gave them a reproductive advantage in the spring, further bolstering goose numbers. Once a critical population mass had been achieved, numbers soared.

Increasingly, like us, Canada geese have become urbanized. Cities and towns provide a utopia of green grass on golf courses, parks, and lawns. Adaptation to an urban environment has included new nesting options, such as the balconies of high-rise apartment buildings. Goslings float down to the pavement and then dodge traffic to rear on flood-control ponds, subdivision lakes, and on rivers.

People may not remember geese as a species at risk and there is some ambivalence about the numbers now noisily occupying public park space and the greasy poop left on fairways, lawns, and sidewalks. A senior biologist, now retired but instrumental in restoration efforts, does not want his name associated with this brilliant conservation success story. Because some, including biologists, now refer to geese disparagingly as "sky carp." Turning on the proverbial tap has allowed geese to recover, but now it has become difficult to turn it down.

Pronghorn antelope nearly followed the path of no return taken by their prairie neighbour, the bison. Antelope numbers declined precipitously with the spread of settlement, loss of native range, fencing that impeded movement, prairie-wide, man-caused range fires, and indiscriminate shooting in the late 1800s and early 1900s.

Settlers turned to sheep over cattle and large operations spread over antelope range. Stocking rates on native prairie were high and overgrazing was prevalent, especially on silver sage, the essential winter survival food for antelope.

If these factors weren't enough, a disastrously hard winter in 1906–1907 hit remaining antelope populations hard and it seemed extinction in Canada was almost inevitable. With provincial urging from Saskatchewan and Alberta, the federal government reacted quickly in 1910, moving some animals to existing national parks, like Banff, in a bid to save the species. This was unsuccessful.

Next was recognition that if antelope were to survive, herds would have to be fenced and protected on their native prairie habitats. Between 1914 and 1915, three National Antelope Parks were set up: Nemiskam and Wawaskesy in Alberta and Menissawok in Saskatchewan. Antelope populations steadily increased in these protected areas and recovery efforts were deemed successful over the next two to three decades. All of these "parks" outlived their utility, with the lands turned back to the provinces.

While it can be argued these conservation measures were effective, there might have been contributing factors in the recovery of antelope. Severe droughts in the early 1920s were compounded by further drought, leading to persistent crop failures in the 1930s. Much of the former antelope range should never have been cultivated and the droughts made the point. As a result, there was a major human depopulation of the arid southeastern portion of Alberta, allowing previously cultivated areas to return to native range.

With the onset of the Second World War, a large piece of settled landscape was expropriated by the federal government to form a military training area. CFB Suffield, which encompasses the previous Wawaskesy National Antelope Park, reverted back to native prairie. Later incorporation of provincial grazing reserves also contributed to protection of antelope range, especially wintering areas with dense sage brush stands.

Antelope populations in Alberta rebounded from a low of less than 2,000 in the early 1900s to an estimated 30,000 by 1945. Current populations are around 19,000, down from over 30,000 in the 1980s. While such numbers might appear to be impressive, they are a far cry from the pre-settlement antelope population.

Severe winter storms, compounded by fences (including from solar farms), highways, and railroads that impede movement, are still a risk to antelope. Antelope are now shoehorned into a much-diminished habitat that is being chipped away at by petroleum development, agricultural expansion, and urban sprawl. The situation with antelope requires constant vigilance.

Politicians promise a chicken in every pot – fishery biologists have worked to put a walleye at the end of every fishing rod. In Alberta we have geography working against us for walleye production. First, there are fewer than 200 lakes that contain walleye. Second, walleye grow slowly and mature late in our cold, northern climate. Finally, walleye are more easily caught in our lakes than in other jurisdictions. This created a perfect storm as angler numbers grew in step with population increases in the province.

A large number of anglers concentrating on a small number of lakes with slow-growing walleye led to a population collapse. It began to take more time to catch a walleye than to change the engine in your truck. The collapse of walleye fisheries by overfishing provides a primer on biology. If you want more of something (such as walleye), you have to let more adults have more babies, grow up, and repeat.

But how do you do that when there is inherent distrust toward government and little support within government for actions thought to be controversial? Some anglers and biologists have an aversion for accepting blame for declines in fish stocks and instead look for alternative reasons for the inability to catch fish.

This follows the axiom that those who want to do nothing can find enough uncertainty to avoid doing anything. In this case, maintaining angling pressure meant the majority of anglers caught nothing. If the goal was to let walleye populations recover so more people could catch more fish, the status quo in fisheries management had to change.

The impasse was met by a combination of computer-modelling simulations (showing what was in the realm of the possible for walleye angling) and stakeholder workshops. Engagement with anglers meant they became part of a decision-making process that was evidence-based. This signalled a shift in culture and in attitudes.

Stakeholders understanding the problem and accepting that some pain was required to make gains prevailed over those who thought of low walleye numbers as the norm, and that there was no problem that needed solving. This overcame a fundamental rule in bureaucracy that "many things may be done, but nothing must be done for the first time."

In 1996 a series of more restrictive walleye size limits and bag limits was implemented. Catch rates increased by at least an order of magnitude and anglers began to see how good fishing could be. Angler surveys, where the impact of regulation change hits the road, showed anglers reporting better fishing than in any time in their memory. Maybe there isn't a walleye at the end of every rod yet, but more anglers are experiencing much better catches from robust walleye populations.

There are some key lessons in the recovery of walleye populations. First is determining the status of a population based on evidence, not opinion, and then identifying the factors that are bottlenecks to recovery. Next, engaging with stakeholders to inform them, to develop trust, and to make them part of decisions on fisheries management allows a process to continue, especially in the face of opposition to change. Last, don't wait to see if things will improve without any action taken – for if you do nothing long enough, soon you will reach a point where nothing can be done.

Conservation successes are important to profile and we can take some measure of satisfaction that some fish and wildlife populations can recover, given the right circumstances, efforts, and will. This can be a template for the work still required, but it shouldn't blind us to the reality that the task is immense, and in many ways requires more than habitat restoration, management changes, or regulatory interventions.

We need to limit our human land-use footprint, which is the biggest risk to biodiversity. We need to be more aware of the issues, be alert to the risks, and be motivated to act and be less complacent about the slow rate of conservation progress.

AN ISLAND OF WILD IN AN AGRICULTURAL SEA

The late J.C. Sproule, an avid upland bird hunter, must have had his own crystal ball, foretelling him of declines in habitat in Southern Alberta. He purchased a quarter section of land south of Rolling Hills in the 1950s. Sproule, a petroleum geologist, didn't plan to farm the land but rather to assure himself of bird-hunting opportunities.

In that era, securing land for future hunting might not have seemed smart or prescient. Primitive flood irrigation created massive seepage areas, thick with willows and cattails. The area around Brooks became a mecca for pheasant hunting. My brother would take me there in the 1960s to hunt birds. It never dawned on us to get beyond hunting the roadside ditches, since the action was so good within steps of the roads and often on the roads. Anything else, including buying land to hunt on, would have seemed superfluous.

That apparently didn't deter Sproule. He and his hunting buddies built a small cabin on the land. They termed it the "shack" because it had few amenities, including no indoor plumbing. Sproule felt indoor plumbing would attract the wives and this place was to be an exclusive male retreat. Sproule's hunting buddies clearly bonded with the place, buying it from the estate following his death in 1970. They formed a foundation and kept up with taxes, water rights, and occasional hunting until the early 1980s when age started to catch up with them.

By this time, irrigation canal rehabilitation and modernization of farming practices had started to catch up with the country, eliminating huge tracts of former upland bird habitat. Sproule's clairvoyance was becoming more and more obvious.

The Sproule Foundation initially contacted Alberta Fish and Wildlife headquarters with questions about how to better manage the property for wildlife. The initial response was a plan to "study" the place for a year, and to accomplish this, they submitted a rather significant budget request to the foundation. Foundation members, all shrewd businesspeople, nearly came unglued at the response.

I became aware of the foundation and the property in a telephone call with the chair of the foundation, who asked me for my input. I was then with the regional Habitat Branch of Fish and Wildlife in Lethbridge. We had several wildlife habitat developments under our belt and more in the wings in concert with Ducks Unlimited.

We met on the property and the potential was immediately obvious, in spite of dying cottonwoods, weeds, and limited winter cover for pheasants. The shack was by this time derelict, housing a family of great horned owls. Our observations suggested the development of three shallow wetland basins for cattail development, an essential for pheasants and deer winter survival. Ducks Unlimited confirmed this potential and provided a modest budget estimate to accomplish the plan. The Sproule Foundation was ecstatic.

The Irrigation District was less supportive of the plan, since we needed water from an adjacent canal. This could have been a major impediment, but once the foundation was told of this, its lawyer provided a terse letter to the Irrigation District. The letter advised that the foundation had water rights, had been keeping them current, and any attempt to block the development would be met with a legal altercation.

Wetland development proceeded, a corn crop was periodically grown on the few cultivated acres, and the local fish and game club was encouraged to oversee and steward the property. Within a few years the foundation offered to sell the property to the province and a land acquisition transaction was completed, making it a Buck for Wildlife site.

The Fish and Wildlife Habitat Branch was subsequently disbanded and the Alberta Conservation Association (ACA) took over from that point. I lost touch with the property and returned to it just recently, after a 30-year hiatus.

It took me a few false starts to find the place again, amid an agricultural landscape of intensive "clean" farming with barely a blade of grass on the fencelines, centre pivots rather than flood irrigation, buried pressure pipelines instead of canals, and the only wildlife cover of note being the shelterbelts around farm buildings.

I stepped onto the property from an ACA parking lot and

immediately my dog flushed a covey of grey partridges. Deer trails and beds punctuated the waist-high grass. Several roosters were boosted from the edge of the thick cattail wetlands. A flock of mallards complained bitterly about the interruption. The old cottonwoods on the edge of the canals transecting the place have a new lease on life. Willows now spread out from the canals, creating an almost impenetrable labyrinth. Spring and summer birdsong must be deafening.

Stepping onto the property was akin to being transported to a place of serenity, quiet, diversity, and wildness, especially in comparison to the surrounding manipulated and domesticated lands. Sproule's property has become an island of wild in an agricultural sea, fulfilling his dream of secure wildlife habitat.

On a sombre note, wildlife need more than isolated islands of habitat. In a way it is unfortunate there have not been more men of vision like J.C. Sproule. Imagine what the rural landscape might resemble with more nodes of wild in what is now an increasingly homogenized, wildlife-unfriendly, and sterile expanse.

These places are not only wildlife refuges but are also an essential balm for the human spirit.

TURNING BACK THE CLOCK FOR SAGE-GROUSE

———

Main Street in Manyberries is deserted. The venerable Southern Ranchman's Inn is locked and shuttered, with kochia weed growing in front of the doors. This is a town one short step away from becoming a ghost town. The Manyberries oil boom has now gone bust. Traffic on Main Street now consists mostly of night hawks, barn swallows (ironically a species at risk), and mourning doves (with a suitable lament for the town).

In recent memory the street was packed with trucks, most with door decals from oil or oil field service companies. Beer flowed in the bar, the café hummed, and the hotel offered the only beds within an hour's drive.

The oil field southeast of the town was a focus for drilling, development, and extraction for over 40 years. Yes, immense profits were made from oil, but an economic boom for some turned out to be an ecological bust for many native critters, greater sage-grouse especially. Some biologists felt the worst place to plunk an oil field was in the middle of prime sage-grouse habitat.

Concerned about the beginning stages of the boom, biologists with the Habitat Branch of Fish and Wildlife undertook a primitive cumulative effects assessment in the early 1980s. Even then the results were sobering.

Resource booms are unrelenting, unrepentant, and concerns over wildlife are brushed off as insignificant. Regulatory approvals for well sites, pipelines, powerlines, batteries of oil tanks, and roads proceeded but with no overarching cumulative notion of effects or of ecological thresholds.

Driving the lease roads up to the early 2000s, of which there were several hundred kilometres within a township and a half of land, meant paying attention to the heavy truck traffic, oil tankers, service rigs, and pickups, all driven as if they were stolen. With such a road density, coupled with relentless daily traffic, there were no secure, quiet havens left for sage-grouse, let alone mule deer and antelope.

If human traffic wasn't enough, all the pumpjacks, power poles, and other oilpatch structures became comfortable perches and nesting sites for ravens, crows, great horned owls, and hawks, all of whom have appetites for sage-grouse. With some accuracy these artificial features led to a predatory invasion against which a declining sage-grouse population had no defences.

Predictably, sage-grouse quickly succumbed to the speed and scale of development. Populations that used to be counted by the hundreds plummeted, virtually overnight, to dangerously low levels. And so here we are with sage-grouse listed as endangered, a short step away from the other "E" word, extirpated. With every resource boom comes an inevitable economic and ecological bust.

Now that the easily (and cheaply) recoverable oil is gone, quiet has descended over the juniper badlands, the native grass uplands, and the sage brush-covered valleys. Joel Nicholson, the senior wildlife biologist from Medicine Hat, kindly offered a tour of the area and I was keen to see how reclamation of the oil field footprint was proceeding.

My generation of biologists was unable to stem the tide of development and wildlife losses – I was hoping to see something positive in a landscape that had taken on the appearance of an industrial Mordor.

What I saw can only be described as transformational. All the pumpjacks were gone (with the exception of two well sites the Alberta Energy Regulator had inexplicably allowed to persist). Most of the power poles had been removed and smaller well site roads, now unused, had started to regain native species, notably silver sage. Oil tanks at the battery site were gone and the site was under active remediation, as were several of the old wells.

The landscape is not back to 1962, when aerial photos showed no human incursions except the CPR rail line between Many-berries and Consul, Saskatchewan. But it is a far cry from a mapping exercise done in the late 1990s, which showed an over-whelming industrial footprint, one that continued to grow in the early 2000s.

Industrial incursions became so pervasive that the area was dropped from a list of candidate Special Places 2000 sites, meant to fill in gaps in Alberta's Natural Regions, remembers Cheryl Bradley, who worked on the program for Southern Al-berta. Progress is now being made on erasing the multiple de-cades of industrial exuberance.

Oil created the boom and the ecological bust. The echo is reclamation of the oil field, of which the scope and scale of work is mind-boggling. There are challenges to reclamation because of the history of construction and, crucially, the aridity of the area. There are hundreds of well sites, some with responsible owners, but many more abandoned ones under the auspices of the Orphan Well Association (OWA).

Samantha Price, an environmental planning specialist with OWA, related the mandate was to quickly return those foot-prints to usable habitats for sage-grouse and other wildlife spe-cies. What has been accomplished to date is nothing short of stunning!

It would be unfair to blame the oil patch for all the ills suf-fered by sage-grouse. Cultivation of grasslands has always been a large and contributing factor. In the mid-1950s a farmer with a quarter section of private land in the centre of what would become the oil field set his son to work breaking, cultivating, and seeding a grain crop. As the story goes, this cultivation was based on the "idle hands do the devil's work" theory to keep a young man from evil-doings. From a wildlife perspective, a chisel plow applied to native grassland is the personification of evil.

When Joel was first introduced to the area in 2000, these 130 acres of cultivation struck him as an ecological outrage and he vowed to see them restored. To his credit, and with a liberal application of persistence and continuity, the course for these lands has been reversed.

This took getting to know the owner, the former kid with the chisel plow, and quietly negotiating for land purchase. Then the Nature Conservancy of Canada (NCC) had to be convinced of the merits of buying cultivated land, not an easy sell. Bob Demulder, then the regional vice-president of the Alberta region, could see how this could fit into a larger recovery strategy for sage-grouse. He made the purchase happen with funds from Barbra Bell, a caring and generous donor.

Reversing 50 years of cultivation, even with appropriate native seed mixtures, has been a challenge says Megan Jensen, NCC's natural area manager for southeastern Alberta. "Drought and weeds made the task seem impossible." Even so, Megan is cautiously optimistic for natural recovery.

I observed some silver sage plants, a hub species for sage-grouse survival, amid a promising catch of native grasses. A translocated sage-grouse hen from Montana nested on the edge of this field a couple of years ago, providing a ray of hope that the old maxim of real estate – location, location, location – works for birds as well.

I'm under no illusion that sage-grouse will magically reappear tomorrow in any semblance of earlier numbers, but turning back the clock on the landscape of the Manyberries oil field is a step in the right direction. Even if the wand of reclamation completely recreates landscape function and integrity, there is no guarantee that many wildlife species will follow.

As Joel pointed out, "Sage-grouse are still on a razor's edge of survival, without a critical population mass to weather all the contingencies hurled at them." Reclamation of the Manyberries oil field is but one initiative on the path to species recovery. Sticking to the path means that other grassland species will benefit, as we saw when we turned off into the oil field and immediately saw a group of ground squirrels alert to a badger, all being watched by an audience of antelope.

Habitat restoration and eventual wildlife species recovery needs spark plugs, people who can trigger action and are committed to getting the job done. All this requires adequate funding and political support. It also means we have to learn from past mistakes and not repeat the resource gold rush mentality that led to wildlife species nearly winking out of existence.

That way we won't continually lose the things we should have never lost in the first place.

RIGHTING HISTORIC WRONGS — RECREATING A CASCADE RIVER

The past didn't go anywhere, it's still with us – disguised, diminished, and discarded, as in a dry river channel. It is a reminder of where we were at a point in time. Utah Phillips, folksinger and poet, reminded us of this when he said if you drop an old rock on your toe, it's the past catching up with you. The past is never past. It sits there, giving us advice on the future, maybe showing us a place to which we need to return.

The extensive manipulation of water in the Bow River watershed for electricity generation is something we now take for granted. Electricity resembles magic, so much so we have lives of ease, comfort, and convenience because of it. But there have been consequences.

Tourists driving north of the townsite of Banff and arriving at Lake Minnewanka might be surprised it isn't a lake anymore but a hydropower reservoir. Three successive dams, culminating with the last in 1941, raised water levels by 30 metres.

The final dam topped off 20 years of political and corporate intrigue between advocates of power production and those attempting to protect national park interests. In some influential jiggery-pokery, the National Parks Act was suspended by the War Measures Act, the rationale being that the power was needed to meet the war effort. How providing power to Banff townsite was part of the vital needs of the Second World War is not clear. As is the usual case, power trumped protection.

Indigenous legend relays that a warrior saw a fish in its waters as long as the lake. There was respect and fear for the resident evil water spirit. I sense we have had more to fear from modern engineering spirits than any malevolent fish spirits.

Two rivers were negatively influenced by engineering spirits to accomplish electrical generation, the Cascade and Ghost rivers. The Cascade River was diverted away from its historic course, drying it up most of the time. Both rivers were home to native westslope cutthroat and bull trout. For a variety of reasons, including the manipulation of river systems for electrical generation, both these species are categorized as threatened.

In the Cascade River, neither cutthroat nor bull trout adapted to a dry channel with periodic trickles of water, estimated to be about 1 per cent of former flows. Several millennia of evolution still have not created a fish that can live without water.

As part of a commitment to recovery of fish species at risk, Parks Canada put a priority on restoring the nine-kilometre section of the Cascade River from Minnewanka Reservoir to the Bow River in their 2010 Banff Park Management Plan. Only now it is Cascade Creek in deference to the reduced flow.

One has to stand in awe of those who proposed rehabilitating a mostly dry channel, some of it clogged with sediment from the occasional trickle, with essentially all the flow diverted. This was the brainchild of the late Charlie Pacas, a Parks Canada fisheries biologist, who did not have a faint heart when it came to righting a historic wrong. Bill Hunt, as the head of Resource Conservation (now retired), took up the torch after Charlie's death.

Sometimes in project implementation nothing succeeds as well as pure, blind luck. In June 2013, before much work was started, an upslope condition resulted in extremely heavy rainfall over a sustained period. Snowmelt was late and the ground was already saturated from several previous days of light rain.

Water levels rose rapidly in Minnewanka Reservoir, to the point that the dam structure was at serious risk of being overwhelmed. TransAlta opened up the emergency floodgates for the first time ever, creating a flood that raced down the old channel of the Cascade River.

Flood waters blew through several crossings, washing them

out and carving a new, wide channel. All the sediment, accumulated over 70 years and over a metre deep, was washed downstream. Yes, infrastructure took a beating, but the flood was also an unintended habitat improvement event, especially for Cascade Creek.

One of the better decisions for project planning and implementation, according to one Parks Canada person, was to retain Dr. Robert Newbury, a "semi-retired" river hydraulics engineer. Bob is the Canadian guru for understanding how streams function and what it takes to repair them. He was given a free hand to design and restore the stream – Charlie's dream.

What Bob was confronted with was a wide ditch in many sections of the stream, with shallow, uniform flow that was not good for trout. The task was to integrate natural, high-quality habitats into built ones, add riffles, rapids, and pools to increase hydraulic complexity, and allow the stream to meander and create channel characteristics that suit aquatic insects and trout. Simple, right?

It started with an assessment of the characteristics of the existing channel using cross-sectional profiles to assess widths, depths, and water velocities at a range of flows. Then it was a question of how closely these characteristics matched the modelled results for the velocity and depth preferences of cutthroat trout and to identify what stream reaches needed a nudge. The geometry and complexity of pool, run, and riffle sites (slope, rock sizes, spacing, pool depths, gravels, velocities, and discharge) were measured and used to design the Cascade reaches.

Bob then walked each reach to determine where the existing good habitats were and to see how these could be integrated with built habitats. This is where, he pointed out, "It becomes a bit of an art, trying to copy a natural stream form in pools, riffles, and meander bends." As a template, he had the natural design of a similar trout stream in the Jumping Pound watershed.

To achieve this for Cascade Creek took heavy metal in the form of a tracked backhoe and a skilled operator, Larry Clark. Volumes of material had to be moved, placed, and adjusted, often with the support of Parks maintenance staff. Sometimes it was the careful placement of boulders, just so, with the considerable finesse of a backhoe bucket.

Every 100 metres the velocities and depths were plotted and compared with preferred cutthroat trout values, and any segments that did not meet these criteria were altered with a combination of pools, riffles, and meanders. The physical structure of the stream channel was completed in 2019.

Once the channel was reconfigured, hundreds of hours of mostly volunteer time went into replanting the riparian zone with a variety of trees, shrubs, grasses, and forbs. As Helen Irwin, who served as the project manager, notes, "Imagine trying to dig a hole in large stream cobble to plant a willow and you have an impression of the labour involved."

Riparian vegetation is the "green" rebar that glues stream banks together, resists erosion, provides a place for sediment to be trapped during high water, and is a source of terrestrial insects for trout. The shading from trees and shrubs also helps maintain low water temperatures, essential for trout.

At the mouth of the stream, near the confluence with the Bow River, a fish barrier was built to keep non-native trout species out so they would not compete with native trout. A fundamentally important part of the project has been the willingness of TransAlta to restore and keep water flowing down the new channel.

Work done to rehabilitate the Cascade River and allow native trout to reoccupy the channel after nearly 80 years is a singularly tangible example of species recovery. Although it is still a work in progress, the essential elements of a stream ecosystem have been reconstructed.

The reality is the work is by no means finished and, in such a dam-regulated system, will require sustained attention and effort. This is the cost of working with severely modified riverine systems to achieve and maintain a self-sustaining native trout fishery. Monitoring by Mark Taylor, aquatic ecologist with Parks Canada, will determine if the trout give it a passing grade.

No one involved with the project would say it was easy (or will be), but the will and persistence displayed should motivate others to consider similar projects. Charlie Pacas's "crazy" dream is a reality and other dreams can be as well. Dreaming is what it takes to recover native trout populations at appropriate scales. The Cascade River rehabilitation appeals to me because of the systems approach used by Bob; it was not a series of Band-Aids.

Recovery efforts for native trout will only be effective if we can turn back the clock and restore the habitats historically occupied by them. Recreating a Cascade River does just that.

HUMAN DIMENSIONS IN SPECIES-AT-RISK RECOVERY

———

Wild critters are in trouble, what with habitat losses and essentially too many of us leading to too few of them. Species-at-risk recovery efforts seem to lie somewhere between hopeless and Herculean. Part of this is the sheer scale of habitat restoration required; there are the looming issues of climate change and always there are bureaucratic, political, and corporate impediments and hurdles.

In the search for villains in the decline of native trout populations, you don't have to look far. Human activity is responsible. Restoring habitat features is an integral part of recovery efforts. Behind the scenes of stream banks rebuilt, sediment sources stabilized, and willows planted are people – people who saw the need and worked out how to accomplish the task.

This process of people coming together, often from disparate backgrounds and agencies, is every bit as fascinating as the reclamation of physical habitats itself. Sometimes the process of doing so is murky. Rocky and Fall creeks, in the watersheds of the Clearwater and Ram rivers, provide the story behind successful recovery endeavours.

Margaret Mead, an American cultural anthropologist, is said to have observed, "Never doubt that a small group of thoughtful, committed citizens can change the world: indeed, it's the only thing that ever has." Evidence strongly suggests this is true for conservation.

There is a saying that some people watch things happen while others make things happen. The reclamation of off-highway vehicle (OHV) trails leading to the recovery of bull trout populations in Rocky and Fall creeks is a stellar example of people making things happen. Although it seems simple – close OHV trails and let bull trout respond to improved habitat conditions – it is rarely a straightforward proposition. Many stars have to be in alignment and mostly those stars are people.

As Jess Reilly, a provincial fisheries biologist who played a key role in the Rocky Creek project, has remarked, "There were many questions to grapple with and lots of moving parts requiring alignment."

In the beginning there must be an assessment of what the potential ecological problems are, the ones that impede the survival of native trout. Progress can be stymied by a welter of potential risks to bull trout. There are many to choose from, but ensuring the right solution aligns with the critical problem is a challenge.

It's said the army of ecological destruction comes by road. The Clearwater and Ram watersheds are replete with roads, trails, seismic lines, and right-of-ways for pipelines and power lines. Roads beget more roads and wheels take advantage of those roads. Vehicle access has unleashed a tsunami of OHV use.

Perversely, the damage has persisted long enough now for there to be a generation of users who no longer recognize what has been lost, what ecological integrity looks like, or what their cumulative role has been in the changes. With no reference points, there is an erroneous assumption that the expanded human footprint of today has always existed and native trout populations were always low.

Each stream had issues, compounded by the insidious growth of a land-use footprint. Both had an OHV trail paralleling and crossing the streams at multiple locations. In the space of 20 kilometres, Rocky Creek had 31 fords crossing it; Fall Creek, 54 fords in just nine kilometres. With constant OHV use each ford bled sediment into the clear waters. The trails produced more sediment when it rained, and ruts created with branching routes sometimes captured a stream segment, diverting water away from the channel.

Elevated levels of sediment delivered to the streams created life-threatening problems, potentially inhibiting the spawning success of bull trout. That was the hypothesis, the beginning of a logical thinking pathway of remedial action to test the assumption.

Unfortunately, OHV enthusiasts seemed oblivious to this reality, even to the point of denying there was a problem. As Mark Twain allegedly quipped, "Denial ain't just a river in Egypt." The urge to deny inconvenient truths is as widespread as it is tiresome. Rocky and Fall creeks are bull trout havens and spawning areas for the greater watersheds. What seemed obvious to biologists as a risk to populations may not have been clear to others. This included the actions of some renegade OHV users who wielded their chain saws to hack through some of the reclamation barriers, undoing essential recovery work.

Rolling back the level and footprint of use was essential to meeting recovery goals. A key step in population recovery of this species at risk was the reclamation of these OHV trails and fords.

It's not enough to identify the ecological problems as the solutions cross jurisdictional boundaries, require staff involvement whose mandates may not directly include bull trout recovery, and involve a suite of land planning and land designation issues, including industrial dispositions. Then there are the political issues, especially if there is more support for continued OHV activity rather than saving native trout. Generally, these impediments to action stifle any meaningful recovery actions.

There can be countervailing actions from some to recovery

proposals. Recovery projects require permits from provincial authorities, and sometimes federal ones, and might, if instream activity is proposed, be subject to timing constraints. In some instances, the regulator seems to have a hard time distinguishing the difference between industry crossing a stream with a pipeline and a conservation group planting willows for habitat restoration. Regulators can be slow to respond to applications, which throws off planning, may delay project implementation unnecessarily, and cause funding to disappear. There can be imperious questioning of restoration techniques despite a long track record of success.

For the bull trout of Rocky and Fall creeks all the stars were in alignment with the right people, in the right place, at the right time. A number of individuals found ways to align priorities among several agencies, fast-track approvals, find avenues for provincial funding, and assemble partnerships with Freshwater Conservation Canada (FCC), which did much of the heavy lifting. The ability to cut through administrative red tape, thwart bureaucracy, and co-operate across the castle walls of departmental silos reminds me of the quote attributed to Bob Geldof of the Live Aid famine relief effort: "Bugger the complexities, let's save lives."

Restoration of species at risk fits with this message. The reality is that institutions are never going to move quickly enough to save imperilled critters. Economic and political aspirations are antithetical to biodiversity concerns. But the actions of individuals, even some working in government and industry (or in spite of it), and those in conservation groups may help to stem the tide.

This is what effective species-at-risk recovery comes down

to – people committed to the task. Not government departments stuffed with bureaucrats who, when they see the light at the end of the tunnel, add more tunnel. Not the footdraggers, apologists, and gatekeepers of industry. Not recovery plans, however essential and well intended. No, not these, but individuals who care, who are resourceful and get things done, who have the skill sets to make collaboration work, people who go well beyond the extra mile, knowing they need to do so for the species they love.

On the list are volunteers who provide lots of sweat equity, watershed groups (e.g., Oldman Watershed Council, Ghost Watershed Alliance Society, Elbow River Partnership, Mighty Peace Watershed Alliance, Athabasca Watershed Council), conservation, stewardship, and environmental groups (notably Cows & Fish, FCC, and the ACA), some in industry and municipal governments with a sense of stewardship, and government biologists.

Recovery tasks can be too great for one group, so several often have to work together on different project aspects; sometimes their efforts are co-ordinated by the Alberta Native Trout Collaborative. Work continues despite efforts being under-resourced and running on a shoestring budget. In the field, on streamside, it's often not more than a dozen people. These are not high-profile projects with local politicians and dignitaries dropping in for a photo-op. Rarely does the group ever include those who caused the problem for trout in the first place.

I'd like to name some of these people who recognize their obligation to wild creatures. It would be nice to give them the credit and recognition they richly deserve for their courage and persistence. But there is risk in missing some, especially volunteers and those who work behind the scenes. As committed individuals you know who you are, you know what you do is important, and you do it because keeping critters from disappearing isn't a job, it's a calling.

THE CURRENCY OF ANGLER CITIZEN SCIENCE

Some anglers are incessant recorders of the minutiae of fishing. This is a way to note important moments, provide bragging rights, and gauge the condition of streams and rivers for repeat engagements. It's also a way to ensure memories reflect what actually happened. As in how big the fish really were, how many were caught, and how long it took to catch them. In *Mark Twain's Own Autobiography*, Twain had it right when he wrote, "If you tell the truth, you don't have to remember anything."

Even biblical verses document this propensity of fishers to count things. In John 21, disciples of Jesus, having learned of his resurrection, didn't immediately rush to greet him. Instead, they pulled their nets and assiduously counted their catch – 153 fish. Not dozens of fish, lots of fish, or over 100, not about 150 but precisely 153 fish.

Imagine this person, their spiritual guide, has been crucified and put in a cave from which he emerges, alive. A miracle, one would think, and worthy of a rush to be with him. No, instead they first count their fish, all 153 of them!

Obsessive behaviour? Maybe, but when it comes to understanding better the range of variability in a fish population, in fish habitat, and to documenting when things come unglued, the records anglers maintain is priceless.

I encountered this when trying to determine the status of bull trout in Southwestern Alberta streams. Systematic fisheries inventories are a recent phenomenon and provide detailed information on fish stocks, growth rates, and distribution for only the last few decades. This information does not provide a glimpse of what fish populations were before settlement and subsequent developments. Without that critical benchmark, we don't have an adequate starting point against which to measure changes.

The oldest angler I interviewed for information on bull trout was born in 1910 and all were born before 1940. Their experiences ranged from the 1920s to the 1960s, with an average of 60 years of fishing experiences. Many had fishing diaries and photographs to back up their memories and convince me they were not relating typical fish stories. These proved to be a treasure trove of information, not just in terms of the number of fish caught and their sizes, but also for reflections on the land. Without these remembrances I could not have correctly assessed the changes in populations – essentially a 70 per cent loss in bull trout distribution in the Oldman watershed.

When coal company consultants assessed the trout population of Gold Creek, beneath the proposed Grassy Mountain coal mine, they had no benchmarks. Their information allowed the company to term the trout population of the stream as "depauperate," apparently containing too few trout to impede mining. This might have been enough to allow the joint federal/provincial panel to conclude there was nothing to be concerned about and coal mining might proceed.

But coal interests hadn't counted on Jim Rennie, a long-term angler of Gold Creek (one of his favourite streams) and his prodigious record-keeping. Jim had records of his catch rates, measured in fish caught per hour, which dated from 1993, with minor breaks until recently.

Catch rates are a surrogate for population size, the assumption being that the greater the population, the greater the catch rate. For Jim, an accomplished, consistent angler and disciplined record keeper, his information eliminates much of the bias in reporting.

In a simple, hand-drawn graph, presented to the panel, Jim showed annual peaks and valleys in the trout population; often the valleys corresponded with floods, with catch rates (i.e., population size) recovering in the year following floods. Despite these fluctuations, Jim's catch rate stayed around ten trout (caught and released) per hour.

Except in 2015, when a coal spoil pile failure related to rainfall and perhaps exploration activity unleashed a slurry of sediment to Gold Creek. Jim's catch rates plummeted to nearly nil, virtually overnight. His estimate, based on this precipitous decline in catch rates, was that Gold Creek had suffered a 95 per cent loss of trout. His point, tellingly made to the panel, was the consultant's work had all been done from 2016 to 2019, after the spill and the population crash. No wonder the coal company was willing to write off the trout of Gold Creek, what few remained.

When no one is watching, and apparently the coal company wasn't, significant losses in fish populations can occur. But Jim was watching and his data was irrefutable.

It's easy to discount angler tales. On creel surveys of the Oldman and Livingstone rivers, when asked, everyone said they had caught at least one fish. But actual measurements of fish in the creel showed that a handful of anglers had caught most of the fish. In reality, most people catch nothing. It leaves you wondering who to believe. Fish tales wither in the face of long-term written records.

When I talked with Jim about his angling records, he obligingly pulled out his fishing diaries, a small pile of them. In those diaries are found his history of fishing, of fish, and of habitat conditions, all painstakingly accumulated from more than 25 streams, rivers, and lakes over a period of five decades.

Most included repeat visits over the years to the same streams, the same stream reaches, the same pools and runs and riffles. Detailed notes on water and air temperatures, flow rates, water quality impressions, insect hatches, species of fish caught, numbers of fish caught per hour, fish health, and best flies used paint a picture over time of the stream.

I asked Jim, "Why take such detailed notes?" His answer was telling: "I knew the fishing I experienced wasn't going to last with the developments I could see encroaching on each watershed. If records aren't kept, how do we know if changes, even trout population crashes, have happened?" What Jim was expressing is, if you've never encountered yesterday, you may think today hasn't changed a bit and tomorrow will be much the same.

It was clear to me that Jim was establishing, with his detailed records, biological benchmarks so changes in these streams and their fish populations could be recognized. So often we don't see or measure changes and we accept that whatever the current condition is, it is the one that has always persisted. That's how we lose watershed integrity, fish and wildlife populations, and recreational opportunities – it slips through our insensitive fingers.

So often governments that we think are monitoring, measuring, and regulating simply aren't. Systematic inventories, collected by resource professionals, are absolutely important. But if the inventory data isn't current, contains substantial gaps, and provides only single snapshots of conditions, its value at showing change is watered down.

This is where the citizen science of people such as Jim provides the best available information to chart changes. Jim's long-term records tell him that the amount of sediment is rising in East Slope streams, water is getting warmer, there are fewer deep pools, and habitat complexity is being homogenized into long reaches with little or no holding water for trout. This translates into fewer fish.

I had to ask Jim how this made him feel as he looked back through his diaries. Not surprisingly, Jim replied it saddened him, made him feel "sick" to know how much had changed on his favourite waters.

This was especially so since he had fished Gold Creek just a couple of days after the coal spoil pile failure. It motivated him to make a submission to the panel that was holding a hearing over the proposed Grassy Mountain coal mine in the Crowsnest Pass.

The panel was very receptive to Jim's message on the trout crash, to the long-term angling record he was able to display. The coal company had no rebuttal, except to downplay the significance of the coal pile failure. The panel clearly saw through this subterfuge because of Jim's evidence.

Unfortunately, much of this essential information, contained in angler diaries, is squirrelled away and not available for review. Many anglers treat this information as proprietary and secret. Jim mentioned he wrestled with whether or not to share his angling records of Gold Creek, since they show what a productive fishery it was before the spoil pile failure. The risk was that if the fishery recovered, it might be overwhelmed by too many other anglers (his recent experiences show little recovery). It's normal to be tight-lipped on good angling spots, but Jim reasoned the public needed to know what had happened and what could persist if mining proceeded.

Our watersheds, our water, and our fish and wildlife populations need more engaged citizen scientists such as Jim and consistent, repeated observations taken over long periods of time. Otherwise, so many changes go unrecognized and get swept under bureaucratic rugs, and the ecosystem declines in integrity.

Memory alone is always another country of imperfect landmarks, but records are a good roadmap of reality. Those who manage our landscapes and our biodiversity assets might find a treasure trove of information in these citizen science observations to inform better outcomes for our watersheds.

It can't come soon enough for the fish.

RETHINKING THE FISHING EXPERIENCE

Fishing means different things to different people, but perhaps not to the fish. Among the list of reasons to fish are escape, reward, interaction, contemplation, competition, and a meal. Fennel Hudson, a British angler and author, touches on this in

A Meaningful Life with, "People fish because they are searching for something. Often it is not for a fish." From that I think when we focus solely on the catch, we miss the bigger picture.

The tangible reward of a fish in the hand or in the pan doesn't measure up against the intangible rewards. It can't and shouldn't. On an outdoors trip I gain more from the colour of the sky, the way waves implacably scour the shore, the auditory gurgle of running water, or the sound of wind rustling the aspen leaves than I do from the momentary thrill of a fish at the end of a line. That fish is as the period at the end of this sentence – a momentary closure but not a defining moment. There is the risk of losing the experience with a focus on the fish.

There was a time I had to have a fishing rod, a gun, or a camera in my hand to give my excursions purpose. I don't know if, in my declining years, I haven't been able to turn my conscience off to fish, or if I've just gotten lazy, but my ego doesn't need a result in hand to brag about, or the experience of fishing doesn't measure up against other elements.

Each of us needs to ask the question – if catching a fish isn't necessary for a quality outdoor experience, why bother trying to catch them? This is something each angler has to wrestle with to answer. There will be no perfect, one-size-fits-all response. Personally, I still get a thrill out of observing fish, knowing they are present, or obsessing over why they aren't.

I get it, there is an electrical impulse that careens down the line when a fish takes the bait. It feels as if you are trying to hold a crazed wild animal on a string. When that happens, we subconsciously re-enact our ancient role as hunter-gatherers. While it may not be as important these days to retain that anachronism, we can't lose people who are advocates for fish, rivers, lakes, water quality, watershed integrity, and species re-covery, whether they fish or not. If we do, one crowd will wait for the hatchery truck beside a dugout and that will signal we've lost everything else.

People gaze rapturously at a sunset, at a forest landscape, or at a shoreline of crashing waves, all with the sublime aspect seen in jigsaw puzzles. Helping people stare into the water and see what lives beneath the surface of that shimmering ribbon is a step toward that advocacy. This may or may not involve fishing.

OK, I've led you to this point for a reason, as in an unavoidable weather system ominously approaching. Habitat loss, climate change, and historic overfishing have created a new abnormal for fish. It is one that does not advantage them.

Maybe we need to rethink our association with and approach to our piscine neighbours in ways that are less extractive and intrusive. When too many of us pursue a declining number of fish, something has to give.

The need for tighter management, effort reduction, and perhaps cessation of angling for current "sport" species signals the end of a time-worn habit of prioritizing our rewards at the expense of the fish. There is a fine line between a sentimental attachment to an ancient activity and the threat of our quarry disappearing. An adaptation to a new phase might mean we continue to associate with fish but do so in different ways.

The next logical step beyond barbless hooks, is no hook at all. Many of us have already perfected this, inadvertently, when a hook breaks off and we fail to notice its absence. Those who intentionally fish with a hookless fly speak of avoiding the game of "who catches the more fish." The action is just as intense, there is less time taken to release a fish, meaning there is more time to fish. For trout fishing, the challenge is getting the fish to rise and bite your fly. Satisfaction in fooling a fish without hooking it also means fish are treated more gently.

While sportfish species are under pressure, we are not yet short of fish. Other species are available for angling if we can change attitudes and perspectives toward them. In addition to 19 sport species, Alberta has an additional 11 species, often termed "rough fish," such as a variety of suckers, that can provide much angling and eating opportunity. Groups like Roughfish.com provide legitimacy, angling tips, contests, and recipes.

Then there is micro-fishing, pursuing the tiny minnows, dace, sculpins, and chubs, most about the size of your little toe. I can only sense the challenge of using specialized rods, size 20 to 30 hooks (about the same size as the tail on the beaver of a Canadian nickel), and tippets thinner than a human hair. Microfishing.com describes the tackle, methods, and goals. Its essence is an appreciation for fish biodiversity – all fish. We have about two dozen fish species available for this extreme and minuscule pursuit.

While I don't fish much anymore, that doesn't stop me from looking for fish. It has become ingrained – whenever I am beside water I look into the depths for fish. I don't need a fishing rod to see into the water. Maybe this is part of my professional life as a fisheries biologist. Part of this is curiosity, part is sensing whether the stream, river, or lake is healthy enough to sustain aquatic life.

Although fish watching isn't anywhere as popular as birdwatching, the principles are the same. Viewing from a bridge, a raft, or a logjam, or peering over a stream bank using polarized sunglasses, a world opens that isn't available through angling. Common sights might include fathead minnow males tending their nests or a food fight between two brook sticklebacks. It could be a school of perch alternately hunting insects or hiding from the big water dog, a northern pike. *Fish of Alberta* by Amanda Joynt and Michael Sullivan has excellent suggestions for fish watching.

I've listened to the enthusiasm of two biologist colleagues, Kenton Neufeld and Elliot Lindsay, for snorkelling and observing fish in a natural state. As both explain, these underwater voyages provide a unique and fascinating view of all of the province's fish fauna.

Kenton writes lyrically about sculpins "stacked in the cracks between the cobbles," plains suckers grazing on algae, all under the watchful eye of a bull trout lurking "in the flickering shadows under fallen trees." All this without the need for a fishing licence and no cost for admission to the show.

Much of this new approach to fish isn't going to appeal to any hook and bullet magazine, funded by advertising a shipload of hunting and fishing paraphernalia. It goes against the economic grain. It likely won't find traction with hunting and fishing organizations whose members still identify and measure themselves against the fish sizes, numbers, and catch rates of others.

What will also continue is an enduring argument over the status of fish populations, their size, health, and distribution. A fog of denial about population loss and declining population trends will complicate any movement toward rethinking the fishing experience.

If we can stretch our minds around a new idea, we might

find our old ideas are unsuitable for a changed and changing environment. Then we can congratulate ourselves for our foresight and prescience.

Rethinking our relationship with fish is a way to ensure fish remain in our future.

THE ANTELOPE CREEK RANCH
Conservation Persistence

———

In 1984 I led a tour of what would become the Antelope Creek Ranch with a group of departmental decision-makers. To say most of that early tour group were skeptical about the prospect of buying flat, treeless prairie for wildlife habitat is no wild exaggeration.

Ducks Unlimited staff knew the ranch west of Brooks was for sale. In fact, much of it had already been sold, broken, and cultivated – the usual fate of native prairie. At the time, prairie – its value, its importance for wildlife, its worth in an unbroken state, and how little was left – wasn't fully appreciated.

Back in the 1980s Southern Alberta was gripped in drought. This is normally dry country, but the drought had turned it to a crisp. Then, a walk across the range was akin to a stroll on pavement – the ground was baked hard, cracks threatened to swallow you, grass height could only be measured with calipers, and the sun punished with its intensity.

Among the group there was a palpable lack of enthusiasm for the idea of purchasing this ranch. It was difficult to paint a picture of what the future could resemble and what we could accomplish. We flushed one poor pintail hen. Her nest was tucked into a depression created by a ground squirrel and it was shaded with two thin sprigs of grass. It was pitiful!

Those of us who could see a future for this bit of sun-blasted prairie found an ally in the late Don Sparrow, the minister of the day of whatever the department was in 1986. His support really put the grease on the skids of the land acquisition proposal. So in 1986 we had a ranch – Fish and Wildlife, Ducks Unlimited, Wildlife Habitat Canada, and the Alberta Fish and Game Association.

There is no record of the work required to assemble a land acquisition proposal, have appraisals done of the land, negotiate with the former owner, cobble together the cash required (from three different pockets), write an agreement that all the funding partners could agree to, and, most importantly, determine a way to recapture surface rights revenues from petroleum development. These revenues were crucial for undertaking conservation work on the ranch. My mind has gone strangely blank on that effort.

So there we had it – 5,500 acres of possibility. The assets at the time included about 4,000 acres of native range, some converted pasture, water rights for irrigation, an old portable irrigation pivot (underneath which was an abandoned carrot crop), some oil wells, and a sprinkling of wetlands. I suppose the assets also included our collective imaginations.

The enormity of it crashed down on us. Now what do we do? How do we manage this ranch? One thing we were clear on – we couldn't do it all ourselves.

Wetland development was something Ducks Unlimited had a long history in – but managing the uplands, especially for nesting cover to realize a gain in waterfowl and other ground-nesting birds, required different expertise. Canada Agriculture range scientists Silver Smoliak and Bob Wroe were asked to help with a plan for the uplands.

Barry Adams (Alberta Public Lands Division) stepped in later to set the course for monitoring recovery of the range. The range management plan, with some tweaks, set the stage for restoration of the native grasslands, using cattle grazing as the tool. The skeptics at the beginning of this odyssey were very surprised where this took us.

Away we went, cats and scrapers building wetlands, fences going up to help restore and manage the rangelands, and thinking about how to utilize all of the ranch's assets. Everyone put a lot of time, effort, and resources into the ranch.

After a number of years, those of us who already had full-time jobs were struggling to keep up with the demands of the ranch. Just the relatively simple act of converting the carrot patch into irrigated pasture was an exercise in time, frustration, and some crop failures. By the early '90s we realized a ranch of this size, with the expectations attached, required a full-time manager.

Bob Kaufman came over from Ducks Unlimited to be the first full-time ranch manager – a role he performed admirably for 12 years. In those 12 years the ranch blossomed, matured, and reached a plateau of success. Theories and plans and prescriptions are great starting points, but it is consistent observation, testing, record-keeping, and learning that proves the worth of the plans.

Managing cattle turned out to be relatively simple compared to riding herd on the activities of the oil industry. Just as we owe a debt of gratitude to the visionaries who started us on this path, we owe many thanks to Bob for helping us stay on the path.

Neil Wilson and Shannon Burnard took over the reins after Bob retired. Being the manager of the Antelope Creek Ranch is no cake walk, but Bob's guiding hand provided a good start. Neil and Shannon have proven to be exceptional managers.

The Antelope Creek Ranch began with a simple premise – the opportunity to acquire, protect, and develop some key wetland habitat in the mixed grass prairie. It was a project – a focus on one piece of land, one type of habitat, with one intent. Because it was a partnership from the beginning – initially more for financial reasons than any other – it set the stage for learning how to work together, to share perspectives (and talents, experience, and resources), and how to evolve together with a common purpose.

That evolution brought us to understand that the fundamentals of managing the ranch shouldn't revolve around products – ducks, beef, pheasants, or oil. Nor should the focus be around activities – industry, grazing, or recreation – but around restoring landscape health and function. A healthy, functioning landscape produces many of those products and supports many of those activities. It was an incremental, cumulative experience in learning, measuring, monitoring, and helping others grasp some ecological principles. It is still a work in progress that may never be done.

A fundamental shift in our thinking also occurred when we realized that the greatest value of the ranch was not what happens within its fences, but what we could use from our experience on the ranch to help others, outside the fence, to shift their perspective and management. The concept of the

Antelope Creek Ranch as a demonstration venue, showing the principles of range management in action and the integration of several land uses in a way to maintain key ecological health, began to dominate our thinking.

As an example, after about 20 years it was estimated that the amount of native range influenced positively by our management of the Antelope Creek Ranch was greater than 600,000 acres. That's not an insignificant return on our investment.

It hasn't been perfect – time and resources have sometimes been in short supply. Some of the components we should have measured we didn't do early enough; others we didn't do enough of to establish a good baseline. I suspect subsequent managers will discover many things we didn't think of at all. Despite that, the trajectory of healing was documented, as was the response of range management to drought, the interaction of wildlife with range management, the critical need for meaningful restoration, and how to convey many of these messages to others.

The real test of the plan is to continue to implement and monitor through the range of natural variation – droughts, insect infestations, wet periods – the full cycle of events that initially built the grassland landscape.

Sadly, few conservation initiatives last. They start with much fanfare, support, and resources. Then, as people change, priorities shift, and as the corporate memory fades, support dwindles. This hasn't happened to the Antelope Creek Ranch over a four-decade span, and I hope it persists into the future. Four decades isn't long for a landscape, but it represents a lifetime for a conservation initiative. The ranch should remind us that in effective conservation work the two essential ingredients of success are continuity and persistence.

I invite you to take a walk on the range of the Antelope Creek Ranch. When you do, note the feeling of a rich, thick broadloom carpet under your feet. That's no accident. It's the result of many years of patient tending and stewarding. Reflect, if you will, on the passage of time required to allow conservation to take root. It's a patient person's business.

Illustration by Liz Saunders

5

The Weedy Garden
of Paradise

*The profiteering drive of commerce owns
no malice or mercy, is incapable of regret,
and takes no prisoners; it is simply an engine
with no objective but to feed itself.*

—Barbara Kingsolver

IF THE TROUT ARE GONE,
IS IT STILL TROUT CREEK?

On a summer's day an unknown photographer focused his Kodak Brownie on four adults and a child out for a day's fishing on Trout Creek. The photograph, now in the Glenbow Archives, is labelled "Fishermen with catch, Trout Creek, Alberta. July, 1902." And what a catch it was – a pile of native cutthroat trout, well over 100, and maybe 50 kilograms in total. Native cutthroat trout lingered, though continuing to decline, over the next century or so in this tiny stream that flows off the east side of the Porcupine Hills in Southwestern Alberta.

They were still present in 2013 when Elliot Lindsay, a biologist with FCC, caught his first cutthroat trout there. When government of Alberta biologists sampled the stream in 2015, they recorded "hundreds" of trout. By 2019 those hundreds had dwindled and FCC caught only two from a subset of the same stream reaches. Unfortunately, contagion with genetic material from non-native rainbow trout was already well established.

Further investigations in 2021 by the Blackfoot Confederacy Tribal Council Native Trout Recovery project, using environmental DNA, failed to find any strong evidence of pure-strain cutthroat trout in the watershed. The population is functionally extirpated, not just teetering. This is extirpation in real time, not ancient history but virtually overnight, with a timeline of just yesterday. It might be as Hemingway's description of bankruptcy in *The Sun Also Rises* – gradual, then sudden.

The loss of a native population of cutthroat trout calls for a postmortem – how could this have happened after the species was designated as threatened, a recovery strategy was implemented, and much fanfare was made of restoration efforts? Call it death by a thousand cuts, starting with the cruellest cut, timber harvest.

The Trout Creek watershed has been extensively logged, with large clear-cuts, creating a web of logging roads and inadequate streamside buffers. Roads begat more recreational traffic, with spirals of OHV trails adding to the linear density and sediment produced. Past cattle grazing may have reduced streamside willows, increasing bank instability.

Climate change brought persistent drought periods. Coupled with hydrologic shifts from logging and the loss of beaver, the watershed has lost much of its ability to store moisture and stream sections periodically dry up. Recent protracted drought conditions, added to creeping hybridization, have been the last straw.

In the past, natural conditions may well have produced similar drought conditions and low or no surface flows. However, there would have been connections with other cutthroat populations in the wider watershed, allowing movement and replenishment under better flows. The problem is now there is no rescue option from downstream sources. Cutthroat trout no longer exist in the lower watershed.

In the departmental and bureaucratic silos of land and resource management reside little chance for rescue, since few see (and are responsible) for the bigger picture – the additive, cumulative impacts. When no one is assigned to watch, no one seems responsible when the essential pieces of landscape and watershed integrity come unglued.

As Vic Adamowicz, a professor at the University of Alberta, observed to me, "Under Alberta's public land management system, the cost of habitat loss is only considered after economics are accounted for, and there is no reason for resource sectors to co-ordinate activities, resulting in destructive cumulative effects."

We inherit the world we allowed to happen. We find out, sometimes too late, the kind of world we create when things are allowed to proceed unhindered. And so the native cutthroat population of Trout Creek, having persisted for at least a dozen millennia, comes to a whimpering end. So ends a population intimately tied to the watershed, having been tested and evolved to deal with the considerable range of natural variation expressed over time beyond human imagination. This we do not mourn, either because we do not care to know, or we do not know to care.

Fortunately, there are a few who do care. Organizations such as FCC and Cows & Fish plug away, increasing awareness about native trout and their plight. Bit by bit, metre by metre, mind by mind, they rebuild battered stream banks, close off excessive OHV trails, work with ranchers on riparian grazing management solutions, and help people see the trout for the trees.

Provincial fisheries biologists work on the development of a composite brood stock of pure-strain cutthroat trout. Once habitat conditions are stabilized and improved, this offers an opportunity to restock the stream and restore the cutthroat population.

To spell "cutthroat trout" you need only arrange 14 letters in the right order. But to make a trout you need a huge array of biotic and abiotic material and assemble it in precisely the right sequence. Beyond water, both quantity and quality, the pieces include intact forest and watershed, aquatic insects, a combination of stream characteristics, the right genetic code, population critical mass, movement ability, grappling with limiting factors, and the time to evolve to fit the stream environment. Even knowing what the essential parts are and how they fit together may not be evident. It is decidedly not the same as baking a cake. That is the challenge for restoring native cutthroat trout to Trout Creek now that they have gone missing.

In spite of the challenges, you can't help but be impressed with the infectious optimism of people such as Elliot Lindsay, with FCC, Amy Berlando, with Cows & Fish, and many provincial fisheries biologists who will not give up on Trout Creek. They will need to think big since real recovery can only happen at a watershed scale. It might require the equivalent of a moon-shot to bring native cutthroat back to the stream.

While much work remains to deal with the proliferation of OHV trails and crossings, as well as riparian grazing management fixes, the fundamental task might be to restore the capability of the watershed to retain and store water. This watershed once had dozens and dozens of beaver dams, effectively drought-proofing the system. When R.B. Miller, Alberta's first fisheries biologist, initially surveyed the watershed in 1948, he commented on the number of beaver dams.

The Burke Creek Ranch has been situated in the Trout Creek watershed since 1890. Rick Burton, the third generation on the ranch, recalls the headwaters and tributaries being wetter and having more beaver dams in the '60s and '70s. Beaver activity is now spotty. But beavers still remain and that is a hopeful sign.

Restoration plans include the installation of multiple beaver dam analogs – structures designed to mimic the form and function of a natural beaver dam – in different reaches of the watershed. These structures are meant to jumpstart the growth of woody shrubs and entice beavers to move in and take over. As Elliot says, "Ultimately, the beaver are probably the ones who will be able to have the might and persistence to kick this watershed out of the rut that it's currently in."

Fingers crossed, I hope habitat restoration, coupled with the availability of pure-strain cutthroat trout for stocking, can someday bring trout back to Trout Creek. With a name such as Trout Creek, it seems as it's the right thing to do. At the same time, some receptivity needs to be built in the minds of those who contributed to the disappearance of cutthroat trout.

If there is no shame in being party to the loss of an ancient element of a watershed, it will happen again, and again.

In an indeterminant future, if all the aquatic stars align, someone may take a picture of a group of anglers on Trout Creek, not with a large stringer of native trout, but with smiles indicating their satisfaction with a day of fishing on a stream brought back to life.

FALTERING STEPS IN SPECIES RECOVERY

Species at risk are those native plants, animals, and fish that are in danger of extirpation or extinction. They exist on a knife edge of survival – most because of human actions. In Alberta there are currently 41 threatened or endangered species. This is a minimum number since more likely exist but have not been assessed and designated. At least five species are now missing from the Alberta landscape. To ensure none of the current listed species at risk disappear, recovery plans are mandated.

As a vision of species recovery as practised in Alberta, consider the prospect of your house on fire. The fire department wheels up, but instead of immediately pouring water on the house to quell the blaze they engage in the following steps:

- There is an assessment made of the extent of the fire, whether it is serious and actually threatens your house and if it warrants further action. There will be delays as your home is designated as a "house at risk," which might allow the process of fighting fire to begin.

- A committee, including "directly affected" people, would then be assembled to weigh this information. In the spirit of inclusiveness, even the arsonist is invited. There would be multiple meetings over time with minutes, status reports, scenario development with mathematical models, additional information requests, and recurring arguments over whether a fire is burning and if your house is, indeed, at risk.
- The fire ministry then would assess the costs of putting out your house fire, as well as the costs and inconvenience that might accrue to your neighbours of these actions.
- If you are lucky, your house will be deemed "at risk," and then recommendations would go to a government minister for review and sign off. There may be jurisdictional issues to sort out over which ministry is "responsible." Some ministries will deny any responsibility or culpability.
- Budget submissions, timelines, and staffing requirements would be made to handle the development of fire-fighting actions for your house. Another group will discuss and debate those actions. Some will want immediate action – others will be gatekeepers, impeding action. A report will finally be prepared. It will be filled with words of sincere intent and be accompanied by recommendations of masterful inactivity.
- There would then be a call for partnerships to undertake and share in the actions required from the

fire-fighting recommendations. Another committee may need to be struck to decide who does what, who is the spokesperson, and who will take credit for any progress. There may be brochures printed.

- Monitoring protocols would be developed to assess the outcomes of the actions.
- Arguments will ensue over when to define the fire as out and declare your house saved.

Then and only then might a few drops of water trickle from fire hoses. Finally, a group of spectators might gather to watch the last wisps of smoke rise from the burnt-out basement, all that's left of your house. They will wonder why it took so long.

I make these tongue-in-cheek observations based on my experience of participating in several species recovery plans, as well as watching and waiting for recovery actions to happen. I tend to agree with Aldo Leopold, who wisely pointed out in *A Sand County Almanac*, "The only progress that counts is that on the actual landscape of the back forty."

As in an ebb tide where water flows back to the ocean, caribou have steadily been pushed farther and farther north by habitats increasingly industrialized, fragmented, and busy in the Eastern Slopes. Declines in caribou populations were witnessed by Henry Stelfox in the Clearwater watershed in the 1930s. They were missing from most of the southern portion of the Eastern Slopes by the 1950s. And the decline continues in their northerly range.

Issues with extensive, industrial-scale logging were noted in the early 1980s; a 1986 caribou restoration plan called for habitat protection; and a 1993 conservation strategy mentioned logging as the biggest threat to caribou survival. A recovery strategy was completed in 2005. Unsurprisingly, the government of Alberta chose not to follow the recommendation for a moratorium on land uses in ranges where caribou were known to be at immediate risk of extirpation.

Much ink has been spilled on the plight of caribou, lots of coffee and doughnuts consumed, and a forest of paper has been used to describe and denote the issues, as well as suggestions for rescuing the species. Some 40 years later, we seem no closer to that essential rescue, or to recognizing that it is a one-way tide in the case of caribou if we do not act now.

Fish species on the edge fare little better. More that two and a half decades have passed since alarms went off for Athabasca rainbow trout, the same for westslope cutthroat trout, and over four decades for bull trout.

Then there are plants, underrepresented in the cauldrons of ecological catastrophe. Too few botanists, with too little time and money, struggle to identify, monitor, and assess risk. Charismatic megafauna, with large, plaintive eyes are the Cinderella species, commanding most effort and resources. It's hard to relate to a plant – you can't look into its eyes.

While it is probably true that few want to read about plants or insects, even in eloquent and urgent tones, we can't live without them. Yet both broad groups are in crisis because of climate change, habitat destruction, invasive species, and overuse of agrochemicals.

If species were capable of questioning our behaviour, it might make a St. Mary River sculpin, a limber pine, or a northern leopard frog wonder about whether there is any real intent to save them and the essential habitats they rely on.

The ponderous machinery of bureaucracy takes so long to set itself in motion. Multiple great wheels and levers and gears, once started, revolve with such a laborious, ponderous, and pained deliberation. When that work on the status of a species is finally complete, with all its surety, firmness, and procedural completeness, then a recovery plan is initiated.

A plan, however well intentioned, does not, in itself, save a threatened fish, bird, or mammal. It is the will, the intent, the resources, and the purposeful action of doing something that may save these imperilled species. Sadly, recovery actions tend to fit into the mode of "doing as little as possible and only as much as necessary."

It is easy to be blinded by the essential futility and uselessness of government planning exercises compared to the sense of achievement one derives from making progress on even one small part. Semantic arguments from bureaucrats and corporate executives over what constitutes "critical" habitat divert one's eyes off the recovery ball.

By the time any recovery actions occur, decades may have passed. It may then be a largely academic exercise as it is often too late for effective action to bring some species back from the brink.

A half-hearted recovery strategy is similar to putting out half a fire – we don't get half the benefits back and we end up poorer as a consequence. You don't walk away from a fire half out, or a species partially recovered. Hewing to the mantra that "you can't go wrong with low expectations" does not lend itself to species recovery.

From our own health we can recognize that an ailment left untreated has a nasty habit of becoming an affliction that is untreatable, maybe fatal. Ignoring the peril a species may be in and deciding not to follow an evidence-based designation to avoid a response that might be uncomfortable, complex, and potentially costly is a cop-out of our collective stewardship responsibility.

Bureaucrats talk of "industry partners," maybe even believing these entities are serious about being part of species recovery. Irony is one of the great cultural resources of Alberta. These are likely the same entities that are responsible for the collapse of species and continue through planning processes and their own political avenues to produce impediments to recovery actions.

When one adds up the procedural, bureaucratic, logistical, political, and economic steps and impediments, it is a wonder anything gets done. Often it is just a few resolute individuals, working in spite of the system, who struggle to implement recovery goals. Sterling examples include westslope cutthroat recovery in Banff National Park and bull trout habitat restoration in the Ram River watershed.

When we see the unwarranted delays in species-at-risk recovery, we need to ask some pointed questions to politicians, economists, corporate executives, investment bankers, and the apologists for unbridled economic growth. Have they calculated the number of species and their habitats that must be condemned to extirpation, degradation, irrelevance, and death to produce one more vote, one more stock dividend, one more fourth-quarter improvement, and one more rich person? What is the metric for this that results in a land made poorer because of a single-minded pursuit of financial wealth?

Beyond a few engaged conservationists, most of the public

is blissfully unaware of species at risk. They might be more aware if instinctually there was a recognition that species on the brink are a cautionary signal for our own survival. Give us a starlet's infidelities, the shopping channel, or the hockey series, and we're all ears and eyes. Trivia takes precedence over tangible, superfluous over substance, and consumer crap over consequences.

But if it were your house burning, you might pay attention.

HOW DID THE FISH CROSS THE ROAD?

———

I watched as a small trout attempted to leap into the flow of a culvert on a road crossing a tiny creek. The downstream lip of the culvert was about 30 centimetres above the water level of a small pool. In the clear water I could see the trout developing speed, launching itself into the tiny waterfall, and then falling back. After several attempts, the exhausted trout swam back downstream, stymied in an attempt to move up the little stream.

As in the riddle "Why did the chicken cross the road?" a fish's reasons are similar – to get to the other side. It could be to find cooler water temperatures in summer heat, a search for more food resources, better habitat, especially deep pools to over-winter in, or to find spawning locations. How a fish crosses the road, or if a fish can cross a road, becomes one of culvert size, length, water velocity, and ability to enter the culvert.

Alberta boasts of having 473,000 kilometres of roads. That's everything from multi-lane paved highways down to narrow resource roads. We have enough road length to get to the moon and part-way back, except there are no stream and river crossings on that journey. In Alberta, those roads intersect on a regular basis with flowing water.

It's estimated there are over 110,000 water course crossings, of which over half are culverts. This may be a considerable underestimate. There is acknowledgement on the part of those who work on this issue that inventorying culverts is a Herculean task. So too is assessing whether a culvert poses a problem for fish passage.

Culverts are the low-cost (read cheap) way to bridge a stream. An engineered bridge is orders of magnitude more expensive, although a fish might say it is well worth the cost. Although bridges can fail, culverts do routinely. They have a reported failure rate somewhere between 30 and 60 per cent.

What culverts fail at mostly is allowing fish passage. They can become like one-way doors. If you're a fish, you can swim downstream, but it's a path of no return. In time, upstream populations become isolated and, at worst, disappear.

A culvert is a corrugated but essentially smooth pipe. There are no refuges from the current where a fish can rest. What this means is a fish must use its burst speed to make the trip in one go. That might work for shorter culverts and some species of fish, but not all.

Research indicates burst speeds are only sustained over short time periods, usually less than 20 seconds. Trout and grayling have relatively high burst speeds compared to cool water species such as walleye, pike, and perch. This also varies by fish size and life stage.

The ability of fish to successfully navigate the length of a culvert also depends on their ability to enter it. Improperly installed culverts can have the downstream ends situated high above the water surface. Although some species of fish have the ability to jump, the combined energy to do that and then swim through the culvert may not be available.

Culverts become "perched" or "hung" as water speeds through a relatively friction-free pipe and develops more energy to erode when it pours out from the end of the pipe. Scour creates a vertical drop in an otherwise continuous channel slope. The stream downcuts below the culvert and the upstream portion becomes disconnected because the road is now an artificial channel control.

According to Mike Myles, an independent fluvial geomorphologist, culverts seem to be consistently undersized to deal with flood flows. Engineering specifications have not kept up with climate change, land use, and the impacts of both on hydrological response. This means culverts have a habit of blowing out during floods, adding to the sediment burden of streams and sometimes further exacerbating the failure to allow fish passage.

It's not as if this is current, breaking news. From *A Manual of the Principles and Practices of Roadmaking, 6th Edition*, dated 1853: "Size must be proportional to the greatest quantity of water which can ever be required to pass, and should be large enough to admit a boy to enter and clean them out." The last part of this old but timely advice indicates that culverts can become blocked with debris, or by beavers, and require regular maintenance.

Connectivity, the ability of fish to access all of a stream that is naturally available, is essential to population survival. Culverts that block fish passage fragment fish populations, restricting them to smaller stream sections, or blocking all the available habitat. This is of particular concern for species at risk. Work done to resolve some of these culvert issues in the Clearwater and Red Deer watersheds has opened up dozens of kilometres of stream for trout population expansion. Electro-fishing often shows trout queuing up below a hanging culvert, waiting for a repair.

Ironically, a hanging culvert can sometimes protect an up-stream population of native trout from competition and hybrid-ization with non-native species. Nothing is ever simple.

It is estimated that up to 40 per cent of culverts are barriers to fish passage. Based on best available information, more than 10,000 culverts currently fall into this category. This could be a serious underestimate since most culverts on small, first-order streams weren't part of the assessment.

The problem is recognized and steps are underway to remedy culverts with fish passage problems. Work progresses with staff from Public Lands, Alberta Transportation, the Alberta Energy Regulator, municipal governments, and fisheries biologists.

Alberta has a Watercourse Crossing Remediation Grant Pro-gram that provides financial help for municipalities to correct sites with fish passage problems. This initiative started in 2021, ran to 2025, and had $11.5 million available for the five-year per-iod. There is also a nifty Watercourse Crossing Inventory App available for anyone to report stream crossing issues. This helps document where the culverts are and the extent of the problem.

Despite the provincial dollars available, there are still two things standing in the way of full resolution – time and money. At the current rate of progress, with an average of 54 cross-ings fixed per year, it is estimated that it could take a century, perhaps two, to resolve the issue fully. You might think of this as putting a Band-Aid on a bullet wound.

In spite of the gloomy projections, some remain optimistic there is a light at the end of the culvert. They point out that fixing culverts isn't rocket science. Compared to other environmental issues this can be a very easy problem to solve. If owners of these crossings took the issue seriously, with time and effort put into resolution, in a few years the wins could be immense.

Corporate and government responsibility, coupled with a stewardship ethic and grounded with legal requirements, can provide significant steps forward, especially to deal with trout species-at-risk recovery efforts. However, not all display those characteristics; there is a lack of regulatory oversight, some roads (and crossings) no longer have "owners," plus many of these roads are well beyond their design best-before dates.

The latter is what faced Freshwater Conservation Canada, with two small tributaries of Waiparous Creek in Southwestern Alberta. Despite the fact that the trickles don't have formal names, bull trout and cutthroat trout didn't care and swam up the flow until soon they were blocked by a series of hanging culverts. Both streams had undersized culverts, multiples of them, at the bottom of steep valleys where cut and fill had been used to level the road. There was a metre drop from the lowermost culverts to the stream.

The fix required substantial engineering and preparation. Before construction, the work sites were isolated with blocking nets, trout were relocated, and the streams were diverted through pipes to dewater the area. All the earth fill was removed, including the old culverts. These were replaced by an open-bottomed metal arch. The fill was replaced but stabilized with reinforced geotextile.

These arches have much greater capacity for passage of flood flows. They also have a natural substrate bottom, affording trout free passage upstream and down. Most importantly, these allow the stream some flexibility in lateral movement, no water velocity barrier to fish passage, and less likelihood of being blocked by debris. Angela Ten, an FCC management biologist, reports that trout have moved upstream to occupy habitat.

Was this expensive? Yes! These remodelled culverts required the combined resources of many donors and funds from the Native Trout Collaborative. Was it worth it?

Some might say that the cost of allowing upstream access to a few trout seems exorbitant. That is the situation when too little thought was applied in the past to protecting native trout. If we want to save and recover at-risk trout species, this is the bill for inattention, ignorance, and greed.

Lord Darlington in *Lady Windermere's Fan* may not have been thinking about fish and the cost of fixing culverts, but his observation, "A cynic is a man who knows the price of everything and the value of nothing," might be the appropriate answer to those questioning the cost. I hope the culvert that blocked the passage of the trout of my memory has been replaced by an open-bottomed arch. If it has, the trout's progeny are now revelling in new habitats.

STOCKING FISH

A 19th-Century Answer to a 21st-Century Problem?

———

The practice of stocking fish probably started with someone transferring a few fish from a place with many to spots perceived to have none. This might have included a stream above a natural barrier like a waterfall, or a barren lake. Like many of our attempts to "fix" the world, this seemed like a good idea. But simply transferring fish was time-consuming and inefficient, so we started to raise them in artificial environments where we could control nature and up the output.

Once the supply chain issue was solved, then came the question – where can we put these fish? This started with a sense that water bodies were being "fished out," depleted with too much angling or commercial harvest. The solution was to replenish these places with hatchery-raised fish, like restocking a grocery store's shelves.

As author Kim Todd writes in *Tinkering with Eden*, "Ponds and lakes, rather than being viewed as complex ecosystems, were treated as outdoor aquariums waiting to be filled."

When the idea of raising fish began, hatcheries seemed like a logical, rational approach – if fish are scarce, just make some more. It seemed to work for just about everything else, so why not fish? Problems began, and are still with us, that hatchery operations can't come close to mimicking what happens in nature.

The province used to operate a lake whitefish hatchery on Lesser Slave Lake. R.B. Miller, Alberta's first fisheries biologist, was the agent of the hatchery's closure, as he wondered why the facility was necessary. Years of research showed "Catches from hatchery-supported age groups were no bigger than those that received no hatchery support." Miller concluded that enough naturally spawned eggs survived to ensure the success of the next generation.

In concert with this was the conclusion that native fish species were incapable of sustaining angling pressure and had to be bolstered with the product of a hatchery. Part of this was a bit of bigotry toward native fish, perceived to be unable to "keep up," a bit unsporting, and not familiar to anglers from other places.

Rarely was it conceded that native fish populations, under a regime of suitable regulations, could keep up with demand, especially if habitat conditions were not degraded at the same time. Stocking of non-native fish species was, and still is, done to entertain anglers. That "entertainment" has had many profound negative consequences. For example, there may be many non-native trout species stocked, but they are all of one flavour, one texture, and one hue. Like factory cheese, compared with our native species.

In aquatic systems of high complexity, interactions, and interrelationships our ability to accurately predict outcomes is severely stretched. It is prudent to let the fish that have adapted to these systems over millennia tell us what they need rather than accept that a non-native species (or a formerly native one with several generations of hatchery dilution) will substitute for that accumulated wisdom.

Think of the operation this way, that only a few fish are used in fish culture to create thousands if not millions of offspring. Think of the implications if it were humans instead of fish. In nature, the pairings are random, creating a wide range of genetic diversity based on generations of experience. It is genetic diversity that assures native populations of their abundance, since in diversity are found the keys to surviving and thriving in a changeable, variable aquatic world.

Without the genetic information about the world, when that world changes, as it does subtly and sometimes chaotically, a hatchery fish may not know what to do and when to do it. Like a worn key that no longer engages with the lock, the messages imbedded in the DNA may be faint or missing.

In waters near population centres, where angling pressure was high, where overwinter habitat was scarce, where periodic fish kills from effluent discharges wiped out populations, it was rationalized that stocking could compensate and provide limited angling for part of a year. This does seem to work, in some situations, but at a very high cost.

Stocking hatchery fish is seen to be a way to take pressure off native fish populations. This is an unproven hypothesis that needs testing. Unfortunately, before any research confirmed or denied this assumption, the decision to build hatcheries had been made. Once that expensive infrastructure was in place, the pressure to maximize the "benefits" of the expenditure became the driving force. The answer was a hatchery – what was the question?

Every water body has inherent limitations to fish production – space, food, temperature, predation – that regulate populations. You can't escape the "reaper." Even the natural system doesn't allow every egg to hatch, or for every fish to survive to adulthood. Mortality might be delayed with hatchery fish, but it is never eliminated. Stocking is a game of musical chairs – we bring in more fish, but we don't make more chairs.

We can't "beat the system" with hatchery fish. Hatchery fish, raised in a benign, artificial environment with abundantly available food, have trouble adjusting and fending for themselves in the natural world. They can die quickly, especially in streams, but out of sight so there isn't evidence of high mortality. This also means the ones that do survive are very costly, but the bookkeeping is opaque.

Stocking sends a message that we can have our cake (development) and eat it too (angling). When we don't recognize ecological limits to our land-use footprints, we assume we can mitigate fish losses through stocking. Investment in habitat, especially restoration of damaged bits and appropriate regulations, is costly in the short term, but when amortized over time, it is insignificant compared to the costs (and failures) of stocking. Hatchery fish are no substitute for conservation. Fish hatcheries have high capital and operating costs compared with natural fish production.

If aquatic habitat has been degraded or is no longer available, stocking will not solve the problem.

Use of hatcheries to create fisheries where none previously existed might have merit, albeit with some ecological costs. If a fishery has to be maintained because natural reproduction fails, the cost to maintain the population is high and perhaps unsustainable.

"Wild" fish have been formed in crucibles of change, with unique water flows, temperatures, food availability, and seasons, especially everything from cement mixer-like turbulence in flood flows to extremely low flows over winter under ice cover. When we use the term "wild," we really have very little idea of the micro-conditions under which these fish exist.

Our history in this landscape is a shadow of a fish's. In the 12,000 or so years of evolution on the Eastern Slopes, and longer for their ancestors, fish have a distinct history that belongs to the place where they currently exist, where the fit is akin to the tumblers on a lock.

Fish culture specialists like to work with tractable species, which is another word for "domesticated." These fish are calm in hatchery situations, respond to handling well, and essentially have lost their wild tendencies. Hatchery fish, like rainbow trout, are animals dressed in the skin of a trout but they are missing much of what makes a trout a trout. They don't have the advantage of a 12,000-year apprenticeship in one place.

Our experience with hatcheries suggests that artificially changing selection pressure will alter native fish genetic outcomes. In short, diversity can be sacrificed for efficiency of production. If you think about it, a streamside technique that improves hatching success by four times equals a loss of natural selection by the same amount. Is that a good trade-off? Our history with hatcheries suggests we're playing with fire in a tinder-dry forest.

A colleague told me of a conversation with a lady from the Old Crow community who was working on Yukon chinook salmon. Her advice was to "leave the fish alone." Fix the habitat, suspend their harvests, and keep hatcheries away from the system. Let healing begin. These sound like wise words.

What worries me, though, is as native fish start winking out because we've changed and destroyed their habitats, we seek other species to compensate for the human-induced void. Anglers didn't complain when the native cutthroat, bull trout, and Athabasca rainbow trout became imperilled. Instead, we stocked non-native rainbows, brook, and brown trout.

As conditions changed in the pothole fisheries, we resorted to tiger trout, a hatchery-manipulated cross between brook and brown trout. The same thing occurred with splake, crosses between lake and brook trout. These are artificial crosses, rarely seen in nature. Some would describe them as "Frankenfish."

There have been calls to stock bass and other non-natives, mostly for variety but also to circumvent changes to our lakes and ponds. It's been suggested that catfish would allow angling to continue in the face of warmer waters, a climate change outcome. What happens when our waterbodies can't even support these species?

Regardless of what you think about hatcheries, they aren't the sole cause of the collapse of native species. While hatcheries and aquaculture have a role to play, we shouldn't give up on our wild fish, and that means rebuilding and conserving them. Hatcheries can and do perform vital conservation and restoration work.

We need all the tools we can muster for fisheries conservation, but tools like hatcheries need to be managed wisely and we need to be wary of overselling or becoming completely reliant on them.

OF ELEPHANTS AND SAVING TROUT

———

In the dilemma of recovery actions for native trout there is a parallel with the parable of the elephant and the blind men. Each blind man felt a different part of the elephant and described the beast based on this limited experience. The answers were simple – this is a snake, a tree trunk, a wall, a rope, or a spear. The complexity of an elephant was reduced to simple explanations, as is the case sometimes with recovery solutions for trout that are at risk.

In rare instances the answer to keeping a species extant will be simple. Removing a hanging culvert to allow trout to reoccupy upstream habitat is an example. Unfortunately, for most struggling populations of bull trout, westslope cutthroat trout, and Athabasca rainbow trout the answers are anything but simple.

Biologists point out there can be 15 to 30 discrete physical, chemical, and biological factors that account for declines in populations of native trout. In the challenge of species recovery efforts there is also a decidedly human dimension. There is conscience and commitment, with a counterweight of unwillingness to rock the boat and picking inoffensive solutions. If anything is obvious, it is complexity – the elephant in the watershed and how we deal with it.

Much as we big-brained humans can research the complexity of the world and the factors that imperil trout, we still have stone-age brains that gravitate to simple solutions. We seek the simple amid a welter of the complex. However, as H.L. Mencken correctly pointed out, "For every complex problem, there's a solution that is simple, neat, and wrong."

Maybe we need to start by acknowledging that simple solutions to complex problems can fail because a complex problem demands you start by admitting that complexity exists.

Karl Popper, an influential philosopher of science, once divided the world into two categories: clocks and clouds. In *Of*

Clouds and Clocks, he described clocks as neat, orderly systems that could be explained in simple terms. Clouds, on the other hand, were "highly irregular, disorderly, and more or less unpredictable" messes.

Native trout recovery would not be in the category of Popper's clocks. We shouldn't pretend that peering deeper into the intricate workings of a watershed and its trout inhabitants will find the exact tool to completely fix something we have broken. There may well not be any simple solutions to the complex problems we have contributed to with land use, non-native species introductions, and climate change.

Despite the protections put in place, unintended consequences and inadequate protocols have led to imperilled species. One of those impacts relates to cumulative effects. So to solve a complex problem, we need to respond in a continuously adaptive way. Maybe we will never understand the problem until it has been solved. Sometimes the act of trying to solve a problem helps point to seemingly unrelated issues. Every attempt reconfigures the situation. But until we break out of the pattern of always doing what we've always done, what we'll always get is what we've always got – not much of a formula for successful recovery.

Several threatened and endangered trout species, in various overlapping combinations, often mixed with non-native species in a variety of watersheds, subject to different land-use pressures and intensities, with multiple ecological needs certainly add to the complexity of recovery efforts. Trout exist in naturally dynamic stream systems, where they have adapted to the range of natural variability. The land-use footprint has made the responses of systems more chaotic, well beyond the range of natural variability. The challenge is to bring stream systems back into a more natural dynamic.

Tackling such a complex problem by breaking it down into smaller, more easily managed pieces may not be effective. Instead, we should start by considering the watershed as a whole. If we can describe it, explain how the different parts of the system work together, and how some interconnections generate their own influences on the wider system, then we will better understand what is broken.

Taking a complex system apart until we find a piece of the problem we can solve means only one piece is ever addressed – the unintended consequences that come from only solving a small part of the problem might negate any effective progress on species recovery. Garrett Hardin, an American ecologist, wisely observed in *The Tragedy of the Commons*, "We can never do merely one thing, therefore we must do several in order that we may bring into being a new stable system."

Not all complexity is related to the physical setting or the associated factors. Many of the issues that have led to species declines have human dimensions related to hidden social, political, or economic trade-offs in resource allocation, land, and water use decisions. Until there is a better level of transparency as well as accountability and responsibility on the part of industry and all government departments for species recovery, many recovery actions will be constrained or rendered ineffective.

This constitutes a "wicked problem," something that is difficult or impossible to solve because of incomplete, contradictory, and shifting bases that are often difficult to recognize. It refers to a problem where there is no single or simple solution. In addition, because of complex interdependencies, the effort to solve one aspect of a wicked problem may reveal or create other problems. There can be organized resistance and irresponsibility from the political, bureaucratic, and corporate worlds. "Wicked" can also denote internal resistance to resolution, for a variety of reasons.

A real or perceived lack of empirical evidence leads to uncertainty about which recovery action is best and the outcomes of such action. There is risk – will the chosen action be positive or negative? This creates risk aversion. No one wants to be part of a failed recovery effort (but equally so, no one should be party to no recovery effort). The fog of uncertainty impairs the ability to see a path forward. More emphasis on what isn't known and less on what is drags out recovery actions.

Paralysis sets in and the displacement behaviour of wanting more information, more research, and more data postpones action. Values, preferences, and prior experiences drive decisions, and those can lead to more and more conservative approaches.

No threshold exists to define when information is sufficient to proceed to an action, and so a vicious circle can be created. At this point we need to take the opportunity to learn effectively by proceeding, using adaptive management and monitoring, and be coached by objective expert opinion so we can break the impasse created by the paralysis of perfection.

There is another aspect to this, which involves shifting benchmarks and the sense that everything can go on a little worse than yesterday but not noticeably different. This ties into what Timothy Snyder, a Yale historian, calls the "politics of inevitability" in *The Road to Unfreedom: Russia, Europe, America*. It's the sense the future is just more of the present, that the laws of progress are known, that there are no alternatives, and that nothing really needs to be done.

Then, as some investigators have termed it, there is the "knowing but not doing" syndrome. This is the perverse situation of knowing what to do but not translating that knowledge into doing something. It is also referred to as the "research-implementation gap."

A step forward is recognizing the gap is real, that there is a problem turning theory into practice. By expanding the scope of practitioners engaged in recovery efforts and widening the net beyond the provincial boundaries, there may well be a light seen at the end of a dark tunnel of uncertainty. Engaging with the academic community and encouraging research on practical, pragmatic solutions would help. A lack of effective monitoring and evaluation of recovery efforts stymies progress. This should provide guidance for further efforts.

As Sandra Steingraber said in *Living Downstream*, "It's time to start looking at alternative paths. From the right to know flows the duty to inquire and the obligation to act."

Alberta biologists have developed a modelling framework for testing the possible outcomes of one recovery action or another. The Cumulative Effects Assessment methodology, better known as the "Joe Model," is a pragmatic approach to threats assessment for fish species at risk and is useful as a robust method for geographically prioritizing recovery actions. The framework of the Joe Model allows the testing of hypotheses based on best available data and the avoidance of scattergun responses to recovery efforts. This provides a much more focused and defensible strategy to move recovery efforts for fish species at risk forward to deal with complexity and uncertainty.

Lastly, a better understanding of the social, political, and economic dimensions of recovery actions would better advance understanding of impediments and possible collaboration.

Adding to uncertainty and fear of failure is the defence of untested or wrong, but simple (and uncontroversial), recovery solutions. This could be categorized as worshipping at the temple of wishful thinking. There was a time we complained we didn't have enough information to make an informed decision. We might be at a point now where we do have enough information, but we fail to act because we might not like where the decision takes us and who will be irritated along the way.

As an example, it seems to me recovery actions have to occur at a watershed scale, which would involve interactions with logging, OHV use, random camping, water management, mining, grazing, and petroleum interests. For trout, it's easier to focus on the immediate stream and stream banks for recovery efforts, to avoid the unpleasantness of a battle with multiple interests.

However, because of a limited focus, these types of actions could have very little meaningful impact toward species recovery. Some authors have termed this the fear of "upsetting important others," which could include politicians, senior staff, and other stakeholders.

The potential to upset others has implications for criticism and loss of trust and can lead to a high degree of controversy and implied (or real) political opposition or pressure. There are multiple stakeholders with conflicting interests to whom resource managers feel accountable to (or are accountable to), as well as legal agreements related to resource use and extraction.

Perversely, administrative silos functionally separate land-use decisions in forestry, energy, and agriculture from species-at-risk protection. This adds to and escalates species declines, affecting recovery needs, recovery effectiveness, and costs. As in the parable of the elephant and the blind men, this creates a blinkered approach to land and water management where each agency only touches one part, thinking that is all there is.

A possible solution to the issues of competing interests and limited recovery funds may well be a broader expansion of responsibility for recovery successes. Instead of a small group of biologists and conservation interests shouldering all of the load for species recovery, there needs to be a recognition that this is a mandated provincial and federal responsibility that cuts across administrative boundaries.

Specifically, if staff in forestry, energy, and agricultural departments were advised that recovery efforts are part of their roles, co-ordination was essential, and performance appraisals would incorporate outcomes for species at risk, this would facilitate recovery efforts. This may be a fantasy, given the very clear, impenetrable silo walls between (and sometimes within) departments.

Engaging all social, economic, and political stakeholders in recovery efforts and tasking them with equal responsibility for positive outcomes would remove many barriers to successful recovery efforts. A mutual investment in outcomes would also spread the economic burden of recovery to all stakeholders. Instead of adding to the recovery costs because of poor resource extraction and use practices, these would be minimized through tighter regulatory standards and loss of future business opportunity with non-compliance.

Just as complexity needs to be embraced, so too does the

concept that biologists alone cannot bring species at risk back from the brink. Until there is a concerted, co-operative effort to share the task among all stakeholders, the outcomes are grim. Economic and social imperatives with their political supports need to reflect a new order of doing business, one where success is based on ecological integrity measured by robust populations of fish and wildlife.

All the land uses that effect species at risk have their own levels of complexity and degrees of uncertainty. Yet these issues did not impede progress on these activities. Recovery actions are delayed because of apprehension about negative outcomes, either from the recovery efforts themselves or on account of others' perceptions of these efforts. Those who want to do nothing, think nothing needs to be done, or fear doing anything can find abundant ammunition to support their intransigence or procrastination. This is not species recovery but rather cataloguing the death rattles of a species.

Species extirpation is what happens when we continually plan for recovery but never implement the plan. It's similar to having a lifeboat but never putting it in the water while the ship is sinking.

Alice, from *Alice in Wonderland*, asks the Cheshire Cat, "Would you tell me, please, which way I ought to go from here?" To which the Cheshire Cat replies, "That depends a good deal on where you want to get to." Alice then responds, "I don't much care where, as long as I get somewhere." There may be much wisdom in this to move forward on the elephant of recovery efforts.

AN ELEGY FOR THE CROWSNEST BULL TROUT

———

"Were there drum rolls, rifles fired in your honour, and a sombre elegy provided to commemorate your loss?" It's a rhetorical question to the departed bull trout in the upper Crowsnest drainage of Southwestern Alberta, and the answer is "no." I can't help but wonder why this happened.

For a species that existed over more than a geological epoch to slip through our fingers in almost a human lifespan without anyone paying attention is a mystery worth exploring. To unravel the mystery requires a journey through geology, hydrology, ecology, history and, inevitably, the human mind.

The landscape of bull trout is one of relative newness, geologically speaking.

Most recently, up to about 13,000 years ago, the Eastern Slopes of Alberta were covered by the Cordilleran ice sheet, while the plains were under the mile-thick Laurentide sheet. Alpine and continental glaciations then shaped the watershed in an epoch that ended a scant 12,000 years or so ago. For the next 11,900 years, give or take a few, other forces, including climate, erosion, fire, drought, floods, and grazing, combined with plant growth, movement, and succession to form the habitats bull trout evolved with and prospered in, and from which many have subsequently disappeared.

Bull trout are a hardy fish, perhaps with ice water in their veins. They currently exist under the influence and at the edge of glaciers elsewhere in Alberta. One can imagine the scene a dozen millennia ago as bull trout queued up at the edge of mountain and continental ice masses, waiting to test the waters for new opportunity. Glacial refuges for these fish existed in the Columbia Basin, the Missouri/Mississippi watershed, and in Yukon.

Bull trout probably crossed the Continental Divide at low spots such as the Crowsnest Pass to occupy new waters. It would have been an interesting time, of alpine glaciers retreating, advancing, and sometimes forming ice dams to allow fish to swim over the Continental Divide. The bull trout were some of Alberta's first explorers and pioneers. Maybe they began as tourists who became marooned in a new environment.

Imagine what these fish found – a raw landscape recently chiselled out of rock, unstable, dynamic, and empty of other fish. Few fish species were up to the migration and southern East Slope streams were dominated by just three species – bull trout, westslope cutthroat trout, and mountain whitefish.

These fish were subject to cold-water temperatures, including multiple months under ice cover and turbulent habitats in steep stream gradients. Their homes were under periodic siege by floods, droughts, and fires. Even the foundations crumbled from time to time with massive landslides, such as the Frank Slide. Yet these creatures survived and thrived in this changing, dynamic landscape. How did these fish make a go of it?

The operative words to explain their success have to be adaptability and flexibility. Like the India rubber man of circus fame, bull trout display an astonishing elasticity to take advantage of the wide variety of habitat choices offered them. In the Crowsnest they encountered a lake (Crowsnest Lake) gouged out by glaciers, with an ice dam downstream.

These pioneering bull trout formed a unique, lake-dwelling population that spawned in several of the Crowsnest River's tributaries and reared in these streams and in the river. Some of them shook the evolutionary dice and took up a riverine lifestyle, detached from the lake. As some of them progressed downstream, they plunged over Lundbreck Falls, never to return to the upper Crowsnest.

The key to their survival (and an ecological bottleneck) was the annual return home to small tributaries to spawn. In these streams are special places where water percolates through the gravels, signalling to bull trout that eggs laid here will survive and hatch. Not many of these places exist. This groundwater is captured as surface flow earlier in the year, the decade, perhaps even the century, and kilometres away from the spawning site.

We still don't understand much about groundwater, hidden as it is from our inspection. It could be related to intact old-growth forest. Old-growth forests are good sponges. They capture, store, and slowly release water. For the Crowsnest bull trout, survival was at a landscape scale, the sum of all of the parts, not just a few in the water.

As we turn the time machine dial backwards, to the 1880s, changes in landscape and fish abundance would already be evident. In the records of the NWMP post at Pincher Creek in 1890 is a notation of concern about declining fish populations. "If only we had been here a few years ago when fish were plentiful," wrote one of the officers.

The Crowsnest Pass might have remained a backwater had it not been for the discovery of coal that coincided with the need for a rail line that could transport the shiny black stuff. The coming of the Crowsnest Pass Railway in 1898 was the beginning of the end for bull trout. In countless other places, the same story has played itself out. With better access comes more people, which begets more human endeavour, which increases access – and the native flora and fauna falter.

As we nudge the time dial forward to 1898, we find that the rail line blocks Blairmore Creek to upstream fish passage. Crowsnest Creek begins to experience multiple perturbations, starting with limestone quarrying in 1903, which, over time, would blanket the stream bottom and part of the substrate of Crowsnest Lake with limestone fines and dust. Later, the stream will suffer channelization, major channel shifts, culvert crossings, and fines and sediment from coal mining. York Creek flows are controlled by a new dam, built about 1910 for municipal water supply.

Concerns about forest fires led to extremely high levels of livestock grazing to reduce fuel loads. Sheep and cattle grazing in the Crowsnest Pass, coupled with overharvest of timber for mine props and railway ties, led to a number of serious floods in the Crowsnest Pass in the 1920s and 1930s. Nez Perce and McGillivray creeks are channelized after severe flooding in Coleman in 1923.

Later, McGillivray Creek receives coal mine effluent in the form of red ferrous oxide, which coats the stream bottom. Gold Creek gets a dam. The list of tinkering with the tributaries marches on, at scales both large and small. Nowhere, it seems, are we ever disposed to let water run downhill without interfering.

The Crowsnest River is not immune to changes and advice either. The list of indignities includes channelization, with some sections of the river shuffled around multiple times in the last 100 years. Disposal of raw sewage, fuel spills, garbage dumping, infilling of the floodplain, and removal of riparian trees were perhaps minor compared to the effect of having several mines process coal on the riverbanks.

Coal fines, dust, and sediment poured into the river for about 75 years. People recall the Crowsnest River running black with coal fines and sediment during spring runoff and after every rainstorm. Slack coal was dumped directly into the river in an attempt to flush it away. It worked, but it was devastating. Duane Radford, who was born in the Pass and went on to be a provincial biologist, recalls the river being a "veritable wasteland" from Coleman to Passburg, a distance of almost 30 kilometres.

For fish that are sight feeders, this can be an issue, but the greater impact was on juvenile bull trout. Bull trout children hide under and behind rocks and can even overwinter within the gravel of an apparently dry stream bed. As sediments accumulate, they tend to cover and cement the stream bottom materials together, smothering everything under an aquatic landslide of mud. There is no place left for the bull trout kids to play, feed, breathe, or survive.

Hungry people filled the Crowsnest Pass, especially in the days of less-than-benevolent mine owners. During strikes at the mines, people turned to hunting and fishing to survive. Angling pressure was very high, both from conventional sources and the use of the "CIL wiggler," a euphemism the miners used for fishing with dynamite. My uncle, an avid outdoorsman and a miner, was appalled at the actions of some of his neighbours, but, as was the case of the day, said nothing to them or the game wardens.

Eighty years of angling took its toll, but it was the transformation of the Crowsnest Pass watershed that proved too much for bull trout. Coal mining and logging affected virtually every portion of the watershed. Those land uses combined with residential development meant that by the 1950s every spawning tributary in the upper watershed, except one, had a dam or a barrier to upstream fish movement across it. One by one, inexorably, the options decreased. It's hard for a bull trout to make other travel plans when it runs into a dam or other obstructions trying to get to its natal stream.

A bull trout female will deposit thousands of eggs in a depression she excavates in the gravels of a stream bottom. Not all will survive to hatch, let alone reach maturity. But in some years things are just right and more will survive to create what fish biologists call a "strong year class," a kind of superior bench strength for the bull trout team over many seasons. These positive blips on the bull trout scale of survival will carry the population through the bad times when the numbers of recruits are low.

A wrench in the gears of bull trout prosperity is us humans. First, we have decreased the number of places accessible to spawning bull trout, reducing the available options. Then, in an act almost as detrimental, we have affected the watershed in ways that disrupted the cycle of good spawning years and recruitment. We removed the essential buffer bull trout had evolved to tackle life in an already unstable, dynamic environment.

The last hope for the Crowsnest bull trout was Allison Creek. What was probably the final act in the bull trout tragedy was related to me by Gordon Kerr, a biologist and former assistant deputy minister of Alberta's Fish and Wildlife Division, whose family has a long history in the area.

Gordon remembers, as a teenager, watching the Highways Department straightening out all the meanders of his favourite trout stream not more than a few fly casts from his parents' home. The rifle-shot straight channel was designed to protect a new bridge over Allison Creek. It's a pity no one knew enough then to protect the bull trout. Unwinding the stream unleashed a massive amount of erosion that formed an impassible gravel bar at the mouth of the creek.

That condition persisted for years after the channelization in 1953. With nowhere else to go to replenish itself, the bull trout population disappeared shortly afterwards. All the doors had closed, effectively ending over 10,000 years of bull trout prosperity in the upper Crowsnest watershed above Lundbreck Falls. A threshold was crossed, a critical mass lost.

The strengths of the bull trout, honed over time and endlessly tested in the crucible of their dynamic environment, turned out to work against them when exposed to a new variable, humans.

Maturing later, a strength in a place where it might take several years to accumulate the energy to produce eggs, means the likelihood of being caught by an angler before then is high. Those secret spawning sites didn't lie concealed long and as bull trout congregated they were highly vulnerable to hook, bullet, net, trap, spear, poison, and dynamite.

Their carnivorous habits (and their size) led to an obtuse sentiment that bull trout were undesirable, competing for the "nobler" trout. It seems man, the summit predator, will allow no other competitor to exist. An attitude prevailed (and still does among some) that bull trout should be eliminated.

In his poignant unpublished essay, "My Grandfather's Trout," Kevin Van Tighem writes, "In the 1950s bull trout were easy protein at best, and junk fish at worst." In a time-tested pattern, first comes the denigration and whatever follows is the rationalization.

At another level, one more telling for the fate of bull trout, was the practice of propping up and defending economic interests, often at the expense of everything else. In fairness, local sportsmen's clubs complained about the pollution, but no local politicians had the spine to stand up to foreign-owned mines and the vested economic interests of local business. The mine owners had simply to threaten to close the mines and go elsewhere to quiet any opposition. This has an eerie similarity to the response from today's energy industry.

One local politician even opined that coal dust was good for trout, for it warmed up the water and allowed trout to move further upstream. Apparently, he had neither a firm grip on the principles of physics or of biology, but he did have a keen grasp of where his financial support lay. That, too, has linkages with contemporary events.

No one really knows when the last lonely bull trout succumbed. It may have been sometime in the 1960s. The disappearance has been complete with no more caught, either by anglers or extensive electrofishing surveys. Maybe the end of the bull trout line was caught by an angler, ignorant of the fact this was the last of its kind. Perhaps it lingered, as Martha, the last passenger pigeon did, filled with loneliness, frustration, and an unrequited longing.

The slippery horde of the upper Crowsnest now only exists as memories in the minds of a few elderly anglers and in old black and white photographs. I have one of those pictures. It shows a smiling child clutching a trout nearly as large as he.

There are no memorials to mark the passing, no tombstones to sit on to ponder why bull trout slipped from our grasp. There were no eulogies for the passing of bull trout in the upper Crowsnest, unlike for other species we have lost. The passenger pigeon, the bison, and the Eskimo curlew all have their mourners in print.

I'm not surprised, for we have an imperfect understanding of the complexity of aquatic systems, of their connections to all living things, and of cumulative effects that insidiously erode the ability of a system to support some species. We don't live in water – we are not of that world. Yet everything we do affects the aquatic world but is beyond our sight and consciousness.

So what did we lose? Sadly, we will never know if the Crowsnest bull trout were the ancestors to populations in the Oldman and Castle watersheds, separated as they had been by Lundbreck Falls, near the mouth of the Crowsnest River. Loss of genetic diversity hamstrings attempts at restoration. We lost an ancient neighbour with an enviable survival record in a turbulent environment. Anglers lost an opportunity to pit themselves against a fish that grew to sizes large enough to frighten small children. The ecosystem lost a precious, perhaps vital, cog. Bull trout are to the aquatic world as a grizzly bear is to the terrestrial one.

But mostly we don't know what we lost because our understanding and comprehension of aquatic systems is so rudimentary. We don't measure, we don't monitor, and we don't pay attention. If we don't pay attention, things go missing. It could include us.

It took just seven decades, roughly a person's lifespan, to wipe out these fish. No one set out to eliminate the Crowsnest bull trout. There was no malevolent plan for extirpation. Perhaps with a plan we could have been more efficient and concluded the job sooner. So many other species have suffered similar fates of benign neglect and the insidious endpoint of long-term cumulative effects. By the very nature of the term "unintended consequences," each separate action and choice made by people was likely viewed as inconsequential.

We can criticize the ignorance and actions of people in the past, of corporate greed, of individual apathy, and of institutions not keeping watch on the natural resources entrusted to them. If only they had connected the dots and in a timely fashion had undertaken a strategy of protecting and preserving some of the unique pieces of biodiversity. One can't, out of hand, condemn the actions of those people bettering themselves in the Crowsnest Pass 50 to 100 years ago. However, their strivings to better their lot are also those that contributed to depriving later generations of bull trout of their lot.

It would have been so much easier to have maintained something that existed, rather than try to restore something that has been lost. Indeed, those people should have done something. Of course, as a cautionary tale, are we and our legislators materially different today? We seem to have more greed and less need than the old coal miners.

Perhaps a memorial to the bull trout is of little consequence now. We do not feel the need to mourn that which we do not understand enough to miss. Tourists might read the inscription, but their thoughts will not flow from the plaque to the fish that no longer exists. The wonder isn't that the bull trout disappeared, but that they survived as long as they did in the Crowsnest.

Bull trout were very good at what they did – survival – despite the odds. We were very good at what we still do – cause things to disappear – even though we should know better. Perhaps that is what should be writ large in a prominent spot, as a reminder not to do it again (and again).

Fish and wildlife are part of our myths, history, lives, and landscapes. Sadly, they can slip to become only a part of our memory, and worse – we may forget them altogether. If a worse thing could be imagined than losing something of value, it must be to forget that something irreplaceable has been lost.

Requiescat in pace, the bull trout of the Crowsnest.

AN EAR TO NATURE

To say the sights and sounds of nature inspire me seems trite and overblown. But there it is. A formation of Canada geese gliding overhead is as beautiful as any idea perfected. But their abundance can render them invisible to change.

As thousands of Canada geese pass over me in scattered flocks, their calls almost obliterate the traffic noise. It's an everyday miracle to which we can be deaf and blind. I doubt that two in a hundred drivers notice the skeins of geese flying over their heads or hear the goose music inside their soundproofed vehicles, or notice a murmuration of mallards that, at times, blots out the background scenery, or mistake an immense flock of snow geese for a blizzard. Yet these are the things that remind us we still live in a place where the exuberance of wildlife can quicken our pulses.

These sights remind me there are still vestiges of what

Alberta must have resembled more than a century and a half ago. It wouldn't have been just herds of bison blanketing the grassland, with a retinue of wolves and grizzly bears. These were the charismatic megafauna, but their visual presence may have been overshadowed by the sheer volume of bird racket.

It must have been deafening. The tinkling trill of a Baird's sparrow, the scolding of a wren, the screech of a ferruginous hawk, a meadowlark's melody, a loud, rolling call of a sandhill crane, a maniacal sora rail, and the cacophony of honks and quacks from waterfowl of every description. Those and a few hundred more chirps, twitters, screeches, hoots, croons, rattles, mutterings, mews, scolds, squawks, whistles, and shrieks. Ear plugs might have been useful.

One might have heard the bugle of the whooping crane, a tall white bird standing over a metre tall. Frank Farley, an Alberta naturalist and farmer, wrote of whooping cranes nesting in the central part of the province up to the 1920s. He felt these birds had a centre of abundance there, not just the occasional occurrence. And then they were nearly gone.

There is a message in the virtual extinction of whooping cranes. We can't take wildlife for granted, assuming they have abundant space and suitable habitat. It's also hubris to think our development footprint is well regulated, thoughtfully and carefully considered, with ecologically appropriate checks and balances. Every drained wetland, each piece of native grassland cultivated, each little copse of aspen woodland bulldozed, and the fragmentation of the landscape into smaller and smaller islands of unconnected and relict habitats pushes our biodiversity treasure closer to the edge.

Spring on the prairie is eerily quiet these days, with the

catastrophic loss of ground-nesting, insect-eating birds. On dozens of dancing grounds, the booming of greater sage-grouse males, proclaiming their fitness to breed, is missing. My home-steading grandparents probably feasted on the pinnated grouse that perched (and feasted) on the rows of wheat stooks. Extir-pation was their fate.

Gone long before my grandparents settled in Central Al-berta was the passenger pigeon. Pigeon Lake, Hills, and Creek are the sole, enigmatic references to this biological phenome-non. My observations of waves of geese and ducks are probably a mere shadow of the exuberance of flocks of passenger pigeons that were reputed to block out the sun.

"Martha," the last remaining passenger pigeon on Earth, died on September 1, 1914, at age 29 in the Cincinnati Zoological Garden. In a memorial to the extinct species, Aldo Leopold wrote in *A Sand County Almanac*:

> Our grandfathers were less well-housed, well-fed, well-clothed than we are. The strivings by which they bettered their lot are also those which deprived us of pigeons. Perhaps now we grieve because we are not sure, in our hearts, that we have gained by the exchange. The gadgets of industry bring us more comfort than the pigeons did, but do they add as much to the glory of spring?

Some may not mourn the loss of wild critters and hardly notice the quiet that descends in their absence. It's easy to sleep in without the interruption of the robin chorus at dawn. That quiet, to me, is akin to a music fancier waking up one morning and there are no symphonies, no rock and roll, no pop – not a note to be heard, even the blues. Imagine not ever again hearing your child, your lover, your friend – something in your surroundings has gone missing.

A summer thunderstorm descends, full of sound and fury, with a pyrotechnical display. And then it's gone. As summer heat parches the ground and leaves us panting for relief, we scan the weather forecasts, wondering when the next storm will arrive. What if it doesn't? People who are inspired by wildlife, who thrill to the sighting of a bird and the sound of its call, wonder the same thing as silence magnifies.

Imagine no bird symphonies, rhapsodies, or sonatas. No solos or duets. When present, these are the indications that the world still retains some wildness, some link to our past. Amid the chorus, this indicates we have ensured enough places remain for the birds to make a living and enliven and enrich us with their songs. Silence speaks otherwise.

It's not enough to have fried chicken, buffalo wings (no actual buffalo are harmed), or mechanically deboned poultry flesh, breaded and deep-fried, then ingeniously marketed as "nuggets." Convenient and abundant as these avian things might be, we need to decide, as Aldo Leopold observed in the memorial to the extinct passenger pigeon, whether we have gained by this exchange for wild places and wildlife.

The wild doesn't feed us anymore, not physically, but it does feed our souls, as music does. Some of us (me included) cannot live without the music of the birds. Is anyone else listening?

Illustration by Liz Saunders

6

Frontier Myth Spinning: Can We Have It All?

Science must begin with myths,
and with the criticism of myths.

—Karl Popper

SPACE: A FRONTIER NO LONGER?

Outer space may still be a frontier, but the space we call wilderness, a place to recreate in Alberta's Eastern Slopes, is getting increasingly crowded. The refrain I hear from people who remember the Eastern Slopes from a previous era echoes Yogi Berra's enigmatic statement, "No one goes there, it's too crowded." I know I'm reluctant to visit there based on my memories of a place much quieter, with less traffic and fewer people.

Some might retort with some accuracy that this is typical complaining from an old grump. There is, however, a yin and yang aspect of growing old. On the minus side is constantly forgetting where you left the car keys. On the plus side are vivid memories of the "good old days" that form a significant benchmark against which to measure changes.

My formative years were spent in the Rocky-Clearwater and Bow-Crow forests, from the late 1950s through to my entry as a biologist in the early 1970s. During family excursions on the Forestry Trunk Road, we would rarely encounter another vehicle. When camping at Ram Falls, we mostly had the place to ourselves. As I started independent hunting, fishing, and hiking journeys it was similar – few other people and you could scan for game from the middle of the road without getting run over. I thought it was paradise.

That might not have been evident to Henry Stelfox, who immigrated to Alberta in 1906 and became a conservationist and unpaid game guardian based near Rocky Mountain House. He would have found the forest reserve in the 1970s crowded by comparison to his earlier memories. Stelfox roamed the upper Clearwater watershed when caribou were still present, prior to the construction of the Forestry Trunk Road in the early 1950s. The Eastern Slopes might have been described as the "Big Empty" in Stelfox's time. Without benchmarks, the sense of paradise shifts and paradise erodes imperceptibly to a shadow of a former time.

History teaches lessons in limits. Alberta has been through an earlier era of abundance. We are now in an era of overexploitation. We need to move the dial to an age of prudent conservation and protection of what's left.

It's said, with evidence, that "the army of ecological destruction comes by road." It might be just as evident that the decline in recreational quality does so as well. Crowding, noise, and declining fish and wildlife populations have those of us with long memories sensing the balance has tipped or is close to it.

At least 20 cumulative effects studies of portions of the Eastern Slopes by government and arm's length organizations provide a compelling picture that road density and the logging footprint will shortly reach or has reached/exceeded ecological thresholds. The risks to water quality, hydrologic response (including more and bigger floods), threatened trout species, and several wildlife species are clear.

It's also clear that recreational interests are at odds with one another. We can't continue to do everything, everywhere, all the time, any time and not start running over each other, literally and figuratively. It's time for a day of reckoning and that includes all of us who recreate in the Eastern Slopes.

Space, once abundant and taken for granted, has shrunk to the point where the Eastern Slopes are not the place to "get away from it all" but rather the place where "all have come to get away." Ian Urquhart, professor emeritus, sums it up with, "To boldly go where too many go now."

Added to a very busy landscape of logging, livestock grazing, petroleum development, gravel mining, and coal exploration (and a few struggling coal mines) are random campers, OHV users, mountain bikers, e-bikers, hikers, anglers, hunters, geocachers, climbers, cross-country skiers, equestrian riders, paddlers, wildlife viewers, photographers, snowmobilers, and drive-through tourists. The landscape is crowded and if the COVID-19 years are any indication, our love affair with the Eastern Slopes isn't over; it is just beginning.

When I started my rambles in the Eastern Slopes, Alberta's population was 1.3 million. Now it's 4.4 million with an average annual growth rate of 1.4 per cent. That sounds low, but the math tells us that in another 25 years an additional two million people with economic and recreational interests will make Alberta home. As in the principle of compound interest, if the Eastern Slopes are busy now, imagine the future.

Fire marshals set capacity limits for buildings, restaurants can only serve those who can find tables and chairs, and there are only so many seats on the bus. There is a direct parallel to the Eastern Slopes – it is not an expanding universe, as is outer space. It is a fixed one with only so much room for our economic and recreational pursuits. The more we ask to do things in the Eastern Slopes, and the more of us doing it, the less capable these landscapes are of providing watershed function, a haven for fish and wildlife, and quality recreational opportunities. Recreation management is not about adding more to the Eastern Slopes but about increasing the quality of recreation by resisting the things that will diminish the experience.

All of us have experienced the frustration of a decline in quality, whether from a product, a service, or an experience. Consider the too many bad trips to the Eastern Slopes because too many people got there before you. It leaves us feeling cheated somehow, that things could be better. But as quality continues to decline, we realize that without an intervention it's just going to get worse.

For decades we have set limits on livestock grazing on public lands through assessments of carrying capacity. If we can do it for cows, we should be able to tackle human carrying capacity in the Eastern Slopes.

Recreational carrying capacity is concerned with determining the number of users that can be accommodated by a given

area without loss in the quality of the natural environment and/
or the recreational experience. It is challenging, but not impossible, to integrate human values into resource management
decisions.

Other jurisdictions facing human population pressures have
addressed how to protect landscapes and essential ecological
functions while at the same time providing quality recreational experiences. A spectrum of options has been used, but the
consistent theme is that other jurisdictions treat recreation as
a land use that requires planning, management, evaluation, and
enforcement.

While there is no magic formula for setting recreational
capacities, the beginnings might be found in the policies that
initially set up the Eastern Slopes into forest reserves, national parks, and provincial parks and protected areas. Watershed
protection, either explicit or implicit, leaps to the front and
becomes a priority for all of these, despite repetitive resource
management decisions that run counter to the good words
and intentions. What we need the Eastern Slopes to be and do
should be the foundation, not just satisfying every want, often
at the expense of sacrificing our needs, such as protecting water.

If we can agree there are ecological capacities that shouldn't
be exceeded, there is a starting point. That is a big if, since
some people refuse to acknowledge their recreational pursuits
diminish environmental quality. Paradigm shifts are hard because Albertans seem hard-wired to view use of the Eastern
Slopes as an entitlement. Despite this, we have been given the
gift of a common problem, how to effectively manage the Eastern Slopes.

To a degree the argument might hinge on how one defines

"quality." Recreational quality can be related to perceptions of crowding or exceeding physical capacity. It can be tied to facility capacity, as in what amenities such as campgrounds, parking lots, or restrooms are available. How one defines quality is also tied to social capacity, freedom of choice, or how one reacts to crowding, competition, noise, and possibly the perception of threats or danger from other recreationalists.

To some, the accumulation of recreational vehicles scattered over every level piece of a streamside meadow, at the hub of a spider's web of muddy OHV trails, with random firepits, hacked off trees, and no toilet facilities might be considered a quality recreational experience. This does not meet the test for environmental quality because of compacted soils, loss of water infiltration, erosion and sediment additions to streams, displacement of wildlife, loss of riparian vegetation, and possible contamination of water quality from no toilet facilities.

Since this is an issue of regional planning, where is the Alberta government headed? Only two of seven regional plans have been published and there are glaring deficiencies in these. The rest are dead in the water and indicate an antipathy to regional planning, the logical place to have discussions on a variety of land uses, including recreation.

In Southern Alberta, the Livingstone-Porcupine Hills (L-PH) Land Footprint Management plan plotted a course to deal with a very busy landscape, akin to continuing to boil a teakettle that is screaming for attention. The issue of road and trail density was addressed with a line in the sand threshold. This was subsequently blown out of the water with the Alberta Energy Regulator approving new coal exploration roads that now exceed the thresholds for linear density.

The recent *Trails Act* is a blatant attempt to circumvent the ecological thresholds for road density and jump over a sub-regional plan that had broad public involvement and consensus. Promised in the L-PH plan was setting spatial footprint thresholds to deal with industrial land uses, especially logging. Years later there is no indication that the spatial footprint is being addressed. Continual failures to address carrying capacity compound over time.

For recreation, the direction seems oblivious to the existing and future recreational pressures in the Eastern Slopes. It's hard to see clearly when there are loonies over your eyes. A government-funded study by the Tourism Industry Association of Alberta in 2021 had six recommendations about growing recreation but made no mention of how to manage growth to protect ecological values or how to maintain recreational quality. We have yet to learn that more is not better.

Would limiting recreational use to enhance recreational experiences be easy to implement in the Eastern Slopes? Hardly! Given our tendency to tolerate redneck concepts of "freedom," this would not be viewed as visionary but as government overreach and overly restrictive.

However, if we took a clear view of crowded parking lots, increasing levels of frustration and anger between recreational interests, biodiversity concerns, an increasingly trashed landscape, and a decline in perceptions of recreational quality, we might at least be moved to start a conversation.

The reality, considering population pressures and expectations, is we are not going back to an era of abundant empty space and fewer people. What we can do is start, with vision and restraint, to embark on a way to salvage recreational experiences in the face of increased population pressures. It's not too late, but it soon will be.

If we don't acknowledge the trends, the fear is we will kill the goose (the Eastern Slopes) that lays the golden eggs (quality recreational experiences).

SHALL WE GATHER AT THE RIVER?

Irrigation and the Future of Southern Alberta's Rivers

———

In the heat dome and severe low flows of 2021, we left smears of colour from our canoe on several barely submerged boulders of one of Alberta's prairie rivers. These low water levels had me reflecting on the recent scheme by Southern Alberta's irrigation sector to expand irrigated acreage. In response, I thought of the old hymn, "Shall We Gather at the River."

The details of this irrigation expansion, now spun as a "modernization" project, are sketchy, perhaps by design. Ten of the 13 Irrigation Districts with funding support from the Province of Alberta and the Canada Infrastructure Bank propose to "modernize" 56 components of irrigation infrastructure and construct (or expand) six off-stream reservoirs, plus build five new onstream dams. The contention is with efficiency gains and new water storage, irrigation can be expanded by 230,000 acres.

Irrigation Districts now hold licences to withdraw half of the average natural annual flow from Southern Alberta's rivers. This doesn't leave much wiggle room for uses outside of irrigation since the other half of the flow in the South Saskatchewan River Basin must be passed on to Saskatchewan. On average, Irrigation Districts withdraw two thirds of their allocation each year. In dry years, they essentially remove everything. The most critical period is in summer when demand is high for other uses of our rivers.

This doesn't bode well for fish populations, for wildlife habitat, for healthy riparian areas, or for people who enjoy our rivers.

Evidence from government's own reports is that Southern Alberta rivers below major irrigation dams and diversions are stressed and some significantly degraded, and the prognosis is for a continual decline in river health. That was the inescapable conclusion even before the proposed irrigation expansion project was announced.

Irrigation Districts (or their precursors) have been diverting water from Southern Alberta's rivers for well over a century through an extensive artificial plumbing network of dams, reservoirs, and irrigation canals. Irrigation works deliver water on demand over vast crop acreages in a landscape that is classified as semi-arid. The cost to develop and maintain this engineering marvel was (and is) largely from the public purse.

Alberta government departments charged with water stewardship turned out to be the agents of water disposal, merely rubber-stamping expansion demands of the irrigation sector. This is analogous to having Dracula guard the blood bank. Other interests are largely ignored and additional allocations are passed out as party favours.

It wasn't until 2006 that the Alberta government finally closed the Bow, Oldman, and South Saskatchewan sub-basins to further allocation. Some have commented this was "too little, too late."

There might be a vague awareness of the environmental costs of irrigation, such as drowned river valleys above dams, rivers starved for water below diversions, and fish dying from habitat disruption. But those costs are far beyond most citizens' mailboxes and sensibilities.

Extracting water from Southern Alberta rivers, even under the present situation, runs into the wall of climate change. The reality is that the effects of climate change are producing less river flow and there is an inevitable limit to growth. There is the impression we have amended the laws of nature in this dry land with complex engineering works and turned on a tap that never runs dry. But we haven't.

According to Dr. John Pomeroy, Canada Research Chair in Water Resources and Climate Change at the University of Saskatchewan, about 80 per cent of flow in the Saskatchewan River Basin comes from the Eastern Slopes, mostly from snowpack, making Southern Alberta's rivers "very vulnerable to climate change."

Pomeroy thinks it is "important to look at the whole thing before expanding irrigation in one part or managing it differently in another part, and we're going to have to do that always with an eye to the mountains." Lessons from south of the border backstop this since over-allocation of water in the Colorado River Basin, coupled with drought, has led US governments to severely curtail water use for irrigation.

Modelling studies of the Oldman River at Lethbridge show drought (a reality under climate change) throws a significant wrench into the works – water needs would exceed supply and droughts that last more than two years could not be mitigated by reservoir storage. This shows that building more reservoirs is, at best, a questionable adaptive strategy. We kid ourselves if we think we can outwit nature instead of adapting to its realities.

There is a way to manage the issues of environmental flows by establishing limits, real ecological limits. An instream flow need (IFN) is a rigorous, science-based recommendation for the amount of water that should flow at any particular time to meet the objectives of river health.

Healthy rivers should have been the goal, but while many waited for the answer from proper IFN research, water managers in the government of Alberta were busy giving away the water that would have assured a measure of ecological integrity. Now, because of allocations to irrigation, too little water is left to meet IFN values.

Our rivers, especially those in Southern Alberta, show the strain of over a century of careless development. Provincial water managers seemed oblivious even after a massive fish kill related to high water temperatures exacerbated by excessive diversions occurred on the Highwood River in 1977. This incident (and others) put irrigation diversions and inadequate instream flows into the broad public consciousness.

But when you've exceeded ecological limits, all that's left are some administrative Band-Aids to give the impression that our rivers are being managed to avoid ecosystem failure. These are rarely met and will not restore health to degraded rivers. In stark terms, Southern Alberta rivers are on life support, without enough water to guarantee a healthy, functioning ecosystem.

Initiatives where investment of public money is proposed, that involve a public resource (water), and that have the potential to significantly impact the public interest in broader matters of ecosystem health require scrutiny. What could be more in the public interest than the health of Southern Alberta's rivers?

Irrigation Districts, with support from government, boldly assert that this initiative does not require any public review. This massive irrigation expansion could occur without a determination of whether or not it is in the public interest.

An independent review, through an environmental impact assessment (EIA) has the potential to clarify a mind-boggling amount of information on public interest matters such as whether or not this expansion of irrigation is from efficiency gains, or just another way to maximize water withdrawals. Is yet another massive injection of public money warranted when the result will be to sacrifice something that is in the broad public interest (healthy rivers) for private enterprise profit (as we see with coal, petroleum, and timber)?

We need to get out of the hydro-illogical cycle, where every dam, reservoir, and efficiency gain is touted as solving the problem of water scarcity, until they are built and then the cry starts for the next one to solve the problem of not addressing limits and so on, *ad infinitum, ad nauseum*.

In the continual focus on downstream structural features no one seems to think about water sources – the headwaters. This is the ultimate "reservoir" for downstream water users and interests. In the headwaters, unsustainable logging, proposed coal mining, and a proliferation of roads and trails drain this natural reservoir too quickly. An EIA with an expanded scope is required to avoid past parochial decisions.

Most significantly, an EIA might allow those not benefitting directly from this scheme to see how other attributes important to a broader public, such as similarly imperilled native grasslands, might be affected.

A review would help us answer the question, "How much is

enough, and have we already exceeded reasonable limits?" A review has the potential to open up new conversations about irrigation, and about how to successfully adapt to changing conditions (and all advice is that adaptation is imperative).

If this scheme is a race to exercise irrigation "rights," to use up all the allocation, who eventually wins the race? It won't be Southern Alberta's rivers and those who cherish them.

Maybe irrigators could resolve to live with a little less water, so the river can have a little more. However, even those that foresee the upcoming crisis seem to accept none of the responsibility for it.

As Cheryl Bradley, an independent biologist who has followed this for years, observes: "There is a palpable reluctance to release water under their [irrigation] licences, perhaps because it would mean relinquishing control over a valuable commodity in short supply." In reality, giving up some of "their" water to let rivers live will not diminish irrigation agriculture.

What does it mean to take so much water out of Southern Alberta rivers? Sadly, these rivers are shadows of what they once were; we know they are degrading, we know what they are degrading from, and we can measure their death throes. Natural justice and a sense of equity need to be injected into plans for irrigation expansion while there is still a chance to salvage a better future for our rivers.

Otherwise, counter to the old hymn, there will be no living river left where we can gather.

BEST LITTLE RANCH BY A DAM SITE

Postmortem on the Human Costs

———

When land is "taken" for a project – a highway, for example – there is some rationalization that this is for the "public good." While there is some basis for this view, Anne and Quentin Stevick have an alternate opinion, based on the forced expropriation of their ranch for the construction of the Oldman Reservoir.

Ranching runs in the Stevick blood. Quentin was raised on a small farm/ranch in north-central North Dakota; Anne on a ranch in the Porcupine Hills. Both dreamt of having a ranch of their own, in spite of the challenges. Dreams are powerful motivators and may cloud reason. Once the couple saw the ranch from the ridge overlooking the Castle River, they were hooked.

Looking at a painting of the ranch done by local artist Sharron Bourassa provides a sense of why Anne and Quentin chose the ranch and why it was so hard to leave it. Buildings sat on a river terrace surrounded by tall trees to break the wind. The Castle River at this point makes a sharp bend to the north, giving a panoramic view up the valley of rolling foothills backstopped by the Front Range of mountains. You can perceive shelter, expanse, and perspective – just the place to put down roots.

What also hooked them was the financial maelstrom of the early 1980s, which saw interest rates skyrocket to over 20 per cent. Channelling Charles Dickens, it was the worst of times to buy land and begin a ranch. Undeterred, they plunged into both building up a ranch and the deep end of serious debt. Both commented in classic cowboy understatement that the first decade was a struggle of blood, sweat, and tears.

Both told me, in separate ways, that such a struggle cemented their attachment to the land. This wasn't just a place to make a buck, but a place to cherish as a home.

At about the time they were looking for a ranch, rumours of building a dam somewhere on the Oldman River were circulating in the community. Three proposed locations were being floated: one in the Gap of the Livingstone Range, one somewhere below the confluences of the Castle, Crowsnest, and Oldman rivers (the "Three Rivers site"), and another, termed the "Brocket site," on the Piikani Reserve. In the grips of the drought of the 1980s, the then Progressive Conservative government of Peter Lougheed announced in August 1980 that a dam would be built but deferred a decision about the location.

It all seemed so speculative, pie in the sky stuff, and Anne and Quentin largely dismissed it as an issue for them. Little did they know!

Fast-forward to August 9, 1984, when then Premier Don Getty surprised most by announcing the dam would be built at the Three Rivers site. Like a sucker punch, no advance warning was provided to those landowners, including Anne and Quentin, who would lose some or all of their land to reservoir development.

The decision to build the dam created rifts in the community. A few people, Anne and Quentin included, poured their hearts, souls, and cash into resisting a project with so little benefit locally. Some businesses drank the political Kool-Aid that included unspecified economic development, a reservoir fishery, a recreational draw, and other mistruths.

Quentin recalled some businesses that he dealt with having "Save Our Water, Dam It" in their windows. Here he and Anne were, about to lose their ranch and these local business owners were completely tone deaf to this reality.

As both recall, the worst seemed to be the inevitable rumours, the speculation, the misinformation, and the interminable waiting for the axe to fall. In retrospect both agree this was benign compared to the actual negotiations.

As Quentin related, "Dealing with Alberta government was like going to Las Vegas, hoping to beat the house." It was less a negotiation than it was a hostage situation. Holding all the cards, making up all the rules, spinning the message to the media, with a divide and conquer strategy, the negotiators held Anne and Quentin to ransom, eventually just wearing them down. Anne said it was akin to surrendering and then having to draft the terms of your own surrender. This time-tested form of "negotiation" still occurs with projects, notably power line routing and wind farm development.

The Stevicks signed a "voluntary" expropriation, which sounds more like a "voluntary" execution.

With tongue partially in cheek, I asked, "Surely, the compensation was fair and equitable?" "Hardly," replied Quentin, "if you recognize there was only one buyer, not a bunch bidding for the ranch. Also, with the financial crash, land prices declined by about half from the time we bought the ranch. So we were forced to sell low in spite of a mortgage based on the much higher value. And we couldn't just move immediately into a turn-key operation, so we lost almost two years of income."

In a minor tribute after dealing with a forced sellout, the

government named one of the wildlife mitigation projects on an oxbow of the Castle River after them. It's one place Quentin can return to from time to time without recurring negative feelings. Wounds may heal, but scars linger as memories.

After a year and a half, they started over on a piece of land southwest of Pincher Creek. It took them nearly 15 years to climb back to the place they had started with the ranch on the Castle River. Both agree it was a significant setback, financially and mentally. Of course, there was no compensation or empathy for the psychological trauma of being evicted from your home.

Beyond the environmental costs of creating a dam that has irrevocably ruined stretches of three beautiful river valleys, there are the individual human impacts of reservoir construction. Multiple families were displaced by the Oldman Dam, and ranches were fragmented to a non-viable status. None of this is tallied in the dam's final price tag.

For all of the rhetoric over the dam's purpose, it was and is to supply water to irrigation farmers in the Lethbridge Northern Irrigation District, a hundred or more kilometres away. The price tag for this was half a billion dollars, public dollars. We can debate to what degree the Oldman Dam had a significant public benefit, or whether the benefit accrued to fewer than 300 downstream farmers, far from the Stevicks' ranch.

An objective academic review of the project might conclude it was one of resource colonialism. This is generally defined as fundamental decisions about resource use being made and implemented in pursuit of economic interests by distant entities. It is an appropriation of land and resources for economic development at the cost of those occupying the land. The colonizers, generally governments and industry (which are hard to tell apart sometimes), make decisions and wield power over which those impacted have little control or voice.

Some scholars argue that tar sands production on Indigenous Peoples' lands is a practice of resource colonialism. Water management in Alberta is another instance of resource colonialism, where landowners in the headwaters have had to sacrifice their land to reservoir development that benefits irrigation farmers far downstream.

The irrigation sector, aided, abetted, and funded by the provincial government, is yet again pursuing more resource colonialism in the form of six new off-stream irrigation reservoirs and five new onstream dams (one is a low head weir) to prop up dreams of irrigation expansion. Clear-cut logging and proposed coal mine developments in the headwaters also fit the mould of resource colonialism. The pattern is riches for some distant entity and costs for the rest of us.

I asked Anne and Quentin how they would have reacted if an irrigation farmer had come to them and said, "I would like to build up my farm, doubling, maybe tripling its value at your expense. Are you all right with that?" I wonder how that irrigation farmer might have felt after having weathered the incredulous stares from both of them.

It's been nearly four decades since the Stevicks were forced to move off their "dream" ranch. When they searched for somewhere new to land, one of the selection decisions was it had to be a place that was unsuitable for dam construction. The Castle River ranch was at an elevation of 1103 metres. The next place was at 1219 metres and their retirement home begins at 1380 metres, extending upwards to 1424 metres. Anne and Quentin have moved higher and higher, beyond the reach of any reservoir development. Once burned, twice shy!

They have re-established their lives but still have periods of anger over the situation they were forced into. None of that is ever calculated in the cost of a dam. Politicians talk of supporting the "hard-working little guy." The reality is that in their propensity to cultivate a business-friendly face, the voice and concerns (and to a degree rights) of the little guy get overlooked.

Anne and Quentin are still skeptical of the sugar-coating applied to the expropriation, the self-serving rationalizations of development being "for the greater good" and "in the public interest." It more resembles the thick layer of mud that now covers most of the old ranch and their early dreams. People are deeply and personally affected by these distant decisions. It suggests that it is necessary to rethink how such decisions are made by appreciating the trauma they cause.

To date, and this is now going on nearly 40 years, Anne and Quentin have not received even one thank you note from the Irrigation District, any of the irrigation farmers, or any other downstream beneficiary of their sacrifice. Makes you think.

DOES GOING GREEN PUT WILDLIFE IN THE RED?

Somewhere there must exist a great ecological ledger, administered by Bob Cratchit-like accountants who toll up the pluses and minuses of our fumbling human endeavours. One critical entry relates to the need to reduce our greenhouse gas emissions to prevent the world from overheating. There is no question we need to transition from fossil fuels to alternate energy sources.

Climate change, the big shift in our world, is a global risk to wildlife and their habitats. Increasing heat is a key factor in declines of the once-common bumble bee, one of our essential plant pollinators. Reduced and warmer streamflows impact native trout. It's hard to find a species in Alberta not affected by climate change. But we shouldn't be blind to the issues renewable energy solutions can cause to wildlife and their habitats. I'm not sure what we should call these solutions when one considers habitat issues, wildlife mortality, and embedded energy costs for infrastructure. Low-carbon, maybe, but not "green."

Wind and solar developments are experiencing an exponential expansion, a literal energy gold rush, due to the recognition of increasing climate change risk and to government subsidies to quicken the rollout of solutions. As befits a relatively new industry, assessing the ecological and biological effects of renewable energy developments is beset by inadequate studies, no long-term monitoring, inadequate baselines, data deficiencies, differing infrastructure types, and variable geographic and landscape differences. All of this confounds simple answers and solutions.

Both solar and wind facilities have footprints and operations that affect wildlife in similar, and sometimes different, ways. There are direct and indirect effects, plus cumulative effects, given these facilities do not exist in isolation from other land uses.

It is clear that wind turbines kill bats and birds through collisions with vanes or through barotrauma, a huge pressure differential that causes internal hemorrhaging. The majority of deaths from such direct mortality occur during migration. Initially, the concern was over birds – raptors and songbirds; however, this has changed. Jason Unruh, the provincial wildlife biologist who reviews renewable energy projects, says, "What was once a bird issue has become a bat issue."

Bat populations are hard to estimate – many species are migratory, all are nocturnal, and most are solitary. What has been noted are precipitous declines in most populations. Most biologists agree that impacts from wind turbines are at a population level – in their words, "really concerning."

Some might question whether the mortality of bats is something of concern. The US Fish and Wildlife Service says, "Bats are one of the most important misunderstood animals." Unjustifiably feared, bats perform vital roles in pest control and pollination, both of which are essential to ecosystem function as well as our economy. If you think mosquitoes are a summer plague now, imagine a world of bug bites without bats.

Less information is available on direct wildlife mortality from solar facilities, not because it doesn't occur, but because little research and monitoring has been undertaken with such a new development. There is a theory that solar panels apparently can resemble bodies of water (a lake effect) and lure birds such as grebes and loons to their deaths. There is no post-construction monitoring or peer-reviewed evidence for this. An emerging issue is that predators such as owls use the infrastructure as elevated perches. This subsidizes these predators at the expense of species adapted to grasslands.

Renewable energy projects don't always kill directly, but there are indirect effects. A recent study of the effects of wind turbines on whooping crane migration published in the March 2021 edition of *Ecological Applications* showed migratory habitat is reduced by wind energy development. For most migrating birds, rest stops and feeding areas are important stepping stones along their flight path. Researchers found whooping cranes avoided wind turbines to a distance of five kilometres. This effectively reduced their access to habitats essential for migration by making some potential stopover areas unusable.

A southwestern Wyoming study of the effects of solar developments on antelope found direct habitat losses of summer and winter ranges. Impervious, wildlife-unfriendly fencing altered both seasonal and annual migration patterns and fragmented habitats. Joel Nicholson, the senior wildlife biologist in Alberta's grasslands, points out there are biological issues associated with movement barriers, including extra energy costs that can increase antelope mortality in winter situations.

Species that are already faced with significant cumulative challenges that include small and declining populations, continued habitat losses, powerline/window collisions, illegal shooting, movement barriers, and other mortality factors may not be able to tolerate the additional risk presented by some of these alternative energy developments.

There are no "silver bullet" solutions, but one obvious alternative is to avoid placing infrastructure in high-risk areas. While this sounds simple, there are complexities that make this very difficult to implement. To assess risk, there needs to be sufficient baseline information on basic biological questions of wildlife presence, numbers, distribution, movement patterns, and the timing of movement through the proposed development areas. Following that is an assessment of the way wildlife species would interact with renewable energy infrastructure.

None of this can be effectively accomplished in the narrow development time frames set by an industry in a rush. Areas of risk to wildlife are often identified after a development has occurred and significant mortality is observed. What results is mostly insight from post-development monitoring, applied elsewhere to new proposals.

Provincial Fish and Wildlife biologists use information from existing sites and what little data is available on wildlife use elsewhere to assess the risk potential from new projects. This assessment is forwarded to the Alberta Utilities Commission, who is the regulator and final arbiter for renewable energy developments.

As an example of just how complex the matter of assessing risk is, one only needs to consider bats. Migratory bats (hoary, silver-haired, and eastern red) take the biggest hit from wind infrastructure, making up 90 per cent of bat mortality in this context. Most of the deaths happen during the fall migration in August and September but, as bat researchers point out, understanding of bat migratory behaviour is extremely limited. What we mostly know about migratory pathways is gleaned from deaths at existing wind towers. An equivalent would be trying to assess wildlife populations by counting roadkill on highways.

Since there seems to be limited appetite in most economic development to wait until we know better the relative risks and rewards, the next step is figuring out how to reduce the risk and ultimately the direct and indirect mortality of wildlife.

Mitigation, sometimes considered to be no more than putting lipstick on a corpse, can be useful, but is not a panacea for the issues renewable energy developments create for wildlife. For bats, an understanding of the temporal and spatial windows through which they fly can provide insight into changes in wind turbine operations.

Dr. Robert Barclay, an expert in bat research at the University of Calgary, and several of his colleagues have investigated ways of potentially reducing mortality. As wind towers become taller, the vanes reach into the airspace used by bats. Minimizing tower height can reduce mortality. Recognizing that bats are nocturnal, fly at low wind speeds, and that their movements are seasonal gives operators the opportunity to curtail turbine use at night, at times when winds are light, and at certain times of the year.

Other wildlife mitigative strategies include ensuring that unrestricted travel avenues exist, both in terms of physical access and reducing avoidance behaviour due to noise and human activity. Changes in habitat conditions with renewable infrastructure, roads, and transmission lines require greater scrutiny as early work suggests lower plant diversity, richness, and evenness, with fewer rare species and more non-native species. Siting these facilities on non-native landscapes and brownfields, and thus avoiding important and connected wildlife habitat, would mitigate some of the negative effects.

Because of a lack of monitoring and research on best management practices, current results for wildlife mitigation are often in conflict, and success rates are variable and are very much site-specific in their nature. As the renewable energy footprint expands, the need to better understand, manage, and mitigate becomes evident.

The intended scale of some solar facilities will be of concern from a wildlife perspective. Plans for solar "farms" of 5,000, 9,000, and even 16,000 acres of enclosed, wildlife-impermeable fenced space will reduce habitat availability and pose serious wildlife movement issues for virtually all wildlife species larger than ground squirrels and mice. There could also be the unintended consequence of losing more native grassland. Incumbent on renewable energy companies, who tout themselves as "green," is showing they are willing to forgo some economic opportunity to minimize wildlife impacts in favour of obtaining social licence for their developments.

Before things get completely out of control, as was the historic case with oil and gas development, it would be useful to undertake regional-scale cumulative effects assessments that could help define the siting requirements and also set appropriate limits on development. Government has a role to play by guiding development through a combination of carrots and sticks. A first step might be to encourage the development of solar facilities in urban areas, with panels arrayed on house roofs and the roofs of office, retail, factory, warehouse, and government buildings.

Yes, we need these low-carbon energy developments to combat climate change, but we have to be smart about facility development. There will inevitably be trade-offs between energy development, land availability and suitability, human constraints, and conservation goals. There will be conflicts, resulting in winners and losers. In a perfect system, human and environmental constraints would limit locations to those where renewables are compatible. But if designs and development criteria don't incorporate steps to limit, minimize, or mitigate for negative effects on wildlife, wildlife will lose.

As a biologist, I worry about the effects of climate change on wildlife. I'm also concerned about how our technological solutions involve trade-offs with no clear picture in mind for the persistence of wildlife. In the shift to renewable energy to limit greenhouse gas emissions, we risk running over wildlife, converting wildlife populations to red ink in the ecological accounts as we attempt to keep up with our high energy demands.

HIDDEN CREEK
Of Bull Trout, Floods, and Logging

———

With an almost magnetic fidelity, bull trout have returned to spawn in Hidden Creek, an Oldman River tributary for thousands of years. This movement was documented through redd counts done between 1995 and 1998. Systematic monitoring resumed in 2008 and has continued annually since. I have returned in late September for years now to find and count bull trout redds. Recently, I have waded the stream with some trepidation.

Hidden Creek used to be the natal epicentre of bull trout spawning for the Oldman River watershed. Logging over the winter of 2012–2013, coupled with a major flood in the spring of 2013, dealt the stream, and bull trout, an almost mortal blow.

Prior to these events, the redd count hovered at around 54 redds per year with a peak of 108. In 2013 post-flood redd numbers dropped slightly from the average to 41. From 2014 to 2019, the average dropped to less than ten redds per year, an 80 per cent reduction.

Bull trout females are the ultimate arbiters of whether a stream possesses the right stuff for spawning. Many must have voted, with their fins, to take a pass on Hidden Creek. Where else they went is a mystery since other streams lack consistent monitoring and are also significantly impacted by logging, roading, motorized recreation, and random camping.

Something about the combination of flood and logging created a perfect storm of changes in Hidden Creek, to the detriment of bull trout spawning. Hidden Creek is not gauged, so the magnitude of the 2013 flood and relation to other flood events is unknown.

Even after major floods in 1995 (the largest on record to date in the watershed) and 2005, bull trout still swarmed to Hidden Creek to take advantage of an abundance of groundwater, clean stream gravels, and low water temperatures. Following the 1995 flood, there was a rapid increase in numbers of redds, and although redd counts were not done immediately following the 2005 flood, they were very high three years following that event.

The North Belly River and Blakiston Creek, both in Waterton Lakes National Park, showed a similar rise in spawning success following the 1995 flood. There is no similar pattern for spawning events for these streams after the 2005 flood.

Comparing bull trout redd counts in Hidden Creek, the North Belly River, Blakiston Creek, and Fall Creek (Ram River tributary), there seems to be no consistent and negative effect of major floods on spawning activity or on redd counts.

Flood impacts on trout might include factors such as flood

timing, flood magnitude, duration of flooding, and flood intensity. For fall spawners, especially bull trout, many of the factors of a spring flood are of a lesser concern except inasmuch as they affect the physical elements crucial for spawning success.

A consistent observation from the years following the 2013 flood in Hidden Creek was the lack of suitably sized gravels for spawning. It was apparent that these smaller gravels had been flushed out of the system, leaving behind only larger rocks and cobble, which are unsuitable for spawning. Very few of the traditional spawning sites had gravels left and only a limited number of these had evidence of spawning. It appeared that the few spawners left were chasing a limited gravel supply.

Erosion from naturally unstable stream banks, coupled with overland flow from logging clear-cuts and roads, coated the stream substrate with sediment for several years following 2013. Even seven years out from 2013 there was still a sediment supply lingering in pools where no sediment used to occur. It doesn't take much sediment to start limiting spawning success. Research suggests as little as 10 per cent over natural background sediment levels has a discernable effect.

Too much sediment likely dissuades a bull trout female from spawning. Even if she does, sediment interferes with the successful incubation of trout eggs laid in the gravels. The interstitial spaces between the gravels are clogged with sediment particles and this can smother the eggs, not allowing an exchange of oxygen-rich water, or the removal of metabolic wastes. Trout fry might be unable to extricate themselves from the sediment-impacted gravel.

Bull trout are late bloomers, becoming sexually mature at about age five. If sediment levels inhibit successful reproduction, it sets the stage for fewer trout to mature and return, over time, to their natal stream. Year class failures echo through the entire watershed.

Although there is no discernible effect from flooding on spawning, there may be a synergistic one resulting from logging. The effects of logging, especially clear-cut harvests, are shown to change the hydrologic response of a watershed.

Removal of the forest canopy, coupled with roads, skid trails, and soil compaction from logging, quickens the response time of snowmelt and rainfall runoff, sometimes by orders of magnitude. Basically, logging results in more water delivered more quickly to a stream. This occurs with any level of forest harvest, but more so with large clear-cuts. Flood peaks are elevated, and this intensifies the magnitude of a flood event. This translates into more energy for erosion and more sediment flushed into streams.

Since flows in Hidden Creek are not monitored, it is difficult to determine to what degree logging increased natural flood flows. What was evident was that the three tributary streams, which flow through cut blocks logged in the winter of 2012–2013, showed substantial new channel incisement, or downcutting. The logging road also intersected all of these streams.

Upstream of the logged area, three additional tributaries of somewhat equal size were inspected – none showed any evidence of recent channel incisement. This would seem to indicate that runoff from the logged areas was substantially enhanced compared to non-logged areas, leading to greater erosion.

Hidden Creek upstream of the logged areas did not have the same accumulations of sediment, and it did not appear that gravel loss was as extreme as in downstream reaches. Unfortunately, the upper portion of Hidden Creek is mostly unavailable for spawning because a waterfall is a major obstruction.

It's troubling that the tributary streams flowing through cut blocks showed only a perfunctory amount of erosion protection. Unlogged buffer zones were minimal, a few metres in width at most. Sediment controls, in the form of sediment fences, were either missing, or poorly installed and unmaintained. These were already overwhelmed by large amounts of sediment by the fall of 2013.

Because of concerns over the logging of Hidden Creek, Forest Service staff apparently did regular winter inspections when logging was occurring, but there seemed to be little subsequent follow-up to ensure erosion protection was in place and functioning. Self-regulation was ineffective, as was agency oversight.

Conclusions are hard to draw without more empirical evidence, but it seems that logging exacerbated the flood flows of 2013, likely caused a substantial amount of erosion from newly logged cut blocks, and increased the erosion of naturally unstable stream banks. This deposited a substantial amount of sediment in the lower reaches of Hidden Creek and scoured out much of the suitably sized spawning gravels.

To compound the problem, runoff from an August 2013 rainstorm turned Hidden Creek into a muddy soup. Other streams in the area subject to the same weather event remained clear, indicating that logging had increased the erosion potential substantially in Hidden Creek.

Bull trout spawned in the autumn of 2013. However, it is unknown whether that spawning effort produced new trout.

Subsequent to 2013, redd counts dropped alarmingly, down to one redd in 2019.

Redd counts in 2020 showed 34 redds, somewhat of a resurgence, but dropped to 19 in 2022, and 15 in 2023. This is still far from the long-term average. It shows the effects of logging can linger and a landscape can hum like an anvil long after the hammer of development has hit.

There may be signs of recovery after six years. This is likely related to flushing of sediments from gravel by subsequent high flow events and the recruitment of new gravels with normal bedload movement. It is easy to leap to a conclusion based on one year of higher redd counts, but only continued monitoring will show whether a positive trend continues.

One winter of logging has equated to at least six years of lost bull trout spawning and population recruitment for much of the Oldman watershed. For a species that is designated as threatened, this is a near-mortal blow. It begs an important question: Can sensitive watersheds fundamental to the survival of trout species at risk be logged without serious impacts to those populations?

Whatever the Forest Service and the forest sector say, Hidden Creek provides an unequivocal answer.

RUMPLEDPOTATOSKIN
Spinning Gold into Straw

———

Aren't we clever? We take a perfectly good food item, the potato, and subject it to a variety of "value added" processing steps. Those transform the potato into artery-clogging, heart-busting snack items devoid of much of the potato's original goodness and nutrition.

The "food" product then goes to stuff an increasingly fat world, not a hungry one. But it is a lucrative thing to do and that seems to be the test applied to such endeavours.

Aren't we clever? We take a piece of native prairie grassland, tested and perfected over 12,000 years in the crucible of time, and plow it up to grow potatoes. The grassland is self-sustaining, drought resistant, requires no fertilizer, and is home to a host of native wildlife. Many of the plant and animal species are at risk because the grasslands of Alberta have been diminished by about 75 per cent over the last 100 years.

E.O. Wilson, the noted American ecologist, observed in a 1985 *Bioscience* article, "The one process now going on that will take millions of years to correct is the loss of species and genetic diversity by the destruction of natural habitats. This is the folly our descendants are least likely to forgive us." It's a tough assignment to recreate a prairie where lightning ignited fires, drought tested plants, and millions of bison grazed.

Aren't we clever? After having successfully turned another piece of perfectly good prairie into potatoes, but suffering much criticism, one "Potato King" discovers a less public, more political route for additional public land purchase.

When the Alberta government is caught in its own web of secrecy, cronyism, and denial it makes a brave face and disingenuously calls its process "open and transparent." The equivalency would be to call a stove lid a picture window.

Aren't we clever? The Alberta government, which it seems never met a buck it didn't worship, worked diligently behind the scenes to sell off 100 more quarter sections of native grassland to allow potatoes to flourish even more (this plan was foiled, although perhaps temporarily).

This is public land that the public has clearly articulated, on every occasion its opinion has been sought, should be retained by the province. One can only stand in awe of this cross-pollination of politics and potatoes. Potatoes trump prairie in the ideological world where business is paramount. How rich will Albertans be when we have converted all our forests, all our soil, all our water resources, and all our minerals into cash?

Aren't we clever? By plowing up the native grassland we think we can spark an even greater economic return from this apparently barren desert. We can not only make the desert bloom, but we can also add wealth to the potato grower, the agrochemical industry, the machinery business, the processor, and the other businesses along the way. You can just sense the gleeful rubbing together of hands waiting for the money to flow.

Mind you, it will take more water from already stressed prairie rivers and all the chemical additions will influence downstream water quality. All we have to do is sell off a piece of our heritage that can never be restored to its original form. It follows a great Canadian tradition – private wealth at public expense.

Aren't we clever? The Alberta government acts similar to a farmer who maintains his high standard of living by selling off another piece of the farm every spring. It has a clearance sale on public land, using a fire sale mentality where short-term dollars in someone's bank account become more important than the health of Alberta's ecological account.

It's not clear if the government is giving business to the environment or giving the environment to business. Either way, our account at the bank of the environment is close to overdrawn.

Aren't we clever? Of course, the argument to plow up native prairie hinges on economics. It just doesn't mean it's the right thing to do. E.F. Schumaker wisely said, "Call a thing immoral or ugly, soul destroying or degradation of man, a peril to the peace of the world or to the well-being of future generations; as long as you have not shown it to be 'uneconomic' you have not questioned its right to exist, grow and prosper."

I wonder, if one stripped away generous land deals, the effect of stressing prairie rivers even more, water quality issues, the hidden agricultural subsidies, the inevitable rise of disease pathogens, and the effect of climate change on potato production and compared the native grassland's ability to produce without any of these, would the potato endeavour still be "economical"?

Aren't we clever? Life imitates the Brothers Grimm's fairy tale, "Rumpelstiltskin." You might remember it from your childhood. In the tale the miller's daughter is imprisoned to spin straw into gold to make good on her father's boast. Today's made-in-Alberta tale (Rumpledpotatoskin) is about the spinning of native grass into Yukon gold potatoes.

In the fairy tale the goblin-like creature magically transforms straw into gold. The role of the goblin in today's docudrama is a dual one, performed by the Alberta government and many Potato Kings. Sadly, the magic is missing. Villains rarely prosper in fairy tales. Rumpelstiltskin, thwarted in his endeavour, is so enraged he drives his foot so far into the ground he creates a chasm into which he tumbles. One can only hope, in the Alberta version, that the goblins also fall into a pit of their own making. If politics and economics continue to trump prairie conservation, the Alberta story will not have a fairy-tale ending.

Aren't we clever? Some might think this is the perfect alchemy, transforming grassland with low economic return into something useful such as french fries and potato chips.

To me it's spinning gold into straw, a grim Alberta variant of an old fairy tale.

RUNNING OUT THE CLOCK ON CARIBOU

Great billows of smoke were used to hide battleships in wartime. Smokescreens are still employed, but to disguise a lack of meaningful activity, especially with the long-running battle to save caribou in Alberta. You can't see the smoke, but it's there in the form of caribou task forces that are ostensibly tasked with saving caribou, but in fact have the opposite intent.

The federal government, the last resort for species at risk, has told the province to produce and deliver on a plan to ensure caribou don't go the way of the passenger pigeon. These caribou task forces are made up of concerned conservation groups and Indigenous Peoples, plus the usual footdraggers of industry. In particular, the timber and energy industries are the ultimate gatekeepers, trying to run out the clock for caribou as they maximize economic opportunity. They are abetted by timorous provincial politicians who hide in plain sight behind the smokescreen of these committees.

Caribou are running out of time. Or time is running out of caribou. This species depends on mature to old-growth forests. This is where lichens, the caribou's main food source, are found. Mature forests don't provide forage for moose and deer – the mainstay for wolves. When timber is harvested, habitat shifts to benefit moose and deer, and the logging roads, seismic lines, oilpatch roads, and pipeline right-of-ways are perfect travel lanes for wolves. Caribou lose.

The pace of resource extraction in the northern foothills and boreal forest is at a stage where no caribou population seems safe and most are declining. Biologists hold little hope if the present trend continues. In the face of this, industry denies, delays, detracts, and deflects from any reasonable solution that would keep caribou on the land.

As John F. Kennedy once said, "Sometimes when there's smoke there's a smoke-making machine."

The timber industry says, "Don't worry, in 80 to 100 years there will be lots of caribou habitat." This would be similar to assuring those in the conference room that oxygen isn't presently available but would be in a day or two. Perhaps it was a lack of oxygen that prompted the industry response. An energy representative replied that the pace of oil and gas extraction had to continue or else, "Where would the government get the financial resources for caribou habitat restoration?" These are not solutions but rather hollow and disingenuous excuses for papering over failure.

In the sitcom, *The Simpsons*, Ned's parents were beatniks, early precursors to hippies. In caring for, raising, and nurturing

Ned, they rejected the conventional norms and disciplines of parental authority and direction. Ned developed symptoms of bad behaviour beyond their control. In desperation, they took him to a child psychologist. The doctor asked what they had tried to change Ned's behaviour. Ned's father, frustrated and desperate for help, said, "We've tried nothing and we're all out of ideas."

This *Simpsons* episode is a perfect metaphor for the lack of progress on caribou conservation. This smokescreen doesn't cover caribou, because there are so few left to disguise.

Politicians and the senior bureaucrats have forgotten who their "tribe" is – it is Albertans and not industry. That misplaced loyalty got us to where we are today with caribou. Utah Phillips, folksinger, raconteur, and anarchist, once said, "The earth is not dying, it is being killed, and those who are killing it have names and addresses." Their names and affiliations are writ large on the phony caribou task forces and, in the background, those who set up these smokescreens to disguise their spineless behaviour.

Doing nothing is not a course of action. Instead, it is a flight from responsibility and accountability. It may be high time for the federal government to step in, to be the adults in the room. The province and its industry allies seem intent on running out the clock on caribou to ensure no appropriate recovery action is taken. Shame on them.

THE GHOST RIVER WATERSHED
Loved or Abused?

———

When you see the mountains, like the Devil's Head, etched into the background of a cobalt-blue sky it is an engraving so stark, so powerful, and yet so subtle it leaves you breathless. From beneath a high viewpoint on Black Rock Mountain, the Ghost River carves its way, meandering through a portion of the Eastern Slopes. The watershed is both remote and accessible, wild and tamed, inviting yet secretive. Sentinel species of the wild still find havens in the watershed, such as native cutthroat and bull trout, wolves, and grizzlies.

Yet, stepping out of the truck under a pall of road dust, I nearly ducked as the sound of gunfire erupted close by. Later I reflected this was not the most inviting introduction to the Ghost River watershed.

When I go exploring, the first thing I do is reach for a map. I picked up a copy of the 2023 *Ghost Public Land Use Zone*, an Alberta government brochure. In addition to a map of the area, with access trails, campgrounds, and boundaries, it laid out all the rules, regulations, and stewardship recommendations. Reading it, I was impressed by the tight package of conservation mandates for the watershed. Not long into a sightseeing trip, the scales began to fall from my eyes.

The name "Ghost" originates from a Stoney legend in which ghosts were seen along the river picking up the skulls of warriors killed in battle against the Cree. The river was initially called "Deadman's River" by the Palliser Expedition. Both the legend and the old name circulated in my skull as I listened to the gunshots.

From the eastern boundary of Banff National Park, through

the Ghost River Wilderness and Don Getty Wildland Provincial Park, flows the Ghost River and its major tributaries, the South Ghost River and Waiparous Creek. Its waters flow into Ghost Lake, a hydropower reservoir located on the Bow River at the confluence of these tributaries.

There are many different visions for the watershed – playground for a large urban centre (Calgary), source of timber, petroleum, hydropower, and forage for livestock, a key watershed, homes, traditional territory, and an inspirational landscape of scenery, space, and biodiversity. Within the watershed are opportunities for recovery efforts for threatened populations of westslope cutthroat and bull trout.

There probably was a point in the past where most of these could be accommodated without eroding the integrity of the watershed. Now the aspirations, commitments, and stressors have grown and work cumulatively to the point the rubber band that is the watershed is liable to snap. Maybe in some parts it already has. A cumulative effects assessment undertaken in 2010–2011 detailed the state of the watershed and the issues that need to be faced. It seems few have.

This is a destination for people who need to escape from the city and jobs, for at least the weekend. It's about cutting loose, with a sedate drive on trails, a hike, mountain biking, or fishing for trout. It is also about throwing off constraints and rules to drink, party, shoot, and hurl yourself at a hillside or mudhole with your OHV. In a sense, the Ghost has become the redneck alternative to Kananaskis Country where some view the rules and regulations as too restrictive.

There comes a point where one has to question the "freedom" to express your recreational urges, especially as the landscape suffers. Random campsites, often beside water, are worn down to the dirt – dusty when dry, muddy when wet. Trees are randomly hacked down for firewood and the risk of a human-caused wildfire is ever-present.

There are no bathroom facilities associated with random campsites, which led authors of the 2010–2011 cumulative effects study to model the amount and impact of excessive human fecal material on water quality. During my visit, I came across a truck pulling a holiday trailer, leaving behind a trail of suspect material from their septic tank.

Much of this happens behind signs that state "No camping." People stake their claims and squat on spots by leaving a trailer parked for lengthy periods. The term "Dogpatch," taken from the name of the town in which the American cartoonist Al Capp set his cartoon, *Lil' Abner*, fits some of these slovenly random sites.

From these informal campsites spiral out a spider's web of OHV trails. Many of the users ignore the "No motorized vehicles beyond this point" signs. The government brochure shows a wealth of designated trails for OHV use. Unfortunately, many are inappropriate for mechanized use, being old seismic lines with unbridged stream crossings. When some of the designated trails are worse than the undesignated ones, it sends an unfortunate message to users.

Linear assessments show there are far more unauthorized trails (about 15 times more), which ignore topography, cross streams and wetlands indiscriminately, and conflict with legitimate recreational use. Ranchers say the Wild West attitude of some OHV users has made parts of their grazing allotments virtually unusable.

Most of the trails, especially old seismic lines, were never intended for continued vehicle use. Constant OHV traffic impedes natural revegetation and the erosion adds to the sediment burden faced by trout populations. Until OHV trails are designed and routed appropriately, the damage will persist.

If you count the bullet holes in signs, it seems the users of these spaces have a distinct aversion to rules. I was told you could tell the new signs by the lack of target practice they showed. When disrespect for rules, other users, and the watershed are so blatant, it speaks volumes on the failure of regulatory oversight.

The government of Alberta has failed miserably to take a stand, show the flag of stewardship, and employ enough staff to patrol the area. I'm told the few that are on watch vacate the Ghost by late afternoon, since that's when the drinking, partying, and gunplay really ramp up. A police presence is non-existent until there is a serious accident or fatality.

All of this makes a mockery of the fine words in the government brochure on the Ghost River. Especially, "Stay on the designated trails. Take your garbage home. Respect other users of the area." If the words aren't coupled with enforcement, the brochure is just a handy firelighter.

The Ghost isn't just about recreation; there is an industrial footprint as well. Logging clear-cuts intersect and overlap with recreational uses. Logging occurs under a Forest Management Agreement, which creates a virtual monopoly for one company. There are legitimate ecological and recreational concerns, but the impression I'm left with is that the logging company works in selective isolation behind a curtain of government-supported economic imperatives.

Sensitive areas for wildlife, concerns about sediment from logging operations on native trout, and meaningful, timely public consultation are dealt with in perfunctory ways. The fallback for most concerns is that these things are accommodated within the timber harvest operating ground rules (OGRs). Unfortunately, there is little empirical evidence the OGRs effectively protect other forest values.

The Ghost is a critical watershed for downstream water users and drinkers, especially the City of Calgary. Connecting the dots between clear-cut logging and hydrologic response, especially increasing flood risk, seems to be a fractious endeavour. If I lived downstream of the Ghost, I would hope someone was looking at the impact of a variety of land uses (logging being the biggest one) on the risk of my basement being flooded.

There is a shift in perspective on the hydrological response to logging, except perhaps by the forestry sector. Forest landscapes become less resilient to handle new, heavy rainfall events (as occurred in 2013) because of clear-cut logging and roads. With clear-cuts (and large wildfires), a watershed contributes runoff more quickly, unlike a mature, intact forest that acts as a sponge.

Intact forests not only moderate runoff, but they also help to reduce the impacts of drought. These forests capture, store, and then slowly release water in times of lower flow and greater water demands. The ability of those forests to be reservoirs for water and serve as moderators of runoff diminishes as the spatial scale of timber harvest increases.

Expert opinion from independent forest hydrologists is that the logging footprint, the so-called Equivalent Clear-cut Area, is becoming too large in most sub-watersheds of the Ghost. Proposed logging plans ignore the reality of ecological thresholds for the spatial footprint. A low threshold of timber removal may not impact the hydrologic response, but exceeding the thresholds is a zero-sum game.

This isn't the only disjunct in our forests. Compared to how many Albertans see forests, the forestry sector and the Forest Service view the forest as simply, maybe exclusively, a source of fibre. As a result, other forest values are consistently overlooked and diminished.

There has been no serious discussion about what we want our forests to be, especially in terms of the mosaic of vegetation types, from grasslands to old-growth forest. The forests of the past, as recalled by the Butters family who have ranched in the Ghost for almost 100 years, had fescue grasslands on dry, south-facing slopes. With fire suppression, conifers have encroached onto those fescue grasslands. Erik Butters, the third generation of the family, has seen this in real time as the grazing capacity of his grazing allotment has been reduced three times over 50 years.

Forest policy compels loggers to replant with conifers, even where grasslands once existed. This is clearly a fibre-oriented policy, not one of forest management. This impacts grazing interests, wildlife habitat, possible wildfire risk reduction, and visual landscapes of interest, creating an eventual monoculture of even-aged, farmed lodgepole pine.

Water is a valuable commodity, and this is especially so for hydropower production and downstream water drinkers. The 2013 flood rendered the Ghost diversion into Lake Minnewanka inoperable, reducing power output. Repairs to the structure, built in 1941 under the *War Measures Act*, should go through today's EIA process. There is no compelling reason now, such as a world war, to avoid a regulatory review and grandfather repairs.

A substantial part of the river is diverted, creating reduced flows for the Ghost, yet no instream flow needs assessment has ever been undertaken. Before any repairs to the diversion occur, there needs to be an assessment for appropriate instream flow amounts to protect the aquatic ecosystem.

The Ghost Watershed Alliance Society (GWAS), FCC, Cows & Fish, some off-road groups (Calgary ATV Riders Association and Trails 4 Tomorrow), and individual ranchers have been engaged in repairing some of the damage to the streams of the watershed. Because of limitations such as funding and volunteer labour capacity, this has amounted to a handful of projects a year.

A variation of the Red Queen's line in Lewis Carroll's *Through the Looking-Glass*, running faster and faster and still falling behind, seems to fit. I have been impressed by the scope of restoration projects these groups have taken on, but the scale and pace of abuse is out of sync with reclamation efforts. Without a stronger presence of government to enforce basic stewardship rules, the prospect of climbing out of the pit of necessary restoration seems problematic.

The GWAS is a not-for-profit watershed group under the provincial government's Water for Life Strategy. Its mandate relates to water quality, healthy aquatic ecosystems, and water quantity to meet a sustainable economy. It has a key role in pulling stakeholders together to meet the province's goals. Despite the organization's importance for both strategic and tactical work, it is underfunded, with loads of responsibility and no authority.

The GWAS tries to provide logical goals for the watershed. If followed, these have a good chance of providing landscape resilience and ecosystem integrity. They translate into clean water, flood and drought protection, biodiversity maintenance, and safe places to recreate.

In lieu of comprehensive land-use planning, guided by science and aided by public consultation, things devolve into various interests grabbing what they can in a free-for-all of intense competition. There is a tendency for land-use interests to think they exist in separate universes. They do not. All are found in one universe called the Ghost watershed. No interest seems inclined to give up one inch of territory, opportunity, or control.

Into the fray steps the GWAS. If the Ghost watershed was a car, most in it would be pushing down on the gas pedal to make it go faster, to wring more out of the ride. Some, perhaps a minority, would be attempting to step on the brakes, recognizing that speed just gets everyone to an eventual accident. A few dedicated groups and individuals would be trying to repair the damage to the car.

The role of the GWAS is to steer the car through a cloud of dust, keeping it between the ditches of abuse, overuse, poor planning, and overall bad behaviour to reach a destination of awareness, care, respect, and stewardship. If the GWAS is to be successful, it requires better and stable financial support and a better balance of responsibility coupled with authority.

I asked Marina Krainer, the executive director of the GWAS,

how she maintains perspective in what seems to be a Herculean task. Her answer was, "We work with all stakeholders to find the best possible solutions. Over time I have noticed, with our awareness programming, monitoring reports and hands-on work, an incremental and positive shift in attitudes toward the watershed and its protection. That keeps me going." I admire her patience and persistence!

At the end of my sightseeing journey into the Ghost, I was left with some troubling thoughts. A wealth of background studies exist to show the outcome of a failure to act. There is no mystery about the need to reduce the footprint of human activity, to refocus logging on a more sustainable pathway, and to restore the ecological function, resilience, and integrity of the watershed. Knowing confers the responsibility to act and to do so in a timely way.

The spirit and intent articulated in the *Ghost Public Land Use Zone* brochure need political support for regulatory, enforcement, and planning efforts. Ignoring ecological limits, coupled with chronically low staff levels, does not deal with the urgency facing the watershed or support the efforts of conservation.

Resources are required immediately to manage and steward the Ghost – to show the flag, to engage in ecological awareness with users, to monitor and regulate land use, and to establish priorities for restoration actions.

Wendell Berry, the farmer/philosopher, wrote in *Life Is a Miracle*, "To treat life as less than a miracle is to give up on it." We can't give up on the Ghost. This place, a watershed of beauty and diversity, needs to be pulled back from chronic abuse and treated with care and respect. If we can't, or won't, it shows we cannot grasp the responsibility and ethics of stewardship.

Illustration by Liz Saunders

7

Writing in the Margins:
Notes to Myself

And the blind man said to the deaf man,
Do you see what I hear?

—Wayne Gerard Trotman

PLASTIC WORDS, DANGEROUS INTENTS

Our language becomes ever more devoid of meaning, and more modular. It resembles the plastic building blocks made famous by Lego; a variety of words stitched together. Read many government and industry press releases and you will see a smorgasbord of words that seem familiar, yet are anything but. Plastic words are malleable and can be made to fit every circumstance. They fill up space and glue together incomprehensible subjects to provide an illusion of clarity and honesty.

In "communication," as practised corporately and politically, we are endlessly enveloped in literary alchemy. Listening to the centrifugal rhetoric of a politician or a fast-talking public-relations type might give you a similar feeling, as junk food appeals to the taste buds but not the feeling of contentment.

Many plastic words began as scientific terms with specialized meanings, such as "ecosystem." Now the word ecosystem has been stripped of its scientific meaning and repurposed for use in real estate, building design, and investment. Words used in this way displace more precise words with ones that sound scientific but actually blur meaning and disable common language.

Appropriating the words of science is an attempt to superficially make the dialogue resemble the terms of science. As one reads word soup with some scientific terms sprinkled in, one can wrongly assume an association with rigorous science. However, the meaning is independent of the original source and the words work to provide an illusion of expertise. The words become so flexible that they cease to be useful and become filler words devoid of any relevant meaning.

A short list of such words and phrases includes balance, growing the economy, trade-offs, mitigation, monitoring, modern, protect, appropriate, progress, communication, (comprehensive) engagement, consultation, inform, responsible (resource development), stringent (environmental protection), best practices, world class, ethical (oil), freedom, feedback, rights, law and order, state-of-the-art, sustainable, wise use, red tape, deregulation, open for business, and in the public interest.

As with Lego blocks, these words can be combined, interchanged, and adapted to explain and justify a variety of actions. Putting several of these words together can give you something resembling this: "We can balance growing the economy with protecting the environment and progress to world-class, even state-of-the-art, sustainable, responsible stewardship through cutting unnecessary red tape yet ensuring comprehensive public engagement and timely consultation, informing best practices and ethical wise use with trade-offs, mitigation, and modern, stringent monitoring and environmental protection."

Not so, you say. A press announcement by a coal company hoping to gain approval to blast the top off a mountain in Southwestern Alberta reads: "[This] project will be a state-of-the-art responsible mining project delivering, via an ethical and secure supply chain, a key resource needed by the world for decades to come." A Government of Alberta press release says, "We gathered feedback to help us develop a modern coal policy that will protect the areas Albertans cherish, while allowing responsible resource development in appropriate areas."

What the hell do the words *responsible*, *protect*, *ethical*, *modern*, and *appropriate* mean in this context? Not much, I would contend. You get the picture – these are code words to soften you up for complacency and acceptance of a bitter pill. These words are hollow shells disguising rigid ideas. The words lack substance, are shallow; the meanings are new and don't taste of anything familiar.

Lewis Carroll must have been thinking of plastic words in this passage from *Through the Looking-Glass*: "'When I use a word,' Humpty Dumpty said, in rather a scornful tone, 'it means just what I choose it to mean – neither more nor less.' 'The question is,' said Alice, 'whether you can make words mean so many different things.'"

Karen Marie Moning, an American author, writes, "Words can be twisted into any shape. Promises can be made to lull the heart and seduce the soul." In the final analysis, these plastic words provide little meaning, and it is actions that speak loudest.

Do not be fooled by those who appropriate words and intentionally bind them together in a fog of respectability meant to change reality.

WHERE THERE'S SMOKE, IS THERE FIRE?

———

Watching and tending campfires is a contemplative affair, especially when the wood is punky and damp. As smoke billows out, I think about the parallel to politics, politicians, and policies. Damp, slightly rotten wood produces little flame, or heat, but much smoke. This creates the illusion of light and warmth, but holding your hand over the fire provides little measurable result.

The smoke envelops, clouds, smothers, and chokes inspection, transparency, or progress. If there is a flame, it is well disguised under the smouldering pallor. It's analogous to political/corporate spin, propaganda, and deflection.

By contrast, well-seasoned, dry wood burns cleanly, with little smoke and an evident flame that provides light and allows you to warm your hands. In a comparable political arena there would exist clarity, transparency, and accountability.

Contemplating something with too much smoke and not enough flame is a signal of inaction or inappropriate actions. Old ideas, soft and sodden, have been around so long that rot permeates and they don't produce much light or progress. As smoke is to punky wood, so too it seems with some politicians with agendas that require concealment, not the purifying light of a blazing campfire.

This can happen with the smudge of communications spin, leaving you feeling you've been smoke-tanned and tainted in the process. It detracts from plunging into the gloom to address the subjects that need attention for shifts in policy and legislation. But we can't be distracted by the smoke from politicians and the corporate world.

It is tempting to pour some accelerant, such as gasoline, on a smouldering campfire. Doing so might provide some momentary light, but it does not do enough for long enough to be of much use. The answer isn't to make more smoke but to pour water on this crumbling pile of barely flammable wood and start over with a new, dry base that has a chance of kindling a blaze of change. This has obvious parallels to why governments need to change, sometimes frequently, and why corporations need to be held to account.

In Alberta we can be under a pall of summer smoke, the tangible form from wildfires giving us burning eyes, runny noses, and a sense we have been forced into the equivalent of a two-pack-a-day smoking habit. We are also subject at all times to the metaphoric smoke of politics, sometimes equally thick and choking. Lungs are made to be filled with air, not smoke, and minds deserve to be exposed to good ideas and the truth, not to toxic ideologies.

To the uninitiated, political smoke is hard to identify. It swirls over you, in ever denser quantities until confusion sets in and the creator of the smoke offers to guide you to the clear air. Beware of a purée of platitudes, a bouquet of bromides, and a gall of gestures. These do not offer clarity but are forms of obscuring smoke.

We seem to be enveloped in smoke from neo-con governments related to the erosion of publicly funded health care; a cavalier attitude to the COVID-19 pandemic; an education curriculum derived from the internet; a sense pension funds are not being managed at arm's length; a balanced budget not based on fiscal prudence but rather a windfall of oil revenue; a dubious push for a provincial police force; weakened environmental regulations and the hype of "no-conflict" and "ethical" oil; and climate change denial and foot-dragging in the face of wicked weather.

With these and other topics of concern to Albertans it seems as someone has started up not only the smoke generator but also the fog machine and the haze creator to obscure the truth amid billows of obfuscation.

Albertans are tired of real smoke and should be equally concerned about the political smoke that obscures the issues facing the province. It's said that politicians are motivated by two things – heat and light. If, like me, you are concerned that too much smoke means little heat and light, it's time to build a new fire.

IS THERE ANY CULTURE LEFT IN AGRICULTURE?

———

The notion of agriculture – nurturing life, growing good food, being close to and working with nature, recognizing the rhythms of the seasons, the independence, being self-sufficient – should be a beautiful one. But it isn't for many farmers caught on the treadmill approach to agriculture. Mounting expenses, indebtedness, poor returns, an amorphous and anonymous market, stress, strain, and especially lack of control detract substantially from the great notion.

Perhaps part of the angst is that the essence of farming appears to have been erased. Perched in an air-conditioned tractor cab, metres off the ground and surveying dials and readouts, a conventional farmer may well be as disconnected from the land as an urban dweller is on a Sunday drive through the same country.

Humans are inveterate tinkerers, from the first of our ancestors who attempted to modify a piece of stone into a better tool, to technocrats splicing a gene into a plant to give it some new virtue. We manipulate, remanufacture, mine, and massage our environment to our own ends and needs. We are on a path to exchange the craft of farming for the chemical state of coaxing life from the equivalent of an enlarged petri dish. Farming seems yoked to the wheel of industry, driven by economies of scale and reverent in the pursuit of wealth. What's missing, despite the contention that the goal is to feed the world, is the connection to food and, by association, to the land.

An industrial approach to agriculture, as is an assembly line for cars or refrigerators, is one of simplification, speed, and replacing human labour with machines. Henry Ford, who perfected the assembly line for car manufacture, said, "Everything can always be done better than it is being done." It's that thinking that leads to the perception that natural systems are inefficient and we can "improve" them.

There is a reductionist tendency in agriculture that attempts to deconstruct complexity, to focus just on the pieces related to economic gain rather than appreciating the virtues of an intact system. We think we know enough about a system to intervene successfully in improving its function. It would be similar to the misplaced hope that taking the back off a finely crafted, intricate Swiss watch and jabbing at the innards blindly with a large screwdriver would improve the function of keeping accurate time. In most farming the logic of nature is usurped by the mandates of business. The two are too often mutually exclusive, and in the case of business, logic is a chimera.

Wendell Berry, the Kentucky farmer and philosopher, said, "An enduring agriculture must never cease to consider and respect and preserve wilderness. The farm can exist only within the wilderness of mystery and natural force. And if the farm is to last and remain in health, the wilderness must survive within the farm." He must have been talking not only about bees, birds, and coyotes but also about setting aside some land to ensure we save the obvious and essential cogs and wheels in addition to the ones we don't know anything about. This wisdom is displayed in only a few scattered farms.

With current agriculture policy the trajectory is set and we have largely landed on an industrial mode of production. The impetus driving farming is one of machinery size, horsepower, speed, and complexity, coupled with the latest and best from the laboratories of the agrochemical corporations.

Large fields are the response to economies of scale. Supersized equipment is the answer to covering the ground quickly. The result is farming of marginal lands, loss of wetlands and other natural features, and a homogenization of the landscape into crop monocultures.

A combination of soil cultivation, chemical use, and

application of artificial fertilizers destroys many natural enemies of pests, eliminates habitat for pollinators, and reduces natural agents of soil fertility. Those ecological goods and services were once provided free of charge. With conventional farming, all of that natural heavy lifting is shifted to the farmer, who has to make expensive substitutions in perpetuity, with dubious results.

Inexorably, the trend and trajectory of agriculture has moved into the questionable maw of agribusiness, an industrial approach to the growing of commodities, not food. The business model is driven by efficiency, which means expansion to larger and larger scales to increase the marginal slice of profit. To do that a farm has to become a Dr. Strangelove place of technology, genetic manipulation, chemical cocktails, imported fertility, and immense, expensive equipment to grow crops saturated in liberal amounts of fossil fuel.

A glance at some of the agrochemicals available today might suggest farms are war zones with herbicide and pesticide names such as "Avenge," "Warrior," and "Sword." Aldo Leopold, the dean of ecological thinkers, observed some eight decades ago in *A Sand County Almanac*, "Agricultural science is largely a race between the emergence of new pests and the emergence of new techniques for their control." Other chemicals with names such as "Freedom," "Harmony," and "Logic" suggest the race is over. The enigmatically named "Alamo" might indicate otherwise. Texans hold this was the place the good guys got massacred in a hopeless, desperate attempt to hold the fort.

If we were to manage sustainably, working with the land (not against it) and thinking ecologically (not solely with an economic outcome), the rule might be to "make the smallest intervention possible." Otherwise, as the ecological maxim states, "we can never do one thing" and we cannot predict what the other effects will be, often until after it is too late to reverse the process.

Maybe the tectonic plates underpinning agriculture need to move, if ever so slightly, backward toward something more sustainable. If we want to continue to eat, someone should refocus on agriculture's origins, at a scale that is much more local. That's where a small number of farms are at – focusing not on train cars of commodities but rather on platefuls of food. The investment community isn't there yet, but the wise money and those who consider food security paramount might now turn their attention toward what conventional agriculture and the agribusiness "experts" have derided as "fringe."

That would be the small-scale, organic, free-range, grass-fed, permaculture, no growth hormones, no antibiotics, pesticide/ herbicide-free, direct marketing, "you pick," artisan, community-based, low-input, and "green" forms of agriculture whose focus is on food production and distribution at local and regional scales. In many ways these represent the antithesis of current agribusiness.

These farms operate mainly with sunshine, biological activity, the recycling of plant and animal material, and the owner's footsteps. These "fringe" farms could be considered a return to where agriculture came from. There we might find sustainable forms of agriculture for the future.

Agricultural landscapes produce commodities, sustain rural residents, and support communities, but we gloss over their other values. These are our watersheds; there is space, a place for wildlife, and a visual tonic from a busy cityscape. A drive through a largely industrialized agricultural landscape, one increasingly depopulated, with monotonous monoculture crops and few natural features, should fill us with concern.

We need islands of unconventional agriculture in the form of smaller, regenerative operations to break up the growing homogenization and industrialization of the landscape. That would breathe some life back into rural Alberta, create some needed ecological buffers, and reverse the increasing silence of a landscape devoid of people and birdsong. It would also put the culture back into agriculture.

RIVER DREAMING

There is dawn time along this river, when the insects are yet cold and quiet. It is a netherworld of semi-wakefulness where consciousness begins to return. Birds begin to exercise and warm up their vocal cords for a day of beseeching, threatening, and conversing. A trout rises slowly to intercept the erratic flight of a mayfly. Ripples from that rise dispel the notion that the current looks almost solid enough for a true believer to walk on water. I know I wouldn't dare. Only the water strider can perform this feat as it dances across the water without breaking the surface tension.

It seems the river slides past at a pace of its own choosing. I know it's more complicated and based on snowmelt, gradient, and the size and absorptive quality of the watershed. I understand the theoretical architecture of river flow, that water ricochets from bank to bank, spiralling like a corkscrew as it goes.

Trout know these currents, know how to exploit them for

food items and resting areas. I'm sure there is a trout road map and the longer you watch, the clearer the watery routes become. Trout aren't lazy but know how to use the energy of the river to conserve theirs.

The tug of the current against my legs reminds me of the primordial force of water, capable of carving down mountains, even the ones that now tear holes in the clouds. Perhaps the river recognizes that I am mostly water and the rest just extraneous flotsam. A pair of bald eagles nest in an immense cottonwood, old enough to remember the early incursion of settlers, miners, and woodchoppers.

I have to remind myself that the tree-cleared air I breathe and the seemingly clean river I wade in are subject to the dust and effluent from those entities spurring on the economy upwind and upstream. Be that as it may, I reflect I'm only going to wade in the river, not drink it. Quenching one's thirst directly from the river would be a serious article of faith, such as believing you could walk on water without incident.

The spring snowmelt is mostly over, and the river is clear enough to see the gravels and cobbles produced in an abrasive eternity of grinding and polishing. Spring rains will shortly obscure the river bottom as the sediment from too many roads, trails, and disturbances bleeds into the runoff. This tugs at my anger receptors as the river tugs at me.

I take a deep breath and try to stay with the moment but reflect on a society so intent on their entitlements they cannot recognize their responsibilities. A blind person will not see a mountain but can detect a change in altitude through deeper and rapid breathing. To them a riparian area might be discernable with cooler temperatures and higher humidity. A shopping centre parking lot has no softness underfoot and the palpable sense of a rush for bargain items.

What this might teach us sighted people is we can employ other senses to gather information on our surroundings. We cannot continue to be blind to the sense we cannot drink the river's water without elaborate treatment, that extreme floods are now more prevalent and native trout are quickly disappearing.

The rainbow trout rising to gobble the mayfly hatch is a transplant who has usurped the spot of native cutthroat trout. Yes, this foreigner does reasonably well in this somewhat diminished habitat, sends an electrifying charge through the line when caught, and produces an occasional memorable meal. It should also set off some alarm bells that the river and its watershed have been changed and that this continues under our tenure. If the trend continues, will even rainbow trout survive?

Back in the moment, I react to all of the rises by casting to the larger splashes. A pale dun fly elicits no response, but a western green drake is pounced on by a motivated trout. Sometimes the process of matching the hatch seems esoteric, maddingly complex, and occasionally it clicks. The point is it is absorbing to participate in what is happening, to become part of the theatre, not just as a spectator. Thoughts of mindless resource exploitation, watershed impacts, and the hollow assurances we can have it all are put on hold momentarily.

Under the best of circumstances that is what fishing does. It can take you away into the world of fish and the rhythm of the water, to a place without artifice (except for your trout flies), where even for a short time you can dream as a river.

THE BIGGEST FISH I EVER CAUGHT WAS PRETTY SMALL
Reflections on Fish, Fishing, and Fishers

———

Some might say the essence of fishing is a jerk at one end of a line waiting for a jerk on the other end. That description seems harsh. Maybe it's a timeless meditation on the hopeful unseen, unknown.

But in listening to and participating in fishing talk it seems there is an endless parade of big fish stories; how a fish was bigger than a small child, or, my favourite, how a bull trout stretched from stirrup to stirrup across a saddle. There is a one-dimensional aspect to these stories based on fish size and numbers caught. Is there something more to fishing?

Of course, the filler material includes bigger ones that got away, what fish were biting on, which in one case was a moose liver set in shallow water to cool, and how long it took to catch a limit. Lively discussions, sometimes trending into argument, rage on over which fish species is the hardest fighter, the trickiest to catch, and makes the most elegant trophy.

Individual fish take on personas, like the "Hulk" or the "Monster." It becomes mano a fisho, a contest of wills, persistence, and guile against a worthy adversary. The extent of planning, logistical arrangements, and gear to accomplish this contest seems unbalanced. It's the equivalent of the Normandy invasion to secure a fish with a brain smaller than your little fingernail. Fish take on an aura that make them seem bigger, smarter, and more elusive than they really are. It makes the catch seem ever more eventful, as in achieving a piscatorial Holy Grail.

There are factions, verging on tribalism, among fishers. Some of this is related to where they fish, either flowing waters or still waters. Differentiations are made between cold-water-dwelling fish, the trout, and cool-water species, such as pike, walleye, and perch. Some angle exclusively with "hardware" – lures made of metal, plastic, or combinations of such materials. Others attempt to motivate fish to bite using "flies," artful constructions of feathers, hair, tinsel, and thread. Sometimes their fishing experience is extended by making their own flies. The truly atavistic use natural materials – worms, grasshoppers, and maggots. Others are catholic in this, fishing wherever there are fish, using whatever will work. The lines merge and diverge.

At one end of the scale, with no comment on evolutionary advancement or hierarchy, are fly fishers. A conversation will wax on with attempts to "match the hatch" with artificial flies that duplicate (one hopes) the aquatic invertebrate complement of mostly stoneflies, mayflies, and caddisflies. These come under a blinding, confusing array of names such as Woolly Bugger, Bitch Creek, and LaFontaine Emergent Sparkle Pupa. The Adams, one of the most popular dry flies, looks like an insect, but as author Mark Kurlansky puts it, "No known insect looks like an Adams."

Of course, there is a distinction between "dry" flies, fished on the surface, versus streamers or nymphs that are presented underwater. These choices then get into the nuances of sinking versus floating lines. Rod lengths, weights, and materials are an esoteric journey to a place of either intense interest or numbing boredom.

Some fly fishers challenge themselves by using smaller and smaller hooks tied to fly line leaders with wispy, thin tippets to catch bigger and bigger trout. A probable endpoint to this is microscopic hooks attached to nanofibres derived from spiders' webs.

Unlike the lightweights of fishing are those select few who fish for lake sturgeon in big prairie rivers such as the South Saskatchewan. Lake sturgeon are an ancient species that have been swimming on the planet for at least 136 million years. That rates them a senior's discount. This species is the largest and longest-lived fish on the North American continent. To catch one involves lobbing a line resembling a winch cable out into a deep pool with a large dab of something smelly impaled on what resembles a grappling hook.

At the other end of the fishing scale are those who fish on lakes and reservoirs, mostly for cool-water species. This is a group more oriented to higher levels of hardware and software technology. To better catch fish, they possess much of the same equipment as the nation's navy. This is used with the same determination displayed by astronauts blasting into space to discern aspects of the cosmos.

Fish finders, underwater cameras, and boat global positioning systems take the guesswork out of fishing. These are sophisticated tools, with sonar coverage providing high-resolution images of bottom details and structures where fish hang out. They will show numbers of fish and relative sizes and allow you to watch a fish's reaction to your bait. Once you find the "hotspots," you can return to the exact spot time and time again. A downside is focusing on a fish finder screen may reduce focus on an oncoming storm.

Somewhat similar to fly fishing there is an insider language used by these lake technophiles that verges on something similar to a secret society. If you are bewildered by advice to stack a flasher on a downrigger, welcome to the club. You can choose to engage in trolling (perfectly acceptable in fishing but not on social media), jigging (but not the dance of the East Coasters), or casting (but not for a movie role). Each will require a different type of rod. You can use a bobber to let you know when a fish is nibbling your marshmallow, corn kernel, or hot dog sliver (and you thought those were for lunch).

Implicit in still-water fishing, unless you have perfected walking on water, is the need for a boat. As you go up the scale from a rowboat to a cabin cruiser you would be best to have a substantial inheritance and/or a job as a corporate mogul. Keep in mind that you will need to tow your boat (or ship, depending on its size) from place to place. The outlay for equipment, before you ever fling some bait into the water, will come in close to the down payment on a house in most large urban centres. This is why some so equipped feel the need to catch many fish to rationalize the investment and to feed their children.

Then there is the Hamlet-like question for all fishers – "to eat, or not to eat." This is the choice, maybe dilemma, between catch and release or catch and keep (to eat). Fish are delicious, so much so that some populations have been eaten up. There is the argument that eating fish is a fundamental part of fishing. In munching on them we make a significant connection with the natural world, and restricting this severs that necessary association. Others point out that some fish populations cannot withstand even the taking of a couple of fillets by each fisher. This debate rages on and the middle ground seems hard to find.

I'm not saying fishers are any more prone to exaggeration than the general population but, when asked, most will say they have caught fish. In reality, most people never catch a fish, big or small. This begs the question – if you never catch anything, why do you persist? Is part of this the off chance a fish will, someday, blunder onto your hook? Hope has an eternal quality. The other, perhaps more compelling reason is that fishing has little to do with catching fish.

My colleague Duane Radford surveyed people fishing on the upper Oldman River in the 1970s and I did a similar survey of fishers on lakes in the Cypress Hills a little later. People were asked what elements were important to them for a day's fishing. Consistently, natural beauty, solitude, and water quality ranked at the top of the list, substantially higher than the ability to catch fish. Catching fish (or not, as most people weren't) was almost at the bottom of a list of factors.

This strongly suggests your surroundings, the experience, seeing other wildlife, and interacting in an intact, healthy landscape are important drivers for people. Fishing is just the mechanism to put you into a setting where you might see yourself as part of the natural world, not apart from it. Fishing is something that we feel we need to do, but as Zane Grey, an ardent sportsman and writer, reflected, "the fish are incidental." Why then do our fishing stories give the impression all we are interested in is the catch?

When we get beyond the minutiae of fishing gear and techniques, the intricate preparation and obsessing over quests, which all lead to embellished fishing stories, we land at something much different than one might think. Our stories might better reflect the real reasons we fish. If we love to fish, we must also love the places to which fish bring us. It would help to have reverence for the fish we pursue. In fishing, fish might be the motivator, the bonus, but they are not the sole reason we engage in such an elaborate dance.

So here's the "hook" – what kind of an interaction do you want with fish? Will it be angling with restrictions, but in a place that appeals to your soul, or waiting for the hatchery truck beside a sterile dugout? Maybe it will be another type of association that doesn't involve fishing. In the discussions and arguments over the pursuit and management of fish these are things for consideration.

STANDING ON THE SHOULDERS OF GIANTS
Martha, Elmer, Francis

In the business of conservation, we are often so intent on staring into the fog called tomorrow, we rarely turn around and look back at the pathway called yesterday stretching behind us. How we got on that pathway, how we gained confidence, momentum, and critical mass is mostly based on those who came before us. All of us stand on the shoulders of some giants – Martha Kostuch, Elmer Kure, and Francis Gardner were three of those giants for me.

Martha

It's the day after Earth Day and I've just heard of Martha's passing. Celebrate Earth one day; celebrate the life of a person who did much in Earth's service the next. Martha asked us not to grieve but to act in her memory. Indeed, we should and will, partly for Martha and mostly because we know it's the right thing. Just as she engaged in initiatives she knew she would not see to fruition, we should follow that lead.

Martha worked tirelessly to ensure that environmental laws were improved and enforced, to push industry to use the best available technology to reduce pollution, to collaboratively develop better policies, and to stop destructive and inappropriate developments. These efforts were huge and often successful. She recognized that laws matter and her triumphant Supreme Court decision in 1992 on environmental assessment was a landmark decision that was incorporated into Canada's legislation. This focused on the Oldman Dam, where she forced the federal government to exercise its constitutional and legal duties.

While it's easy to make things personal, she concentrated on the issue, not the person. Her focus was to resolve those issues that impede progress on environmental protection, not on personal attacks on those with whom she disagreed.

Someone wise said the ultimate test of a person's conscience may be their willingness to sacrifice something today for future generations whose words of thanks will not be heard. Martha stiffened our collective spines for advocacy, for promoting fairness and equity, and for speaking (and acting) forcefully, intelligently, and ethically for the environment.

I think of these words of Gandhi when I think of Martha: "First they ignore you, then they laugh at you, then they fight you, then you win." In so many ways, Martha won. For her persistence in the face of ridicule and adversity and the path she created we give thanks.

Elmer

When we look at the dash that represents Elmer's life from 1921 to 2012 it doesn't provide a sense of his vast contribution to conservation. It's not so much the long list of initiatives he worked on but how he managed to accomplish so much for conservation.

In Elmer's long life he was witness to many changes on the landscape. As a farmer he accepted he was part of some of those changes, but he was always aware of the balance between benefits and costs. I think that put Elmer in a rare position to see both sides of the equation, of land uses and land-use issues. His extensive reading made him an informed individual, giving him a sense of perspective, of balance, and of alternatives. He used those skills extensively to inform, negotiate, and when no balance could be found, to draw lines in the sand.

Elmer was part of the Alberta Fish and Game Association and was a key figure in conservation efforts before many current environmental and conservation groups were functional. He capably represented conservation interests during the time the original Eastern Slopes Policy was being written. Elmer was a driving force behind the first Buck for Wildlife project, the restoration of the North Raven River.

In 1964 Elmer came to the Fish and Game Club of which I was a member. Introduced as a farmer from a community just south of where I grew up, he was articulate and talked on another type of killing. He had just finished reading a book that was an epiphany for him. The book was, of course, *Silent Spring* by Rachel Carson. He talked at length on what he had learned about the effects of herbicides and pesticides on wildlife.

I still remember the evening that Elmer spoke. He didn't

back down from the arguments that dead birds were the price of progress. I recall Elmer saying that the price of progress was too high. That evening Elmer Kure led me, eventually, to become a biologist.

Francis

It's the little things sometimes. One of the first things I noticed about Francis was the early version of a multi-tool, a set of locking pliers, that he wore on his belt. I don't know what it was about that tool, but it gave me the impression Francis was a fixer of things. And, in many ways, that tool was a metaphor for who Francis was, a fixer of equipment, of situations, and of landscapes.

If there was one thing that stood out in his role as a fixer, it was his tackling of a fundamental human condition and failing – greed. I think this is where he and I began to find resonance. Among many, Francis was one of the few not consumed by the persistent drive to wring and extract more out of the land than it could reasonably provide. His pithy observation was, "Greed comes naturally, but conservation has to be learned." Early on, our philosophies aligned on this issue.

In conversations and in forums he was inspiring, although sometimes frustrating, because he usually took the long view, looked at the big picture, and reviewed the scene from 10,000 feet. I suppose some of this came from his love of flying, where these attributes are important and part of a survival strategy. When Francis talked of pilots running out of "airspeed, altitude, and ideas," I took it as an analogy about the problem of short-term planning, or the lack of effective planning to guide us on the landscape to a sustainable endpoint.

Concepts such as stewardship get bandied about and pulled out, akin to rabbits from a hat, to shore up ideas or defend a position. But stewardship isn't magic, nor does it happen without commitment, effort, and persistence. When I went looking for the underpinnings and examples of stewardship to write about the concept, I came to the mailbox overlooking Mt. Sentinel Ranch, Francis's ranch.

As Francis observed, "If the land isn't healthy, neither my family nor the ranch will be." It's a circle and part of that circle is clean water, habitat maintenance, biodiversity, and recreational opportunity.

We have a set of coasters made by Francis of slices of old, very old, diamond willow from the ranch. The growth rings are tight, almost indiscernible without a magnifying glass. They represent a lot of living, as did Francis's life. Sometimes though, we need to peer through a magnifying glass to discern the things that make a person special and memorable.

The contributions to conservation made by Martha, Elmer, and Francis were many and are an enduring legacy to their work, integrity, and commitment. The best of conservation successes are the ones hardly noticed. A clear stream with a rising trout, a woodlot harbouring a grouse, a white-tailed deer, a patch of lady slippers, and an intact piece of prairie grassland. These three giants were part of making so many of those things happen.

They were also part of something larger. Healthy landscapes, fish, and wildlife only persist when people appreciate and take responsibility for them. That is their legacy, one of a quest for stewardship and the torch is now passed to us.

Alberta is, no doubt, a better place because of their efforts.

Illustration by Liz Saunders

8

Paying Attention and Dialling In

*The only difference between being
uninformed and misinformed is that one
is your choice and the other is theirs.*

—Frank Sonnenberg

A RIVER'S GIFT — OURS TO LOSE

A river never abandons its people. Even in drought, with little flow, it still serves us as best it can. But it would seem — through excessive withdrawals, pollution, and headwaters malfeasance that exacerbates floods and intensifies droughts — we have abandoned our rivers, especially the ones in Southern Alberta.

Rivers are a gift of nature. We would do well to remember that fact. We should live in radical amazement and gratitude toward rivers. They provide us a substance more precious, more essential than oil. We can live without "Western Canadian Select," the crudest crude oil, but not without clean, pristine water flowing through intact riparian forests alive with birdsong.

We would be wise to know a river's moods, recognize its power, yield graciously to its strength, and be thankful for the bounty provided. Instead, we harness, straitjacket, divert, abscond with flow, and return to the river our waste.

A river twists, turns, and flows, ancient yet ageless and unstoppable. Take it for granted and you will be deceived into believing it will always be there for you, supplying all your needs. Dam it, dredge it, smother its banks with concrete, and it will still flood you or succumb to drought. Study it wisely, reflectively, and don't for a moment think you can tell from its surface what its inner state might be.

Wade Davis, in *Magdalena: River of Dreams*, points out there are something approaching 800,000 dams worldwide and on average every 12 hours sees the construction of another dam. Dam decommissioning and deconstruction are still minor activities. It would seem that dam building proceeds on the rationale that construction is possible – to attempt to control the uncontrollable – and so it will be done.

Dam promotors remind one of Oliver Twist in the Charles Dickens novel of the same name. There, the small boy comes forward, bowl in hand, and begs Mr. Bumble for gruel with the famous request, "Please sir, I want some more."

We need to get out of the spiral of, "The answer is a dam, what was the question?"

We build structural solutions (dams) to meet our immediate needs, not the needs of the future. The future still has to look after itself. That way we generate continual problems that follow us into the future, instead of dealing with them in real time, as in the spectre of climate change and reduced river flows.

In the Book of Job in the Old Testament of the Bible is found the passage: "Man puts his hand to the flinty rock and overturns mountains by the roots. He cuts out channels in the rocks and his eye sees every precious thing. He dams up the streams so they do not trickle, and the thing that is hidden he brings out to light. But where shall wisdom be found? And where is the place of understanding? Man does not know its worth." I had no idea damming rivers meted such damning criticism in biblical terms. It seems as if God sides with natural landscapes. Engineers, politicians, and dam proponents, pay attention!

Ancient Anasazi farmers in the desert southwest of the United States once held a fragile tenure on an arid land they considered productive. Their rudimentary and primitive irrigation systems were suitable for producing subsistence levels of corn and squash. This was the centre of their universe and, yet, likely because of changes in climate, especially drought conditions, they abandoned the area. They moved, apparently to areas with less water uncertainty. If they had taken a page from today's dam lobbyists, they would have agitated for someone else to underwrite the costs of making their valleys verdant.

There are always schemes afoot to control water resources. In times of economic uncertainty, when the provincial or federal purse is stretched with other priorities, the lobby for more dams goes underground. There, like groundwater, the lobby sits and bides its time, waiting for the moment to surface again.

Humans have always been more adept at inventing tools than contemplating the implications of those tools and then using them wisely. It is easier to manipulate a river by building a dam than to step back and predict all of the complex consequences this will have for the wider ecological system, as well as economic and social systems. We don't deal with the issue of increasing demand for water with conservation and restraint. Instead, like the Red Queen in *Through the Looking-Glass*, we continue to run faster and faster to increase the supply of water just to stay in the same place.

Southern Alberta's rivers (and their watersheds) show the strain of over a century of careless development, of dealing only with the supply side of the equation. We are still a way away from a general acceptance that water was already working to support ecosystems and economies before we engineered rivers to maximize their benefits to us. We seem stuck in a mentality that we can engineer our way out of a situation of climate change-influenced reduced flows.

Dams choke rivers, sometimes to death. Reservoirs impounded by dams flood some of the most ecologically important and productive pieces of the landscape – riparian areas. Water is manipulated so that levels in reservoirs dramatically rise and fall, exposing bare valley walls. Wave and wind erosion turn the water in reservoirs turbid. Sediment from erosion then darkens and taints the river's flow downstream.

Reservoirs resemble giant bathtubs, continually filled and drained by water managers. The entire reservoir volume of water might be exchanged several times a year, unlike natural lakes where the water might take decades or longer to be changed. This means the aquatic system in a reservoir remains impoverished and never equates to the naturally higher productivity of a lake or the river channel that was destroyed to construct the reservoir.

Flows downstream of dams and diversions rarely resemble natural ones, and can be much lower, especially during periods of naturally low flow. This severely challenges the aquatic environment and fish. It is physically impossible in over-allocated rivers to divide flows to accommodate the needs of fish and other aquatic life and the demands for irrigation agriculture and power production.

Gabriel Garcia Marquez, in *The General in His Labyrinth*, wrote "The fish will have to learn to walk, because the water will be gone." He certainly was speaking of the impacts of dams on fish. As it is with most dams, fish would have to walk to survive, since their upstream passage to spawning beds is blocked, interrupting their ability to meet their life cycle requirements.

Bob Hawke, a former Australian prime minister, might well have summed up the issue with dams in a statement about a proposal to dam a river in Tasmania. Without mincing words he said, "This project is an ecological obscenity and an economic absurdity."

Rivers bring life, give life, and maintain life. We can manipulate, control, and tinker with them to a degree, but the gift-giving of rivers has limits. Unfortunately, those water managers who foresee the upcoming crisis in climate change and reduced flows still accept none of the responsibility for setting limits. It is the inevitable tension between an extractive economy and one that recognizes our reliance on intact ecosystems.

Margaret Atwood, in *Payback: Debt and the Shadow Side of Wealth*, speaks to this with "Nature is an expert in cost-benefit analysis. Although she does her accounting a little differently. As for debts, she always collects in the long run."

The gifts of a river are ours to lose, or to keep. But to keep them we will need to temper our wants with our needs.

MORE DEVELOPMENT, LESS ENVIRONMENT

First, there is the big lie – we need to prop up the economy and grow it so we can protect the environment. Alberta must become an even leaner, meaner, open-for-business machine. The narrative that we can't have environmental protection without a vibrant economy is a Trojan horse to rationalize watering down, sidestepping, and eliminating environment policy. In other words, we have to mine, cut, and extract more of our natural resources to protect a diminishing amount of our Alberta landscape. To save a hand, we have to cut off a foot.

This sort of government always has an excuse. When the economy is booming, there isn't time to protect environmental assets – in an economic crash there is no cash for these trivial and frivolous actions. We are told we must reduce the impediments to business through dubious concepts such as "Regulatory Enhancement" and "Red Tape Reduction."

These are smooth terms, fine-tuned by the merchants of spin to disguise a process of undermining environmental protection. You might think ecosystem bits and functions are better protected. You'd be wrong! In political parlance it is about removing impediments to development – that spells deregulation.

The presentation of our choices, given our faltering economy, as "it's the environment or the economy" is a Hobson's choice, a false and misleading dichotomy. We can't ignore the economy, but to ignore the environment (or give it lip service instead of real protection) will bite us badly.

Reputationally, jurisdictions suffer when ethical investors bail from a Wild West business model (as some already have). Landscapes with ecological integrity protect and buffer us from floods, drought, and biodiversity loss, as well as provide a suite of economic advantages for recreation, agriculture, and tourism. Squander that and we undermine the most sustainable parts of our economy in favour of a short-term liquidation sale.

Revving up the motors of business inevitably means redlining the capacity of the landscape. Our landscapes have a threshold for human activity beyond which things start to unravel and disappear. For the Alberta public, the majority of whom are concerned about the natural environment, water quality, biodiversity, and open space, proposed changes to the rules governing environmental stewardship should be viewed with alarm. More development with less constraints will inevitably lead to less environment.

The rationale for the weakening of environmental rules seems based on three precepts. First, environmental regulations are obstacles and impediments strangling economic opportunity and competitiveness. No objective analysis is available from either the Alberta government or industry to substantiate this, suggesting that these political and business perceptions are out of touch with reality. As Mark Twain observed, "One gets such wholesale returns of conjecture out of such a trifling investment of fact." The implication that protecting the environment is too expensive and anti-business is tenuous at best and mostly hyperbole. One study indicates the relative magnitude and scope of the economic costs of environmental regulation are well under 2 per cent when compared to other business cost factors. Can this really be the make-or-break decision relating to competitiveness? The evidence, if one takes the time to search it out, suggests following this path will impose real environmental losses, with no meaningful economic gains. What a bargain!

Second, the process will be transformed from proactive to reactive – instead of avoiding problems with front-end work, we will try to cope with the aftermath. The mantra includes "Let's do it fast," and "let's make it easy." From this follows, "We'll probably break a few things." Never, it seems, do we get to ask the more important question: "Is this the right thing to do?"

Industry may perceive the current referral system as cumbersome, but unless they develop much higher environmental standards themselves, failure is certain. Industry and government seem to adhere to the axiom "if the minimum is good enough, we don't ever have to rise above it."

Third, and last, this initiative is based on the mistaken and erroneous belief that we can have our cake and eat it too. Environmental quality diminishes in a crowded, busy industrial landscape, which is what much of Alberta is starting to resemble. The reality is we end up with crumbs.

Business and government might have some valid arguments about how standards are applied. But the result of frustration with multiple windows of application and apparent redundancy is a misguided political campaign against the costs of protecting the environment. There is intelligence in tinkering with the administration of land-use referrals. It is quite another thing to weaken the application of good rules.

Much of the issue could be fixed by the bolstering of staff in departments that have an environmental mandate. Unfortunately, this option is anathema to right-wing governments. The sheer scope, complexity, and intricacy of industrial land use in landscapes with existing cumulative impacts, fragmentation, and significant loss of ecological functions and pieces cries out for more boots on the ground, not fewer.

We would be better served – the Alberta government, the Alberta public, and industry – with professionals working in the public interest and employed by the public. Consider a cadre of resource professionals as the best insurance policy we might invest in to ensure Alberta's ecosystems don't crumple around our heads.

We can choose to cut more trees, mine more coal, or extract more oil and gas, but we can't have all of these and still retain functional, ecologically intact landscapes. A gain in any of the former is a loss in the latter. It's not even clear if more cutting, digging, or drilling is economically beneficial for Albertans, given the dismal track record of undercharging for rents, royalties, and reclamation levies. We taxpayers are already stuck with the bill for abandoned oil and gas wells because of this flawed governance.

Chafing against environmental legislation and policies leads to a disturbing institutional blindness of single purpose and narrow focus. Prosperity and environmental quality need not be strangers, but with Alberta's focus on the former, it comes at the expense of the latter. It seems to be a one-way street to an ecologically impoverished province.

Watering down the rules under the guise of regulatory enhancement and red tape reduction results in the Alberta government running with scissors – a fall will hurt all of us.

MITIGATION TONIC

———

A tonic is a nostrum, something that is purported to be good for all that ails you (and if nothing ails you it's good for that too). As in the advertisement for a 19th-century patent medicine that read, "Takes hold of the vitals and elevates the soul. It opens the faculties, clears the canals of the heart and improves the feeling of contentedness – 5 cents a glass." My mother favoured tonics – what I remember about them is they tasted bad and you didn't want a repeat engagement.

They seem cheaper than real medicine, avoid all that contradictory science, and allow one to continue a lifestyle with habits of excess. It is really liberating to not be burdened with insight and knowledge, to simply blindly trust that something works as stated.

Tonics are patent medicines, promoted and sold as medical cures, and do not work as advertised. In ancient times these were called *nostrum remedium* ("our remedy" in Latin). Today's penchant for mitigation, an unrealistic remedy for our development fever, fits the same mould.

The elixirs and tonics of the patent medicine era had high purchase costs even though they were concocted of cheap materials. The ingredients included turpentine, camphor, grain alcohol, cocaine, and opium. Alcohol and opiates dulled the senses, giving the impression the medicine was working. Turpentine and camphor probably covered the smell of deception. Mitigation similarly blinds us to loss, refocuses our attention, and whips up zeal for unsatisfactory substitutes.

The remedies proved inadequate to cover the bewildering array of medical conditions, diseases, afflictions, and symptoms.

Given the slow state of evidence-based research into real cures and preventatives, many early pharmacists and charlatans (the term "snake oil salesman" comes from this period) put together concoctions of substances to meet patient demands for "something to take." With mitigation, and the many salesmen to peddle the product, we may not be far removed from the era of patent medicine.

A mitigation tonic promotes the advantages of a compensatory mechanism for a loss of ecosystem services, functions, habitat, or biodiversity. It's a panacea shielding us from the grim reality and pain of loss. Mitigation tonic is the one-stop, one-size cure for land-use ailments. It's supposedly able to cure just about everything. When the accepted answer to development isn't no, all that's required is to have faith and blindly apply mitigation as necessary to the affected parts of the landscape.

The tonic is supposed to compensate for the exponential over-consumption of natural resources by an increasing human population with machine slaves fuelled by the fire of petroleum and other commodities. At the same time, primary systems that provide ecosystem services such as air, water, and food are all going downhill. Applying a mitigation tonic means we can continue to do everything, everywhere, all the time, any time, and do so at a revved-up pace without having to worry about the consequences.

There should be a warning label, or at least a full disclosure of the contents. It's suggested that any mitigation effort or project have the following attached in recognition of honesty, accuracy, and fairness:

Caution: Techno-fix Mitigation Tonic

Always seek the advice of a competent, objective professional before starting treatment. Extended use may be damaging and permanent. Stop treatment if symptoms of excessive and cumulative land-use effects persist. Always evaluate before repeating treatment. This product may not be right for every situation.

May contain spin, hype, empty hyperbole, platitudes, political meddling, corporate pressure, cosmetic solutions, false advertising, false optimism, baseless hope, empty promises, faith-based solutions, unproven technology, inadequate evaluation, no biological benchmarks, junk science, inequities in compensation, public naivety, hidden costs, partial truths, half-truths, and lies.

Side effects include blindness to impacts, self-deception, unrealistic expectations, unrealized costs, unrecognized effects, unintended consequences, unfulfilled plans, failure to implement, inadequate measurement, lack of avoidance strategies, increased human footprint, biodiversity declines, species loss, fragmented landscapes, incremental losses, cumulative impacts, lost future opportunity, reputational failure, repetitive use without effect, suspension of reality.

The real medicine isn't an ineffective tonic, doesn't act as a sedative, and isn't a panacea. If taken – and it will taste bad – it will clear our vision, opening the faculties for information, balance, restraint, and consequences. That will help us connect the dots between us, land-use pressures, and the essentials of the landscape disappearing quickly under the footprint of economic development. It will rock us out of symptoms of complacency, false optimism, and defensive apathy toward unrestrained development.

Mostly, it will put mitigation into its proper role as a last-ditch, cosmetic, and ineffectual attempt to rationalize our inability to say no. Mitigation has become the triumph of hope over experience. The process inevitably starts with brave words and positive intent that then slip, inexorably, into fudging and equivocating about the outcomes. Instead of that slide down a slippery slope of compromise, we need first to employ the precautionary principle, judged in part by cumulative effects analysis.

We need to stop the seductive delusion that all our land-use issues have solutions, that our pace of development can continue, and we can salvage ecosystems. Embedded in this is the expectation that the industrial/urban footprint can be restored or compensated for in some inexplicable fashion.

The greatest of delusions is we can have it all. The optimism that comes with mitigation is akin to having a bad cold – if you wait long enough the feeling will end.

Mitigation might be viewed as the cure-all for what ails you, when what ails you cannot be cured.

ARE YOU BEING SERVED?

———

Fracking, extracting oil from tar sands, carbon capture, selenium from coal mining, lithium extraction, small modular nuclear reactors, irrigation expansion, more logging, renewable energy developments, and abandoned well sites – all form a short list of planned or ongoing activities in which the public has an interest.

How well is the public being served to understand the implications of these activities and the technologies involved? As writer Steven Magee said, somewhat tongue-in-cheek, "There really should be a legal requirement for skydiving customers to be fully informed about the age and failure history of the parachute that they are using prior to the jump."

In the essential conversations we need to have on these and more developments, before we jump, we might begin by separating faith-based approaches, the sales hype, from results, or evidence-based forms of information. Many of us, and not just scientists, have cast our faith not in magic, a higher power, or wishful thinking, but in the power of double-blind testing – objective, independent, and ethical science.

So it would be helpful to have the empirical evidence on development schemes that provides clarity on social, economic, and environmental effects. That would help us understand risk and uncertainty. Risk is associated with something going badly wrong. Uncertainty involves outcomes of any kind.

A better understanding of the technology implied in these developments and its application would be part of risk assessment. In his book *Flirting with Disaster*, Marc Gerstein points out that, contrary to the belief of many nontechnical people, most technology is "unruly." That is, the technology servant is not always well behaved, understood, or applied, even by its designers, let alone its users.

As author Mark Kurlansky points out in *Cod: A Biography*

of the Fish That Changed the World, "But technology never reverses itself. It creates new technology to confront new sets of problems." It is also evident there may be unanticipated problems created by the last wave of technology.

Designers and users might not understand all the conditions that cause radical changes in performance, nor do they fully appreciate the reactions among components they have not had the opportunity to observe. This unfamiliarity is especially prevalent with emerging technologies that haven't had time to accumulate a substantial body of experience through use in varied conditions and in complex arenas that possess potential interactions that cannot be (or have not been) exhaustively tested.

In both design and circumstances, contemporary systems involve a bewildering array and blend of people, expectations, experience ranges, technology, and idiosyncratic events. Failures arise from an interaction of elements – increasing the reliability of the parts will not necessarily remedy the vulnerability of the whole.

Ordinary accidents, failures, and problems are more complex than they seem. Human error is often blamed. Yes, it is a factor and cannot be discounted. However, contributing factors, especially design and uncertainties involved with applying a technology in a wide variety of circumstances, magnify the risk.

Dangers arise when regulators develop financial and political ties to the entities they are supposed to be regulating and watching. When politicians and the bureaucracy see an entity as a "client," it encourages a perspective that they need to please rather than to question development, objectively assess the technology, and regulate the industry in the interests of the public. It also means risk is not appropriately assessed and made clear.

In Alberta it is doubtful whether anyone would call the government a disinterested, objective, and neutral party in discussions over economic development. Many would contend the Alberta government has ceded its role as an arbiter by being less than an honest broker of information. When the watchdogs are asleep, compromised, or inept, we all pay a price for that lack of oversight and attention.

RUST NEVER SLEEPS
(WITH APOLOGIES TO NEIL YOUNG)

Albertans live in some classic landscapes. If we could climb some stupendous ladder and gaze to all of the points of the compass, that might be apparent.

There are the remains of the native prairie, its tawny skin stretched tightly over a treeless expanse. The rolling fescue grasslands of the foothills are rich, verdant, and unmistakably alluring. Wooded islands of remaining aspen parkland are alive with the variegated colours of autumn. Cloaked in a blanket of endless greenery is the vastness of the boreal forest. The bordering jewels, the mountains, are a naked and serene backbone of twisted and tortured rock and ice. From west to east and to the north run sinuous ribbons of water, connected like veins in a leaf. Amid this, without a sense of order, are splashes of blue, the receptacles gouged out by glaciers. Yes, these landscapes are classics, the envy of others.

They are the original "oldies," created and moulded by tectonic activity and mile-high glaciers, unrelentingly aided by the forces of erosion, deposition, plant succession, fire, flood, drought, and grazing. These landscapes pleased the buffalo that sustained the first inhabitants and the beaver whose rich pelt lured the first immigrants from Europe here. To the eventual chagrin of the first inhabitants, the European visitors didn't leave. Once here and tasting the riches and the opportunity, we stayed.

We discovered that beyond the fur and the fish there were forests waiting for the axe, soil so rich it was unbelievable, and water – for harnessing, irrigating, and manufacturing. It wasn't just the surfeit of riches. It was also the freedom to stand tall, separate, and individual on a landscape of our choosing that by coincidence was choice. We love this place called Alberta.

Albertans also love their sheet metal, not only sculpted in the form of modern SUVs, trucks, and sleek sedans, but also the oldies. These are classics too. There are the unforgettable lines of a '57 Chevy or a '64 Mustang, resplendent in acres of chrome and gleaming paint. Beckoning to us and to some innermost rebel is a 1950 Indian Chief motorcycle, with valanced fenders and metal burnished to an incredible hue. These classics draw us to them, stirring our blood and, even for non-enthusiasts, creating a sense of nostalgia for the rarity, the quality, and the memory of simpler, perhaps better, times.

One of the challenges in the care of those classic vehicles, in addition to the risk of an accident, is the maintenance to keep that vintage tin from being attacked by rust. Rust is the great leveller of metal – insidious, cumulative, and notoriously effective. Prevention is the keynote here. Otherwise, the cost of repair or the problems of replacement are onerous. Some parts are no longer available.

We've got some rust spots on our classic Alberta landscapes. Some are pinpricks that warn us of incipient problems. Others are a growing blot of corrosion. Most of the prairie grasslands disappeared under the plow in the first 50 years of Alberta's existence as a province. Much of the transformation occurred during the homestead era when immigrants were lured to this landscape by government-sponsored visions of land ownership, freedom, and self-sufficiency. Many discovered the lie too late. This wasn't farming country, especially at the 160-acre scale.

The remains of this marvellously drought-adapted world have been continually chipped at since, some by recurring delusions of cereal crop production and others by pasture "improvements," hoping to best the last 12,000 years of plant evolution. At a smaller scale, an insidious assault on "old-growth" prairie happens daily with every oil and gas well, sometimes renewal energy projects, and the welter of accompanying roads, pipelines, power lines, and non-native plants.

Foothills largely escaped the plow, but they haven't evaded the chainsaw, the starter castle, the drilling rigs, or the piston heads. The "Green Zone," an ironic nickname given the current level of exploitation, was the original answer to the protection of Alberta's watersheds, especially the headwaters of every major river system for the Prairie provinces.

The forest reserve concept was a wise and forward-looking designation, with accompanying policy, to assure downstream water users (and drinkers) of quality and quantity. Somewhere along the way, exportable products as in dimensional lumber, gas, and coal dampened the enthusiasm for an emphasis on watershed.

Along the eastern fringe of the foothills, urban sprawl threatens to link up with rampant rural residential development, which itself is spreading from the gates of Waterton Lakes National Park northward to Edson. Many Albertans are mobilizing over concerns we've proven ourselves good at taking landscapes apart but have failed in our attempts to put them back together again.

The aspen parkland was a tension zone, ecologically, between the prairie grasslands and the forest environments. It was also culturally between the tribes of plains and forest Indigenous Peoples. As in the prairie, little of the original quality and quantity has survived our tenure. In living history, the landscape produced a cornucopia of wild fruit, game birds, and fish from nearby lakes. In the blank perfection of today's fields, interrupted occasionally by a one-tree-width fenceline, there are few opportunities for hunting or gathering.

Lakes have seen declines in fish populations, perhaps coincident with dropping water levels that exacerbate the naturally high-nutrient regimes added to by shoreline developments. The recurring droughts of recent times, instead of sending a message on the value of wetlands, have, ironically, allowed the cultivation and loss of more of them. Many of the remaining intact pieces of the aspen parkland are under attack from non-native plant invasions.

The boreal forest covers an area larger than the combined area of Alberta's other landscapes, yet it is more out of sight and regrettably more out of mind than the others. Boreal forests are said to be the "lungs" of our land because they produce oxygen and absorb carbon dioxide. They actively store carbon and serve as a partial break on global warming. How does Alberta treat this treasure? Unfortunately, we have auctioned it off as a resource ripe for liquidation.

Instead of a climate brake, the boreal forest is largely controlled by a series of multinational corporations, answerable to their stockholders and not to Albertans. We have put the forest's future in the hands of the marketplace, a notoriously fickle entity for resource conservation and protection over the long haul.

Large holes are being dug in the boreal forest near Fort McMurray to assuage the insatiable appetite of the American markets for oil. To give a sense of magnitude to the holes being dug in the tar sands, very soon the disturbed area will be as large as Lac La Biche, one of the few Alberta lakes big enough to identify on a road map. In even a couple of decades, the area will exceed that of Lesser Slave Lake. More to the point, every barrel of oil produced by wringing the bitumen clean with steam takes several barrels of water. As a result, the mighty Athabasca River downstream of Fort McMurray may be transformed into a creek.

Mountain landscapes are the flagship of Alberta's tourism effort, the images luring people, presumably with deep pockets, to spend time and money in the midst of the province's best. Yet it is here that some would propose mountaintop-removing coal strip mines.

As one watches the incredible vistas portrayed by the Tourism Department of Alberta, there isn't a single oil derrick, feedlot, logging clear-cut, coal mine, or lake stained with a toxic algal bloom in sight. Perhaps most of the footage is shot in our mountain national parks, which are not free of issues either, mostly related to the industry of recreation and transportation networks.

In an essay called "Old Mortality," Robert Louis Stevenson, the 19th-century author of *Treasure Island*, wrote that we all eventually have to sit down to a game of consequences. He would not have known of the place later to be called Alberta, but there are some parallels to the fantasy world he created in his fiction about a place with buried riches. What isn't a fantasy is that we can't drink water safely from surface sources in this province of treasure anymore. A history of land-use choices and decisions translates into a haunting legacy for something as common and as irreplaceable as water.

Rust never sleeps, it spreads, and as the spots join the underlying integrity of the structure is compromised and threatened. Ask a bridge engineer, or the owner of a classic car about that truism. If the province of Alberta were, in the parlance of car sales, a previously owned unit, it might behoove the current owners to take a second look at not only the integrity of the external surface but also the structural framework.

If the rusts spots are pointed out, the status of the corrosion established, and the consequences of inaction apparent, the reasonable thing to do is stop and repair the damage. That's what owners of classic vehicles do.

Our classic Alberta landscapes deserve the same treatment, for many of the same reasons. The major difference is that classic cars don't sustain us, while classic landscapes do. In the Neverland of billion-dollar surpluses there is a tendency to think we can buy our way out of those nagging environmental problems.

We tout the perspective that we are in the black economically, but the reality is we are awash in red ink, ecologically speaking. The challenge to us in the field of biology is to chart the ecological costs of doing business and to help people understand the value of Alberta's classic landscapes.

Rusty cars soon lose their resale value and, as the rot permeates the metal, safety and roadworthiness deteriorate. Inevitably, pieces fall off and seize and the car becomes a lump of brown orphaned in the backyard or put at curbside for disposal. Rusty landscapes lose their regenerative abilities, many of the ecological services become impaired or go missing, and they become less attractive as places to live, work, or recreate. In the case of both cars and landscapes, maintenance is about care, appreciation, and awareness of the costs and consequences of inaction. Failure leads to the loss of either mechanical or ecological services, and in both cases, we end up stranded.

If we don't help people focus on a future that revolves around environmental quality (instead of economic excess), we'll end up where we're headed. That destination doesn't appeal to me.

FIGHTING THE FIRES
OF ENVIRONMENTAL CONCERNS

Conservation is failing for a variety of reasons, including poor resourcing, resolve, and a lack of fighting capability in dealing with environmental challenges. It's hard to raise enough capital for conservation projects, even for the most visible, newsworthy, and cuddly animals, because people still fail to see a connection between themselves, what they do (often contributing to habitat losses), and their essential role in conservation.

Yes, people can be charitable and give to numerous worthwhile causes, but rarely do they give to conservation concerns – somewhat less than 3 per cent of all giving. You can give, and should, to humanitarian causes, ones dealing with famine relief, to heart and cancer research, but all of these causes and concerns have, at the root, an environmental link.

In the end, if conservation isn't funded appropriately (both privately and publicly), it won't matter how many human health research initiatives, food aid, or other causes have been supported if we haven't dealt with basic environmental issues such as water conservation, improvements in water quality, reducing soil erosion, making air quality better, reversing biodiversity loss and, of course, combating climate change.

Changing attitudes and behaviours with awareness and options can help, but often the sense is that individual actions are cancelled out by government and corporate inaction, or contrary actions. It seems that the motivation to act and respond only comes when we are teetering on the edge of an abyss. Then all the alarmist cries become real. Two world wars should have taught us that reaction.

Staring into an unknown and uncertain future while clinging to a cliff edge should persuade us that a step backward is infinitely better than a step forward. It should remind us that this is a point where the options become limited and uncomfortable, and many have been precluded or are unavailable.

If we viewed threats to the environment (such as climate change) as an imminent world war, complete with nuclear weapons, or a Black Death-like world pandemic (wait, didn't we just have one?), or maybe an asteroid on a collision course with us (such as the one that wiped out the dinosaurs and just about every other living thing), we might be more focused on what we need to do.

As the shadow of the asteroid (or other threats) looms larger, there are those who deny the evidence, closing their eyes, ears, and minds to the obvious. Others are cynical, maybe secretly believing we are on a collision course, but nonetheless choosing to party as there will be no tomorrow (a self-fulfilling prophecy). For the majority of us, the status quo is a seemingly comfortable and safe trap. The changes are so gradual, so quietly incremental, and maybe geographically distant that these are not top-of-mind issues.

This reluctance to face the issues squarely is, in large part, aided and abetted by our politicians and the corporate world, where a good deal of blame for our situation lies (not that we as individuals are blameless). The corporate sector tends to sit together in their own business bubble, sipping their own bathwater from golden goblets. They rail against taxes, land-use plans, and environmental regulations. What they champion is that government just needs to get out of their way – the free-market argument, except when it comes to generous subsidies and minimal regulations.

We need government regulatory oversight for the same reasons we need traffic lights: to control the flow of traffic. Unfortunately, especially in the agriculture, petroleum, and timber sectors, the traffic lights seem to be stuck on green.

We need political will to drag us out of complacency. Yet politicians are too timorous to provide real change because the benefits will come long after they are out of the picture, based on the four-year election cycle. There will be costs to bear to get us to a better, even a survivable, future, but the sacrifices will hurt politicians in the short term, for they will shoulder most of the derision, skepticism, and criticism. None of the changes necessary are easy to explain and put on a platform for successful re-election.

Collectively, maybe we think there is a poor return on investment in conservation, or a lack of tangible returns. Does that investment pay a dividend? Yes, not necessarily an individual one, but one we all share.

To make this evident, a necessary change is to reboot the concept of wealth. Essentials such as air, water, soil, and biodiversity are a common good – they need to be commonly protected. If they are not, which is the result of economic activity that transfers profit to private interests and downloads many of the costs to the environment, we all suffer. That includes all of us, everywhere, regardless of socio-economic status. A gold lifeboat is useless without water.

Change isn't necessary – survival isn't mandatory or guaranteed. This requires work, commitment, and sacrifice. We need to avail ourselves of the evidence provided by science, even imperfect as it sometimes seems to be. Knowledge is a step to understanding, and understanding can lead us into plans and strategies that may provide us and our descendants a future.

But it's easier to watch Netflix or a hockey game than to immerse ourselves in an article on biodiversity loss, decarbonization, energy efficiency, and the implications for us. Curiously, I understand this, but our ancestral heritage would suggest that an oncoming threat (maybe from a sabre-toothed tiger) needs to be dealt with now, not after we've reclined on the sofa.

Yes, writing a cheque for a conservation cause will help, but what is essential is a change in our consumer habits, our lifestyles, our political choices, and our personal advocacy. If we don't speak up and remain instead the silent majority, we may well become the silenced majority. Forcing our politicians and the corporate world to fix the big stuff, the parts that only they can do, will make our small stuff meaningful and we may dodge, deflect, or delay the bullet headed our way.

Nothing we do at this point will create a utopia – we've already blown past that option. All we can hope for is our world might be a little less dystopian.

ARGUMENTUM AD HOMINEM

———

"I suppose Fitch lives in a cardboard box and uses no modern amenities." This is the flavour of many responses to my concerns about land use and the impacts on the environment. It is a dismissive response to any thought of stewardship, conservation, or environmental alarm. By attempting to demean me and my argument by irrelevantly directing the attack at me and making it about me, these critics hope in some way to diminish my point.

These responses follow a similar, usually tendentious pattern. Any concerns over unsustainable logging will be met with a question of whether or not I live in a house made of wood. If I write about issues with the petroleum industry, I will be pilloried for driving a car. Exposing the problems in mining, especially coal, will bring forth a litany of vitriol about my use of steel (forged in furnaces burning the black stuff). Writing about our rivers receding into tiny trickles because of irrigation agriculture will result in being asked if I eat.

Presumably my legitimacy to speak on these issues can only be based on living in a cave, which I constructed with a sharp stick, wearing only animal skins that I trapped with vines, and walking everywhere barefoot, summer and winter.

The use of *argumentum ad hominem* seems linked to those who really want to believe in some of the hype of prevailing land-use schemes. They are unwilling to buy anything that scrutinizes, objectively reviews, or critiques their dreams. When you've drunk the purple Kool-Aid of growth at any cost, you are resolute in support, even though the cost may outweigh the benefits. "In the country of the blind," the philosopher Desideratus Erasmus commented in *Adagia*, "one-eye is king." When politicians and individuals bury their head in the sand, ignorance rules the country.

Ignorance is sometimes a choice, of not wanting to know. It closes the ears, the eyes, and the senses. The absence of knowing means you can ignore the existence of evidence, of fact. As Dave Christiansen, a colleague, often reminds me, "However well intentioned, speaking to the deaf is futile." It is not the inability to see and to hear, it is the choice not to, and to react negatively to anyone attempting to provide a different message.

Observation and critical thinking aided by some understanding of ecological principles might provide us a better pathway forward than shouting at each other in capital letters. Don Gayton writes tellingly on this in *The Wheatgrass Mechanism*: "It is our nature to be free-form, hot-dog, and eclectic; we live holism. So reductionist science, if nothing else, is probably a useful foil to lives full of concatenated events. A method to test things one at a time, as a check on ourselves."

Evidence-based decision making about checks and balances, ecological thresholds, and cumulative effects might help us stop racing through landscape traffic lights that we seem to think never turn red.

In our rush to fill up the landscape with money-making schemes we might pause long enough to take in some natural lessons. One is allelopathy. One plant species will suppress the growth of others due to the release of toxic substances. It can include auto-allelopathy where the first generation of a plant species inhibits growth and survival of the second generation. Plant examples that use these strategies include kochia, knapweed, and cheatgrass.

Some land uses and their intensity resemble allelopathy. One is blasting the tops off mountains to expose a coal seam. This exposes many toxic substances such as selenium, arsenic, cadmium, lead, mercury, and polycyclic aromatic hydrocarbons. Calcite and extreme amounts of sediment are also released. Mining essentially sterilizes a portion of the landscape and has negative impacts on watersheds downstream. The impacts of coal mining can persist for decades, if not centuries.

Rendering essential watersheds unstable hydrologically by unsustainable logging practices has demonstrable negative impacts on native fish and wildlife populations, on flood risk for downstream communities, and on both water quality and quantity for human populations. A landscape ravaged by clearcut logging no longer holds much appeal for outdoor recreation.

The positive feedback loop from continued (and expanded) petroleum extraction and use exacerbates climate change impacts such as flooding, drought, wildfires, and excessive heat. All ratchet up concerns about our own survival. Our inability to acknowledge the connections means we continue down a dangerous path. The legacy of land and water impacted by toxic petroleum development spills, exposed by Kevin Timoney in *Hidden Scourge*, is equally disturbing.

We need to talk about these and many more issues, to have reasoned dialogue about what we expect our future to resemble, and whether we stick to current paths or develop new ones. Name calling, personal attacks, and nonsensical arguments will not solve the dilemmas inherent in our growth-at-all-costs model.

Taking a page from one of my detractors, the prospect of living in a cardboard box without any modern amenities isn't a future I find solace in, as I'm sure some in the world who now live in those circumstances find. If we continue to trade off landscape integrity, resilience, and the indicators of those essentials, such as native fish, we might find ourselves in similar circumstances.

We can be rich, at least in the short term, with large bank accounts and inflated stock portfolios. Or we can be wealthy over the long haul, edging toward maintaining intact, diverse, and essential landscapes and ecosystem services. As Don Gayton said to me, we have to develop the sense and the courage to draw the line between the sustainable and the unacceptable.

Invective toward concerns on land-use issues may find favour with a few. But, as General Eric Shinseki said, "If you don't like change, you'll like irrelevance even less."

WEATHERING ANXIETY AND GRIEF

———

Against white cumulus clouds roiling in a slow boil, a redtail hawk soared on a rising wind. Never once flapping its wings but dipping and weaving with the gusty winds, it tacked forward. A weather front with inky blue-black clouds rolled in from the north on a chilly wind. The plus-30°C air was shoved aside, to my relief. I could both feel and taste the cooler air of the front as it passed over the cabin. A sudden drop in temperature and the quality of the air seemed fresher, energized. The hawk, inexplicably pursued by a flock of waxwings, disappeared into the gloom of the approaching front.

From sweating to shivering in minutes, as in a fridge door opening. Under a roof the spectacle is partly pure entertainment. But with the drought-parched grass tinder-dry and waiting for some casually tossed cigarette butt, hot exhaust from an OHV, or a lightning stab, there is also a palpable sense of anxiety.

To hell with BBQs, town parades, and golf games – let it rain, rain hard, rain long, soak the earth. Because coming in with the wind is a little fragment of ash, from nowhere close, I hope. Probably lofted on the winds from fires in BC. Anxiety escalates – climate or eco-anxiety. In the article "Understanding and Coping with Eco-anxiety," which is available on the Mental Health Commission of Canada's website, the American Psychological Association has defined this as "a chronic fear of environmental doom."

The weather system huffed and puffed, sending chairs flying. Dark clouds, so full of promise, delivered a few sprinkles. The rain hardly registered in the dust. It's enough to persuade you to wash the car, hang out clothes on the line, or take a hike without your raincoat. Anything to tempt the rain gods.

But, I think, if it rains too hard, forests ravaged by clear-cut logging can't hold the rain. Then somebody's basement is going to get wet, or a bridge will get washed out. Receiving streams and rivers can't hold it all. Stream banks get eroded, the channels widen, and when water levels go down, they go way down so the water is shallow. Then the water warms up too quickly and native trout suffer. Trout have suffered enough, so much so they are missing in many of their old haunts. This makes me sad.

What makes me even sadder is that we can't seem to come to grips with connecting the dots, especially limits. The ever-expanding footprint of logging, of roads and OHV trails that dissect the landscape, of cultivation of native grassland, of draining our rivers for irrigation, of oil and gas extraction, and of urban sprawl. I could go on, but this puts me on the edge of either crying or raging. The rampant greed, thoughtlessness, destruction, and inability to think ahead for other generations mystifies, frustrates, and angers me.

It seems the places most in peril are the ones of great natural beauty, biodiversity havens and ones ecologically intact. Once we put them through the development shredder, they are rendered barely recognizable, akin to seeing an old friend ravaged by disease.

Because I am old enough to remember intact places and have listened to those older than me wax on about fish and game abundance, I can see the extent of changes, of losses, and of damage. Acid drips on my soul. Even when I find out there is a name for this feeling of homesickness for something that no longer exists – solastalgia – it doesn't modify my eco-grief. It does help that others have experienced this deep feeling of grief for our landscapes, plants, and wildlife.

Routinely, when destructive development threatens an intact landscape, we ask for the rationale and press for environmental impact assessments. To further prevent these losses, we have lobbied for better land-use planning, cumulative effects assessments, the setting of ecological thresholds, and timely, progressive reclamation standards. But we end up fighting rearguard actions over and over. It's draining and it adds to the sense the cards are stacked against a reasonable, rational, ecological approach.

In "Understanding and Coping with Eco-anxiety," the Mental Health Commission of Canada summarizes these feelings with, "The natural environment is changing, and people are worried about what it means for the future. That worry, which is increasingly becoming severe enough to cause distress and dysfunction."

Even though 75 per cent of people living in Canada consider climate change a global emergency, there is a combination of denial (most notably among some federal and provincial politicians) and the fatalistic thought that it's too late to do anything about it. The problem with deniers and their kin in the corporate and political world is summarized in Dornbusch's Law, which states, "Crises take longer to arrive than can be imagined, but when they do come, they happen faster than possibly can be imagined." How many "wake up" calls do we need?

I know I harbour anger and a level of frustration toward governments that have not done enough (or anything) to curb the tsunami of climate change, manifested in catastrophic wild-fires, floods, and droughts we have been experiencing. Equally so, I feel the anger directed at older generations, mine for example, for misusing the time and influence to alter the trajectory we are now on.

This also leads me to a combination of guilt and further anger over our individual carbon footprints. Our economy, our policies, advertising, and perhaps even our psyches, are geared to consumption. This exceeds Earth's ability to supply the raw materials and deal with the environmental costs of production, transportation, and waste disposal. We desperately need some full-cost accounting to show us a possible way out of this over-extension of the global natural bank account.

Alan Moore, in *The Watchmen*, said in what could be a response to eco-anxiety, "In an era of stress and anxiety, when the present seems unstable and the future unlikely, the natural response is to retreat and withdraw from reality, taking recourse either in fantasies of the future or in modified visions of a half-imagined past." Sound familiar, considering observations of how some people are reacting to the environmental crisis we are facing?

Short of some kind of technological and unlikely miracle, there isn't a quick cure for our environmental muddle, especially the climate change one. While it's true the corporate and political world have a lot to answer for, that tends to absolve us as individuals of responsibility. Each of us has to acknowledge a level of responsibility and step up to the plate with solutions within our sphere.

I acknowledge my role in our environmental pickle. Yes, I live in a house made of wood, drive an internal combustion engine car, and eat bananas flown in from Ecuador. That is a first step for all of us to take. I rely on acknowledged experts to inform my thinking on topics of an environmental nature and then use my writing to inform others. Without reliance on science and critical thinking it is easy to fall down the rabbit holes revealed by conspiracy theorists, denialists, false experts, misinformation, and distortion.

Part of our angst is we have little control over most external circumstances. We can choose how to respond though. Each of us can take actions and have control of some aspect that can reduce eco-anxiety, maybe even grief. In *Sing You Home*, author Jodi Picoult writes, "Anxiety's like a rocking chair. It gives you something to do, but it doesn't get you very far."

If we have investments, we have the choice of where to invest, refusing to put our money into things that continue to pollute, eat up our landscape, and exacerbate climate change. We can live more simply and sustainably by resisting the urge (and advertising) to be bigger consumers. Since the energy cost of transporting food far outweighs the energy in it, we can eat closer to home by patronizing local food growers, especially the ones involved in regenerative agriculture. When we vote, we should think several generations ahead, not what fills our pockets today.

When I think of growing up in the 1950s and '60s, we didn't have much, didn't seem to miss it, and I don't think I was emotionally scarred by not having the latest toy or nice clothing or exotic travel. I'm reminded of the tongue-in-cheek statement, "No one is going to stand up at your funeral and say, 'He drove a really nice car and had expensive golf clubs.' Don't make life about stuff."

I strive to reduce my footprint, albeit sometimes unsuccessfully. Changing our lifestyles and overly consumptive habits isn't about perfection but about being aware of not only the price sticker, but also the sticker shock – the environmental cost of our activities and purchases. Then it's working toward a goal of reducing our footprint, as well as feelings of guilt and anxiety about our future. Collectively, that can make a difference.

Then the only thing left is to pressure government and the corporate world to do their part.

LESSONS LEARNED IN CONSERVATION

Often the enduring lessons we learn come from failure rather than success. Nature is a hard teacher – the test is given first, and the lesson follows.

Experience convinces me pain is an aid to learning. It helps us avoid doing the same things over and over, hoping for different results. Or at least it should, since the one thing we should learn from painful mistakes is to stop making them.

There have been many missteps in conservation. Some have included financial incentives with no follow-up behavioural shifts, ineffective legislation with the hollow threat of regulatory enforcement, and failed generic prescriptions for change from less than credible outside sources. One fundamental flaw has been the lack of continuity and persistence – sticking to something long enough to see results. All fail in one way or another to build the case for conservation because responsibility for care of landscapes and watersheds has not been successfully conferred.

The pathway to effective conservation actions is not prescribed, predetermined, or predictable. But there are common elements that seem to be part of conservation successes and, sadly, failures. One element of the conservation pathway is awareness, creating a cumulative body of knowledge in individuals, in industry, in government, and in the community as the foundation for conservation actions. As a farmer once told me, "If I know, it helps me to care and caring means I have to do something."

The hard lessons should make us better at conservation actions and lead to additional successes. Maybe these cannot be taught so much as experienced. Drawing on those experiences may help others avoid a lot of pain.

Ten lessons, acquired from much accumulated scar tissue, are:

1. **If you don't do anything, nothing happens.**

   Someone has to step up to the plate. Engaging in a conversation and persistence in continuing to talk means there is a chance we can form a constituency who knows and cares and also gives us hope that habitats might improve because conservation actions are likely to be contemplated or made. A conversation begins a sharing of information about the natural world, especially if it is a non-threatening, non-confrontational awareness effort. This helps people understand some of the ecological processes that shape the landscape they live on and make a living from. Moving beyond misconceptions, suspicion, denial, and conflict creates a pathway to trust, acceptance, and co-operation.

2. **Without motivation, most people continue to do nothing.**
   Doing nothing is comfortable. If people are not given the opportunity to see what is in the realm of the possible for them, their operations, and their neighbours for change, it won't be considered. Acceptance is enhanced because people perceive the initiative and messages are about them and for them as opposed to being externally driven and disconnected. When message-deliverers develop working long-term relationships, this helps to share diverse experiences, talents, and perspectives on how to tackle problems.

3. **There's never time to do anything until you realize it's time to do something.**
   Change is hard. Receptivity begins with ecological awareness, a place to begin sensitizing individuals to recognize elements of their environment and the state of their watersheds, landscapes, and even backyards. The goal is ecological literacy. Literacy is the ability to see and respond to choice, opportunity, risk, or options in land management decisions. Changes to land management are driven by informed decisions that are, in part, based on a greater appreciation of ecological function and process. A selling feature is that

individuals, communities, local governments, and industry can minimize risk, avoid liability, and maintain future options in making ecologically appropriate land management decisions.

4. **With a little motivation, a few people do something.**

   Awareness is a capacity-building initiative. It gives people more information, in the correct format, to allow actions to be contemplated and acted on. Early innovators who make a management change begin to see positive results. This creates a template for others to see what might be possible if they, too, take the first step. The reasons for positive action may result from enhanced awareness, motivated self-interest, concern about legislation, marketing opportunity, or altruism. The net effect will be a return to a landscape that maintains critical ecological function.

5. **Where is the best place to start? Somewhere!**

   There are many choices and opportunities for action and many are good ones with which to begin. But too many times too many choices freeze a response. Then there is a retreat into the default plan of doing nothing because there is too much to do and the task seems impossible. Picking something to work on and proceeding breaks the impasse.

6. **Until you start doing something you aren't going to know what works.**

   Even the best plans have aspects of uncertainty and unpredictability. Outcomes are not programmed or guaranteed. Events and circumstances along the way change the predicted outcome in some ways. The surest way to determine the fit of a solution is to begin to undertake some aspect of it. This is the essence of adaptive management – doing, checking, reflecting, modifying, and continuing.

7. **Once there is a realization something needs to be done, many things start to happen.**

   A synergy is created that allows conservation actions to be contemplated, often at bigger landscape scales. It's like a snowball rolling downhill, picking up speed and getting bigger. This leads to an understanding of the utility of awareness, cumulative effects, tool development, evaluations of ecological health, an increased stewardship ethic, and commitment. Working at the community level provides a foundation for these activities to proceed.

8. **In spite of evidence to the contrary, a few people persist in thinking that nothing needs to be done.**

   Not everyone is easily convinced. Evidence of poor landscape health, fish and wildlife declines, and changes in water quality and quantity are viewed with skepticism. Because of the often slow, insidious, and cumulative nature of changes it is difficult to recognize and acknowledge them. It can take extra effort to find references and photographs of the past to compare to the present to change minds.

9. **Those who want to do nothing can find enough uncertainty to avoid doing anything.**
   Many use the excuse that everything isn't yet clear and predictable. Breaking the pattern of the status quo is difficult given excuses like cost, economic forces, lack of time, distrust, perceptions of lost opportunities, and uncertain operational changes. In many cases, persevering with awareness pays off with a shift in perspective that breaks the inertia. Sometimes the level of uncertainty is an impediment for action.

10. **If you do nothing long enough, soon you will reach a point that nothing can be done.**
    By themselves things seldom get better. Only proactive participation and action produce positive results. Once a system has deteriorated beyond a certain point, where all the necessary pieces for restoration are missing, ecosystem function is extremely difficult to restore. There is a need to create a sense of urgency, to encourage people to start something before it is too late to do anything without high costs and a dubious outcome.

"It always seems impossible until it's done," Nelson Mandela said wisely, and he who knew this from bitter experience. Progress on conservation and stewardship seems impossible because it involves working with people, helping them see their world through different eyes, and motivating change.

Awareness leads to understanding, a necessary prelude to accepting responsibility for change. Acceptance of the information and the issues provides a pathway to the adoption of management changes. Adoption of different management represents commitment. The act of change provides the opportunity for a different and probably better trajectory in landscape health. The progression, starting at awareness, embodies all the elements of stewardship.

When do things get better? When enough people grasp the situation, take responsibility, speak up, and change the dial on what they do.

THE "DO NOTHING" STRATEGY FOR WILDLIFE

The phone rang, as is the usual case, in the middle of a meal. My negative reaction was partially mollified by the soft female voice asking if I was the head of the house. I quietly answered "yes," hoping my wife wouldn't hear. It was a call from a national conservation organization that had teamed with a major credit card company. As it was explained to me, if I signed up for a card, a percentage of my purchases would go to the conservation organization to help fund more good work.

"Imagine," said the lady, "the more you spend the better it will be for conservation." Alarms bells began to toll. To clarify

I asked, "So the more stuff I buy, the more things I do that are channelled through my credit card, the better off wildlife will be, and more habitat will be saved?" "Yes!" was the enthusiastic response. "But," I said, "wouldn't all that activity caused by me buying more stuff actually cause habitat to decline and wildlife to suffer?"

"After all," I went on, "stuff has a cost outside of what I pay for it – the impact on the environment of more oil pumped, trees cut, minerals mined, factories built, roads constructed, trucks operated, stores opened, water diverted, and so on. The more I spend, the more I consume. The more I consume, the more I am responsible for using up the natural environment your organization is trying to protect."

I was really warming to the subject when the initial sweet voice turned sour and snarled, "I guess you don't care about conservation." She then hung up on me.

"But," I struggled to say into a phone receiver already dead in my hand, "I do care." Many of us do. Bird identification guides outsell Bibles. Wildlife shows are some of the most popular TV programs. I just don't think you can put conservation on a credit card. Consuming our way to a better world seems self-defeating, like making war for peace.

I believe we have developed a societal blindness to our consumptive, or more to the point, over-consumptive habits. "The split between what we think and what we do is profound," says Wendell Berry, the Kentucky farmer and philosopher. In our myopia we can't connect the dots between consumption and loss of valued pieces of the natural world. It is a truism in nature that everything is connected.

What is it about human nature, especially we North

Americans, that drives us to keep acquiring stuff? We feed mostly our wants, far in excess of our needs. That's not a vision for tomorrow but rather an obsession with today. A quote from *Punch*, the British magazine of humour and satire, sums this up with characteristic tone: "I am not hungry; but thank goodness, I am greedy." Owning more stuff may provide a short-term version of pleasure, but embedded in each item is a loss for wildlife.

The drive for material goods infects us and is driven by the power of advertising and messaging about consumer products. These render many of our older societal values quaint and irrelevant. It is a manipulation of people's world view from solvency, thrift, conservation, postponement of desire, and community fidelity to self-definition through purchases, instant gratification of urges, and emphasis on the individual, especially social status and image. It's a perceptible shift to a "me first" mentality with a pathological "right now" attitude.

The shift from consumption to consumerism has created a "consumer class" where "self-denial is something to do when you're old, not now." This class, which consists of many of us, has diets of highly processed food, a desire for bigger houses, more and bigger cars (Hummers anyone?), higher levels of debt, and lifestyles devoted to the accumulation of nonessential goods. It might also be said we are self-absorbed, disconnected from natural systems, ecologically illiterate and, when confronted by reality, denialists.

We delude ourselves with "lifestyle" – living life with style – a pursuit with regrettable consequences. Every time the topic is discussed in the media of today it looks more like "living life with stuff" – expensive, often trivial stuff. "It is not even affluent in any meaningful sense, because its abundance is dependent on sources that are being rapidly exhausted by its methods," says Wendell Berry.

Disposable this, plastic that, cheaply made goods with built-in obsolescence (or breakability), all of which lead to a "throw away" mentality. There is enormous waste in the way we consume.

Consumerism is touted by our political leaders as a solution to a struggling economy. The short-sightedness embedded in the admonishment to spend more is breathtakingly stupid, not only ecologically but also in terms of the debt load carried by citizens who follow this rubric. It is the inability to see the economy as a wholly owned subsidiary of the environment.

Political- and media-driven agendas for consumerism may seem good for the economy, but the Worldwatch Institute, in its annual report *State of the World 2004*, indicates "unprecedented consumer appetite is undermining natural systems." A 1998 United Nations *Human Development Report* emphatically states, "Runaway growth in consumption in the last 50 years is putting strains on the environment never before seen." More recently, the Worldwatch Institute indicates 37 per cent of species could become extinct due to climate change that is directly linked to our consumptive habits.

C.D.H. Clarke and T. Madson, in *Waterfowl Tomorrow* (1964), concluded, "The consummate offence to wildlife is not hunting, but the extirpation of species by an indifferent technology in which wildlife is wiped out – not by man's passion – but by his single-minded devotion to a material world in which creatures have no place." With the additional, expanding footprint of our development and consumer zeal, here, there, and everywhere, we subtract from our ecological bank account and that of wildlife.

It happens with every swipe of the credit card. As that plastic facsimile for wealth warms with our use of it, we don't realize we are adding to our ecological mortgage. Earth holds that mortgage, and it rises astronomically because we have made few and sometimes no payments to bring down our indebtedness.

The apogee of consumerism must be Kurt Vonnegut's character Eliot Rosewater, in *God Bless You, Mr. Rosewater*, who said, "Grab much too much or you'll get nothing at all."

Many of our landscapes, especially the prairie grasslands, challenge conventional economics because they will not tolerate overload. But our consumerism drives the need to wring even more from these places. Eventually, something has to give – the first thing to go is wildlife. Unfortunately, our landscape, and its wealth of biodiversity, is poorly adapted to a growth-dependent economy.

So if you really want to do something for wildlife, consider doing nothing. Do nothing that diminishes habitat. Consider that doing nothing means relieving the relentless pressure on natural resources caused by rampant consumerism.

Think before you buy. Will your life be measurably enriched with this purchase, or will it merely add to an overflowing closet, cupboard, or garage? Buy quality products that last, both physically and psychologically.

Practice being a skeptic – question authority. Don't blindly follow the dogma of government that it is our patriotic duty to consume. What is our responsibility is conserving the natural resources (wildlife included) entrusted to our care. Tune out the advertising that is generally about persuading us to buy stuff we don't need, don't want, for more than its value.

Ask for the details, read the fine print, push for full cost accounting on resource development projects. Carefully consider your investment portfolio. Does it aid and abet those activities that imperil landscapes and wildlife? Allowing the corporate world to externalize costs to the environment is a recipe for wildlife losses.

Follow the money. Who benefits, who loses? Ask that the real costs of consumer products, especially the externalized costs, be disclosed. Support "green taxes" that penalize those who wish to profit at Earth's expense or can't be bothered to make responsible choices.

A little introspection might focus on how good most of us have it. Very little of our sense of well-being is connected to possessions but rather health, safety, relationships, meaningful work, and a quality environment. Reacquaint yourself with your community and who lives in it. You might find a rich supply of engagement and entertainment among your nearby neighbours.

In an ironic twist, prosperity, whether it is the spark for increased consumption or caused by it, reportedly isn't making people happier or healthier. Increased consumption comes with a high price and not just for the junk we buy. The cure is to lower levels of consumption, forging a path to a higher quality of life, using fewer raw materials in the living of one's life, and decreasing the footprint of our consumption.

Douglas Chadwick, a science writer, observed about these alternatives, "All are part of the challenge of learning as a modern society how to live the good life on earth without abusing the generosity of our hostess." Wendell Berry suggests in *The Unsettling of America* that we consider "an economy of necessities rather than an economy based upon anxiety, fantasy, luxury and idle wishing."

The battle to maintain wildlife (and their habitats) won't be waged solely with protest signs, by chaining ourselves to trees, or by writing letters to politicians. The fight will be won (or lost) at supermarkets, shopping malls, classrooms, fast food outlets, car lots, gas pumps, polling booths, and finally in the hearts and minds of consumers.

Now, if nothing I have said moves you and if you must buy the stuff anyway, well then at least get one of those fancy credit cards where a conservation group gets a cut of your consumer zeal. You could choose to make a tax-deductible donation to aid some conservation work. The reality is we humans will remain consumers. We have to for survival, yet our disposable income allows us to make choices about and contributions to conservation.

What is critical for wildlife (and the planet) is a shift away from our over-consumptive, wasteful habits. A donation to conservation, well-intentioned as it might be, without an attitudinal and behavioural shift might be "virtual" or "feel good" conservation, but largely ineffectual for wildlife. It doesn't mitigate, compensate, or take us off the hook for bad behaviour.

If acquiring more stuff eventually equates to less natural capital then it might follow that a smaller economy would equate to better maintenance of wild species and spaces. If we buy less, consume less (especially of the resource products whose extraction threatens species and spaces), and generally do less as individuals (especially activities that further threaten imperilled species), that puts us a step closer to keeping the full array of biodiversity.

When you see a bumper sticker that says, "Do nothing, for wildlife," don't be alarmed. Doing nothing (or less than we currently do) would be a positive thing for wildlife and the planet. As J.B. MacKinnon points out in *The Day the World Stops Shopping*, humans had the choice of two distinct paths to meet our wants and needs. "The first was to produce much; the second was to want little."

The environmental community is accused of endless rants and pointless polemics without solid solutions to the dilemmas that face us. Well, this is different. Here is a practical, pragmatic, simple, cheap, and easily adapted solution. All that is required is that we change ourselves.

Yes, plant a tree, recycle, and support environmental organizations. But also buy less, consume less, and live on a healthier Earth longer. Connect the dots. This may be said about maintaining biodiversity – the truism that if we want a better world, we will have to become better people.

PLACES OF THE HEART THAT TOUCH THE SOUL

———

In a vivid memory, fog cloaked the breach in the Livingstone Mountain Range, through which the Oldman River has cut a deep passage. The rudimentary S-curve carving a channel through the folded and faulted bedrock represents time beyond our comprehension. Even against rock the water is implacable. Truck-sized boulders, part of the clawing of water through the weak spot in the mountains, show the river isn't finished yet.

Each of us harbours places of memory, of joy, and of sublime delight. They flood our senses from time to time. Then some of those places become part of you.

They attach themselves to your soul, as does a limpet clinging to a rocky ocean shore. When you leave those places, indiscernible pieces, traces, leave with you. Sometimes with the passage of time the feeling seems to fade, with faint memories remaining.

Never really gone, never really forgotten, places that stir the heart seem ephemeral, like phantoms. But with a gentle nudge, there they are, tempting us to reconcile with them. Every time I drive through the "Gap" in the Livingstone Range, feelings of antiquity and persistence are refreshed. I am also reminded the place transcends my limited sense of time.

A salmon-red sunset filled the western sky, so vibrant it seemed Photoshopped. In dark relief were the Sweetgrass Hills, just over the Alberta border in Montana. It created a surreal sense of expanse so compelling I could feel myself shrinking in comparison to the broad sweep of sky.

Humility isn't a bad thing for us humans to experience, maybe every day. This is doubly so for the beauty, scale, and transcendent feeling places provide. Whenever I want to escape the artifacts of human creation, I go to that primordial sunset in my mind.

It was an untouched, unroaded, unlogged trout stream. Every foot of upstream passage was thwarted by a downed log, a tangle of understory shrubs, or a pool of unwadeable water. Ancient spruce, much older than Canada, tipped toward the water. Some had already toppled, with their root masses some five metres in diameter either damming the stream or lodging parallel to the flow. These key logs accumulated smaller trees and limbs in an indecipherable jumble.

Trout, big trout, lollygagged in the slow current created by all the obstructions in the water. Beneath the log jams, safe from every predator, including me, were smaller trout, hugging the shadowed water. Each piece of gravel seemed magnified in water clear as a windowpane.

The matrix of trees, logs, understory, overstory, and a convoluted channel that dipped and wove itself between, around, and over the logjams seemed chaotic. A jumbled mass of unrelated pieces, of disarray and of unnecessary complexity. It took a while to see it wasn't chaotic; indeed, it was a serene tableau.

It was like the interior mechanism of an enormous natural clock. All the spare parts were present, the mechanism tapped out the time of ancient processes to the syncopated rhythms of indigenous seconds and minutes, a model of symmetry and efficiency where everything mattered, everything was essential, and nothing was redundant.

I suppose in the fullness of time, with enough scientific measuring equipment available, it might be possible to parse out what some of the pieces do, how some fit together, and how all the pieces move in a dance over time to reposition themselves. But the explanation would be a pale facsimile of the whole. There are things we will never see, feel, or prove.

The stream knew the formulas, the pattern, the instructions, the logistics, the construction, and the maintenance schedule. It finally dawned on me the best we humans could do would be to stand back and ensure the watershed has integrity and let the stream, which knew its business better than us, get on with it.

These are some of the places that touch my soul. Some I can

go back to, reminiscent of a visit with an old friend. Some have been gobbled up with our frenetic, frantic desire to extract all the economic benefits. Left behind are the crushed bodies, skeletons, and empty shells of what once was.

Some of my places of the heart are gone. These now-tortured landscapes trigger an ache in my heart. A logging clear-cut, a coal strip mine, a cow-blasted meadow, ploughed-up prairie grassland, or a hillside rutted with OHV trails all grate like coarse-grit sandpaper on my soul. The reason it hurts is because, at least for me, my soul is connected to some of those places.

As more of those places of the heart disappear, I'm afraid I will be a body without a soul. That's why I speak up, not only for places of my heart, but perhaps of yours too. If there was a way to create a window to one's soul so others could look in and see the grief when a place of the heart is trashed, it might make more sense why we are so aggrieved.

The late José Saramago, a Portuguese writer, said, "Inside us is something that has no name, that something is what we are." I would go further and say that we are, in some vital way, the places that touch the heart and attach themselves to our souls.

Find the places that touch you and hang on to them. They both anchor and make us whole.

Illustration by Liz Saunders

Epilogue:
Phantoms in Photographs

History is a watercourse. A river in
the mind. A precarious pattern we
make from the flow of time, as we try
to write our names on the water.
—Lyall Watson

We live with and are surrounded by the ghosts of wild species and the places they lived. Some we knew before they disappeared. Some disappeared long before our paths would have crossed. A few, a scant few, have been resurrected from a close call with an ethereal future.

Then there are the ones that sadly we do not recall, cannot remember, of which we retain little history of their existence. There are also the ones that seem destined to become ghosts because we seem unwilling, unmotivated, to rescue them before they drift off to become wraiths.

Old photographs can speak to us, providing context for our world and perhaps speak about us with the changes that our cumulative wishes and desires have created. I've pored over hundreds of photographs from local museums, provincial archives, and family albums. These are snapshots of a time – with faded sepia tones and still crisp black and white prints – that provide a record of lost memories, ghosts of the past.

The images are a window on the past, often a haunting one. But ghosts don't haunt us. They are there because in some cases we won't, we shouldn't, let go of them. In these photos are the ghosts of past landscapes, of fish and wildlife populations, and the hubris that changed, sometimes forever, the place we now live.

Some might argue there are no ghosts, just fanciful tall tales to entertain and fool us into believing big changes and losses have happened. It would be hard to fake the stories embedded in these images.

A picture might not convey the full reality of the situation. It is just a moment frozen in time, but a story develops with the spark of that one image.

What is portrayed in the pictures forces us to come to some reconciliation with the changes that have happened, which we scarcely pay attention to because of the passage of time and imperfect memory. Three archival photographs stand out to me for the stories they tell about the lost worlds of earlier eras and our forgetfulness of the past.

The first image is a stark black and white winter scene in 1882. Eight bison carcasses dot the snow-covered prairie. A Sharps rifle, the favourite of bison hunters, leans against one of the dead animals. Two hides lie flat, pegged to the ground, just as they would have been pulled off the animals. The date suggests the event would have occurred in the dying days of the great slaughter of plains bison.

It was the juncture between one form of resource exploitation and depletion and the beginning of the next. It signalled the death rattles of one economy that had sustained Indigenous Peoples for thousands of years. Within two decades came the mining of the prairie soils for farming, the further disruption of a landscape finely tuned to the vagaries of weather and moisture. Included was the heartache for those settlers who believed the lies of the federal government, the railway companies, and promoters that you could get rich on 160 acres of arid land.

When I look at the image and what message it conveys, I wonder, did we learn anything from the elimination of bison from the plains? Was it simply the cost of "civilizing" the landscape? Has the passage of time erased any thought of the lessons we might have learned?

In *The Ecological Buffalo*, Wes Olson points out the interconnectedness of the prairie landscape and other species with bison – that bison defined the landscape and vice versa. Without bison, the landscape has lost a vital ingredient. What we might learn is, lose enough of the essential cogs, toggles, and gears and what is left is the ghost of a landscape. The soul of it appears to be living, but it is gone in real and functional terms.

The next image is from 1902. Four men and a child pose with two long stringers of trout and an additional pile of trout on the ground in front of them. It appears to be the result of just one day's fishing. Stacked firearms and cartridge belts suggest these were wilder days and you went armed for a fishing trip.

The fish are cutthroat trout, well over 100 of them, maybe 50 kilograms in total. These were the predominantly native trout, years before the stocking of non-native rainbow trout occurred and diluted the wildness. Just out of sight is the stream these trout were yarded out of, conveniently called Trout Creek. It flows off the east side of the Porcupine Hills in Southwestern Alberta.

There is a certain sadness in the archival image of such an

exuberance of wild trout. Today these fish are categorized as threatened, with population numbers so low there is major concern for their survival. To achieve a similar catch to that of the one depicted in the 1902 photograph would completely deplete the population of a single stream, maybe several streams, where the trout still hang on precipitously by a fin. These fish are becoming the aquatic equivalents of the bison.

It is hard for today's anglers and fisheries biologists to conceive of such prolific productivity from a tiny creek across which you can jump. If we don't know where we started, the benchmark quietly moves and our goals become based on a diminished state. It sets up a sense the future is just more of the present, that we understand the laws of progress, that there are no alternatives and therefore nothing really needs to be done. In the politics of inevitability, as Timothy Snyder, a Yale historian writes in *The Road to Unfreedom: Russia, Europe, America*, we need not fear ecological collapse, we needn't concern ourselves with inaction; technology will solve everything.

In reality, native trout follow an annual cycle that has been forged over time, dictated by genetics and nursed by the ebb and flow of streams and rivers. Block, modify, or tinker with the cycle and the consequences are dire. That includes turning the watersheds that sustain trout into scabrous openings and scarred earth.

An image from the Highwood River in 1911 depicts a log jam reported to be 11 kilometres long. You can't see the river – a jumbled mass of cut logs jam the channel from bank to bank and beyond a bend in the river. The sheer scale of it suggests the resource-rich nature of the forests of the Eastern Slopes, including a cornucopia of trout.

Early federal civil servants envisioned the Eastern Slopes as first and primarily a place for watershed protection. Use of the timber was a secondary consideration, in spite of what the 1911 scene implies. Logging was selective, horses provided the motive power to move logs to the rivers, and rivers were used to float logs to sawmills.

It is likely that the early logging footprint was minimal, impacts on water quality and the hydrologic regime insignificant, although the impact of log drives on rivers might have been periodically devastating. In many ways, we are fortunate that those early loggers had only axes and crosscut saws – not chain saws, feller bunchers, bulldozers, and skidders.

Today's industrial-scale logging, with massive clear-cuts, a tangled web of roads, and a corporate and bureaucratic indifference to other forest values has completely flipped the vision for watershed protection as a priority.

An extensive and growing logging footprint disrupts the ability of forests to capture, store, and slowly release water. Clear-cuts and roads exacerbate spring floods, increasing the frequency and severity of flooding, especially to downstream communities. Drought often follows. Sediment bleeds from these areas, increasing the risk to aquatic life, especially native trout. In large part because of this logging footprint, native trout are now mostly shadowy phantoms up and down the Eastern Slopes.

These three old photographs provide benchmarks for us to consider. The reality is the cumulative impact of many logging cut blocks, well sites, roads, pipelines, dams, mines, water diversions, drained wetlands, rural subdivisions, urban sprawl, and cultivation of native grasslands has significantly changed the health, function, and resiliency of the landscape. Ecological lines in the sand may be faint but they are still real. Once these are crossed, the consequences are profound and restoration becomes prohibitively expensive, challenging, fraught with uncertainties, and in many cases, impossible.

When we fail to look back and recognize the intact ecosystems of the past and their abundant biodiversity in contrast to today's depleted, damaged, and missing ones, we set ourselves up to continue the trend. We forfeit the future, mostly for an economic imperative that ignores the reality of ecological values.

Pondering those old photographs might persuade us to refrain from altering or developing some places where past expressions of landscape integrity and biodiversity still exist. It might spur us to repair the places we have damaged.

A retrospective look is part of remembering our origins and who we are. Each of us harbours places and things (such as photographs) that function as touchstones, sacred locations, and important memories. Whether or not these exist individually or societally, they are the strands and threads that connect us with our pasts and guide us to our futures. It would be wise to keep as many guideposts as we can.

The plaque on a statue at York University reads, "A fish only recognizes water when it discovers air." Those guideposts help us recognize what we have, what we've lost. Photographs can be a powerful check on the collective amnesia that things never change, diminish, or disappear.

As Charles M. Russell, an American storyteller and artist of the Old West, asserted, "The iron heel of civilization has stamped out nations of men, but it has never been able to wipe out pictures." The photographs are there reminding us we can and *must* do better to avoid making further ghosts of our landscapes.

All we need to do is open our eyes.

Acknowledgements

Ideas come on many wings, especially from concepts of influential writers like Andrew Nikiforuk, Candace Savage, Trevor Herriot, Kevin Van Tighem, Edward Struzik, and Don Gayton. This doesn't diminish the long influence of Aldo Leopold, Rachel Carson, Wendell Berry, and Stan Rowe, who are my touchstones.

In everyday conversation also comes the grist for my writing. Key to this has been my long-time interactions with Allan Locke, Ian Dyson, the late Gerry Ehlert, Greg Hale, Dave Christiansen, Harry Stelfox, Jim Stelfox, Kim Green, Brian Joubert, Jeffery Lockwood, and Jessica Reilly. Each helped sort out memories and essential facts and weighed in on my perspectives.

These essays and stories hold up a mirror to our world in the hope some, maybe many, might approach its beauty, complexity, and fragility with more care and responsibility. Writing *Conservation Confidential* was not an easy task. I hope reading it is an easier one.

The illustrations that grace the cover of the book and set off each chapter represent the artistic talents of Liz Saunders, of Sandpiper Ecological Research and Illustrations. I am also appreciative of the continued support from Don Gorman and the staff of Rocky Mountain Books.

My wife, Cheryl Bradley, continues to support my scribbling with insights, inspiration, and affirmation.

Suggested Reading

Atwood, Margaret. *Burning Questions: Essays & Occasional Pieces, 2004–2022*. McClelland and Stewart, 2022.

Atwood, Margaret. *Payback: Debt and the Shadow Side of Wealth*. CBC Massey Lectures series. House of Anansi Press, 2007.

Berry, Wendell. *The Gift of Good Land: Further Essays Cultural and Agricultural*. North Point Press, 1981.

Carson, Rachel. *Silent Spring*. Fawcett Publications, 1962.

Davis, Wade. *Magdalena: River of Dreams*. Knopf Canada, 2020.

de Villiers, Marq. *Water: The Fate of Our Most Precious Resource*. Stoddart Publishing Co. Limited, 1999.

Erasmus, Peter. *Buffalo Days and Nights*. Fifth House, 2015.

Gayton, Don. *The Wheatgrass Mechanism: Science and Imagination in the Western Canadian Landscape*. Fifth House, 1990.

Kurlansky, Mark. *Cod: A Biography of the Fish That Changed the World*. Vintage Canada, 1998.

Leopold, Aldo. *For the Health of the Land: Previously Unpublished Essays and Other Writings*. Island Press, 1999.

Leopold, Aldo. *A Sand County Almanac: And Sketches Here and There*. Sierra Club/Ballentine Books, 1966.

MacKinnon, J.B. *The Day the World Stops Shopping: How Ending Consumerism Gives Us a Better Life and a Greener World*. Vintage Canada, 2022.

MacKinnon, J.B. *The Once and Future World: Nature As It Was, As It Is, As It Could Be*. Random House Canada, 2013.

Maclean, Norman. *A River Runs through It*. University of Chicago Press, 1976.

Miller, R.B. *A Cool Curving World*. Longmans Canada Limited, 1962.

Olson, Wes, and Johane Janelle. *The Ecological Buffalo: On the Trail of a Keystone Species*. University of Regina Press, 2022.

Rowe, Stan. *Home Place: Essays on Ecology*. NeWest Press, 2002.

Timoney, Kevin P. *Hidden Scourge: Exposing the Truth about Fossil Fuel Industry Spills*. McGill-Queen's University Press, 2021.

Van Tighem, Kevin. *Heart Waters: Sources of the Bow River*. Rocky Mountain Books, 2015.

Wilson, Edward O. *Half-Earth: Our Planet's Fight for Life*. Liveright Publishing Corporation, 2016.

Wood, Kerry. *A Nature Guide for Farmers*. H.R. Larson Publishing Company, 1947.

About the Author

Lorne Fitch has been a biologist for over 50 years. He has criss-crossed the province, learned the landscape, investigated fish and wildlife populations, and engaged with ranchers, farmers, industry, and bureaucrats over conservation. His insights are the result of much scar tissue. He is a professional biologist, a retired provincial fish and wildlife scientist, and a former adjunct professor at the University of Calgary. He is also the co-founder of the riparian stewardship initiative called Cows & Fish. For his work on conservation, he has been part of three Alberta Emerald awards, an Alberta Order of the Bighorn Award, and a Canadian Environmental Gold Award, with additional recognition from the Wildlife Society, the Society for Range Management, the Alberta Society of Professional Biologists, the Western Association of Fish and Wildlife Agencies, and the Alberta Wilderness Association. His other books with RMB are *Streams of Consequence: Dispatches from the Conservation World* and *Travels Up the Creek: A Biologist's Search for a Paddle*. Lorne lives in Lethbridge, Alberta.